Whistle
Up the Inlet

D0039991

Whistle
Up the Inlet

THE UNION STEAMSHIP STORY

by
Gerald A. Rushton

J.J. Douglas Ltd., Vancouver, 1974

Copyright © Gerald A. Rushton, 1974

First paperback printing 1978

All rights reserved. No part of this book may be reproduced or transmitted in any form by any means without permission in writing from the publisher, except by a reviewer, who may quote brief passages in a review.

Douglas & McIntyre Ltd.
1875 Welch Street
North Vancouver, B.C.

Canadian Shared Cataloguing in Publication Data

Rushton, Gerald A., 1898-
    Whistle up the Inlet

        Includes index.
        ISBN 0-88894-057-2
        ISBN 0-88894-186-2 pa.

        1. Union Steamship Company - History.
I. Title.
HE635.7.U5R8   387.5'06'5711

Design by Sally Bryer
Jacket design by Nancy Legue-Grout
Typesetting by B.C. Monthly Typesetting Service
Printed and bound in Canada by The Hunter Rose Company

Dedicated
to the
Union Steamship men, afloat and ashore,
who left a memorable tradition with the coast
people of British Columbia and the
City of Vancouver in particular

FOREWORD

When I was a boy growing up in England geography, as it was then called in school, was one of my pet subjects because of its pleasant air of mystery and adventure. Map-drawing of distant lands was a positive delight. I remember that a wavy line sufficed admirably to portray the indented west coast of Canada from the Alaskan bulge to the Strait of Juan de Fuca.

One Saturday my father took me to the Liverpool office of the Welsford Company, which he managed, and as a special treat allowed me to decode a cable from the Union Steamship Company of British Columbia. I was intrigued by its contents, which reported a profit of $38,000 for a single month. He also gave me an illustrated folder, with a map insert, entitled *North By West in the Sunlight*, about the ports of call and exciting voyages of the small red-funnelled ships. I knew they were much smaller than most of the Mersey steam-packets on which I had holidayed to Llandudno or Douglas. Little did I then think that it would be my destiny to spend thirty-eight years after World War I in the service of that Company, and become eye-witness to events throughout its middle and closing years.

It has been my objective to relate the whole Union story from the time when the Company battled great odds to serve the first British Columbia coastal settlements. In doing so, I have tried to preserve something of the atmosphere in which this enterprise developed, as the small, hardy vessels penetrated uncharted bays and became indispensable to the early logging, fishing and mining outposts.

Although this account spans the lifetime of the Union fleet from 1889 to 1959, it is not a Company history in the sense of recording annual statements. Such financial comments are restricted to making the procession of events reasonably intelligible. Neither is it possible in covering such a period of time to include personal reference to all the captains and marine and engineer officers, nor to more than a portion of the intrepid and dedicated men, afloat and ashore, who participated in this maritime saga.

In retrospect, I believe the story covers a "pioneer happening" that could never recur in this way. The Union ships were a phenomenon in our coastal history, and several of the stories would be considered incredible if written as fiction. Perhaps, too, the unselfish devotion of several generations of Union Steamship men to an ideal of good service would strike the modern school of one-upmanship as unbelievable. The love-match between the coast settlers and the ships can best be understood in the context of how it developed and why.

For the most part I have let the story unwind itself, drawing on my own involvement only to fill in background or to provide continuity. Impressions conveyed of people or events usually accord with the feelings of the time, but are not intended as other than a personal assessment. For "ship buffs" I have included in the appendix an all-time roster of the Union ships together with a record of the over one hundred master mariners who commanded them.

The writing of this book has been a labour of love and has fulfilled a sense of duty to many colleagues.

ACKNOWLEDGEMENTS

I wish to express my thanks to the Misses Constance and Mary Darling for access to the private papers of their father, Henry Darling, and also to Frank R. Barnsley, son of John Barnsley, for special information concerning the Boscowitz Company.

For their personal narratives of certain episodes I am much indebted to the late Captain Andrew Johnstone and to Captains John Park, John Muir, Harry Roach, Angus McNeill, Thomas Lucas, Ray Perry and the veteran Chief Engineer Fred E. Smith; and, for his earlier notes, to the late Captain W. L. Yates, I further acknowledge the help of Captains William McCombe, John R. Browne and Dean F. Eaton, as well as the advice of former Union shore colleagues, including Harold N. Crompton, Edwin G. Enwright, Alan P. Thomas and Stuart W. Jenkins.

For the background of several early incidents I have referred to Jessie M. Van der Berg's history, which the Company commissioned privately in 1942. In the trading sequence I have consulted Lewis & Dryden's *Marine History of the Pacific Northwest* and the 1790 journal of John Meares and Hudson's Bay records, in addition to making a search of British Admiralty documents.

My appreciation goes to the Vancouver Maritime Museum whose facilities were so generously made available to me, and especially to Mr. Leonard McCann, assistant curator, for his invaluable help in research; also to the Northwest History section of the Vancouver Public Library and the Vancouver City Archives for permitting examination of newspapers and documents; and to the recently retired provincial archivist, Mr. Willard E. Ireland, and my old friend, Mr. Lloyd Stadum of the Puget Sound Maritime Historical Society of Seattle, for reference to their records.

I am also indebted to early-day Vancouver newspapers and the later columns of the Vancouver *Province*, whose Norman Hacking is himself a maritime historian; and the Vancouver *Sun*, whose marine editor, the late Charles Defieux, had looked forward to the completion of this project.

I am grateful to the Canada Council (Canadian Horizons Programme) for a secretarial grant to assist in the research and final preparation for publication.

It is difficult to convey the force of history without visual aids. Fortunately, the life of the Union Steamship Company encompassed an era of growing interest in photography. Without exception, the Company's basic fleet has been recorded on film, though some of the photographs have been exceedingly difficult to track down.

I am especially indebted to Mrs. J. Crookall for the use of a number of historic photographs from the collection of the late James Crookall. Others who helped greatly in locating rare photographs were: Mrs. H. S. Putnam with the collection of her father, the late Robert M. Logan; Mrs. R. Wilson, Robert F. and Angus Wilson, widow and sons of the late Captain Robert Wilson; Mrs. E. M. Sheppard, widow of the late Captain Ernest Sheppard; Miss Elizabeth Walker of the Vancouver Public Library; Mr. Joe D. Williamson of Winslow, Washington, and Mr. Lloyd Stadum of Seattle.

Among organizations not already mentioned, who assisted in the photographic research, were: the World Ship Society of Western Canada; the Historic Photo Division of the Vancouver Public Library and the Provincial Archives in Victoria.

Many of the photographs selected for this book were preserved from special events during my Union Steamship service days. The Company's archives, photographic and general, are now a matter of public record and have been placed where they can be of aid to the interested researcher: in the Vancouver City Archives and the Vancouver Maritime Museum.

Finally, I owe much to my wife for her valued suggestions and proofreading of the text, and for her forbearance in being imposed upon by a would-be historian.

GERALD A. RUSHTON

June 1974   Vancouver, B.C.

CONTENTS

Remember those early days when a steam whistle was heard? Everybody immediately hollered "Steamboat" and rushed down the winding corduroy road called Center Street to the small wharf with its small warehouse to see the old *Camosun* tie up . . . . The pioneers held a sort of fondness for the Union Company perhaps for the reason it was the first steamship company to operate in the Province.

Resources (Prince Rupert), August 1921

CHAPTER 1

1778-1889

Exploration of the Pacific Northwest
Early Days on Burrard Inlet
The Founding of Vancouver's Pioneer Line

To Captain Cook, among other great and public
benefits we are indebted for the commerce
JOHN MEARES

The Union Steamship Company of British Columbia came into being on July 1, 1889, and was incorporated on November 16 of that year to meet increasingly urgent demands for safe "transportation by water to the outlying new settlements, sawmills, logging camps, stone quarries, agricultural and mining districts." It was the first steamship line to operate from a "home base" out of the new city of Vancouver. Its story is intimately linked with those of the pioneer settlements and the industrial growth of coastal British Columbia.

As an indication of the immense scope of their activities, more than fifty Union ships traversed the channels of the northwest coast — chiefly the inside waterways extending over four thousand miles of actual shore line — during a period of seventy years. This was longer than the Hudson's Bay Company's fleet was in existence. The unique role of the Union vessels cannot be seen in proper perspective without examining the experience and events of early B.C. coast trading, and the maritime background and circumstances that surrounded the launching of the Union Steamship Company's bold venture.

After the arrival of Captain James Cook in 1778 at Nootka, followed to the coast by "Trader" John Meares in 1786 and Captain Charles William Barkley in 1787, over a century elapsed before the port of Vancouver came to life on the forested and almost unpeopled shores of Burrard Inlet. It was the last and finest harbourage to be

1

commercially developed within radius of the Strait of Juan de Fuca, Puget Sound and the Strait of Georgia.

On September 20, 1788, a significant trading event took place when a small schooner, christened *North West America* and flying the British ensign, slid down the slip ways of ex-Navy Lieutenant Meares at Nootka. It was the first vessel built in British Columbia. In the unfamiliar task of launching a ship, someone forgot to put an anchor cable on board and the small vessel almost disappeared out of the harbour before she was taken in tow and anchored alongside two of Meares's ships — the *Felice* and the *Iphigenia*. Chiefs Maquinna and Callicum were there with a large number of Indians; so was an American, Captain Robert Gray, who was to discover the Columbia River entrance four years later. Gray was astonished to find that Meares had not only established a trading post, but also was in the process of launching a ship.

The complete vindication of British Columbia's first trader in the "Spanish Incident" by Prime Minister William Pitt in turn brought Captain George Vancouver of the Royal Navy in the yawl of the *Discovery* into Burrard Inlet on June 13, 1792, in his mission to take possession for Great Britain and chart the coast. After voyaging for seven years under the eye of Captain Cook, he was superbly qualified for this assignment. Although several Spanish galleons had visited these waters — Don José Maria Narvaez in the goleta *Santa Saturnina* sailed round English Bay and narrowly missed the entrance of the First Narrows in 1791 — the coast channels of British Columbia were first properly delineated from 1792 to 1794 by Captain Vancouver and his highly skilled officers.

Earlier navigational data, after Captain Cook's visit, had been gleaned from the trading voyages of Captain George Dixon in the *Queen Charlotte* and Nathaniel Portlock in the *King George*, as well as from John Meares's own book, *Voyages Made in the Years 1788 & 1789 . . . to the North West Coast of America*, published in 1790. A good deal more data were still locked away in the secret archives of the Spanish Navy in Madrid, including the record of a galleon wrecked in the location of the Hawaiian Islands, which had been forgotten since the sixteenth century. There is a strange intermingling of English and Spanish names on the charts. When navigating north, Captain Vancouver retained some of the names bestowed on capes and channels by Caamano and other Spanish captains; other places he named for well-known personages in the British naval and public life of his time.

It was not only the Spaniards who were serious contenders with the British and Americans in the race to capture the northwest coast trade. In 1806 — five years before the Americans established a fur trading base at Astoria with the vessel *Tonquin* sent from New York by John Jacob Astor — Alexander Baranoff, founder of St. Michael (old Sitka) and governor of the powerful Russian American Company, planned to occupy the mouth of the Columbia River. The scheme was abandoned, but published maps of his company's territory included everything from south of the Columbia River to the Bering Strait in the Russian zone. Baranoff actually obtained, in 1812, a supply base in Bodega Bay, north of San Francisco, where Sir Francis Drake once landed. This he established as a foothold in California where he could procure salt meat from the wild range cattle for the Alaska settlements. The last and most northerly of the twenty-one Spanish missions — the Mission San Francisco Solano near Sonoma — was founded in 1823 to hold the Russians in check. This trading post and fort remained under the Russian flag until as late as 1841, but American expansion in California and Oregon prevented the establishment of a permanent Russian settlement.

In the intervening century, many outside events spurred marine activities on the Columbia River, in Puget Sound and on the Fraser River, but they touched the shores of Burrard Inlet last, and then only lightly.

Following amalgamation of the North West Company and the Hudson's Bay Company, Fort Vancouver was founded in 1825 by Governor George Simpson to replace Fort George, at a strategic spot on the north bank of the Columbia at the head of deep-water navigation where Vancouver, Washington, now stands. The site chosen for the Hudson's Bay western depot was five miles east of where the Willamette joins the Columbia. It is not generally realized that this was the first home port for our coast ships, apart from Nootka, and that this up-river port remained in British possession until 1846.

In 1826, a group of carpenters, brought from the Orkney Islands, constructed the Hudson Bay schooner *Vancouver* — the first vessel ever built on the Columbia. An earlier vessel, the brig *William and Ann*, was tragically lost with all hands in February 1828 when she grounded on the river bar and broke up on Clatsop Spit. There exists a log of a trading voyage made by the *Vancouver* to the Fraser River in 1830 and a manifest of the motley cargo she discharged at Fort Langley: such diverse commodities as salt, nails, gunpowder, molasses, kettles, tobacco, rum, guns and shot, even a mill-wheel and oxen. She loaded up salmon in casks, shingles, beaver skins and furs. And when she

3

saluted the fort, a wad out of her cannon killed one of the fort men. Another vessel, the *Cadboro*, came out to Fort Vancouver from England, where she had been built in 1827. Like all the early vessels that plied the coast, she was well armed with six cannon and carried a crew of thirty-five men. Her trading trips between Nootka and the Columbia River were very profitable, and, of course, Cadboro Bay was named for this ship.

By the early 1830s the Hudson's Bay Company had founded a chain of defended posts at such Indian centres as Fort Simpson on the Nass River and Fort McLoughlin near Bella Bella. As many as fourteen thousand Indians once traded at Fort Simpson, a necessary defensive post against raids by the feared Haidas from the Queen Charlotte Islands. The trading company's famed 101-foot *Beaver*, built at Black-wall on the Thames was designed to take over some of the functions of the posts by making regular calls up the coast. Her launching on May 2, 1835, followed by her departure, with a farewell salute of guns, from Gravesend on August 27, 1835, for the mysterious Pacific coast, excited considerable interest in England. She had as an escort the Hudson's Bay bark *Columbia*, which maintained contact throughout the long voyage, sometimes exchanging victuals and medical supplies and even crew members. Under Captain D. Home, the *Beaver* safely reached Fort Vancouver on April 10, 1836 via the Sandwich (later Hawaiian) Islands. She was the first steamer to arrive in the Pacific northwest, although she made this voyage under canvas, rigged out as a sailing ship; her engines were in place but the paddlewheels were not attached. Little did anyone then dream that the steamer fitting out under the guns of Fort Vancouver would end her days fifty-two years later outside a port of the same name — a city yet to be founded — two hundred miles to the north of the Columbia River.

The *Beaver* regularly serviced all the trading posts from Fort Langley north for most of the next decade. The Hudson's Bay Company, with a fleet of six vessels, had leased from the Russian-American Company the trading rights in southeast Alaska, where they collected their rich fur cargoes. Each year the *Beaver* made at least one Alaska trip with a full load of goods to pay "the Russian rent."

However, in 1842, with American emigrant trains pouring into the valleys of the Columbia and Willamette, Chief Factor (later Sir James) Douglas prepared for the abandonment of Fort Vancouver, for navigational as well as political reasons. The Bay of Camosack, or Fort Camosun, on Vancouver Island was selected as the Hudson's Bay

4

Company's new headquarters, and was renamed Victoria in 1843. From a shipping standpoint no one can question their prudence in consolidating all their interests at Victoria, apart from the constant hazards of the Columbia River bar which was without the pilotage and buoyed channels of later days. Besides, the Hudson's Bay Company's trading volume on the Fraser River, where they had a fishing monopoly, loomed larger each year. Their coastal fleet was augmented in August 1853 by the steamship *Otter*, second only in fame to the *Beaver*, whose work she was designed to assist. She was 20 feet longer and was propelled by a set of twin direct-acting condensing engines, although she had three masts and was rigged with auxiliary sails.

The gold strike on the Fraser in the 1850s again altered the shipping picture and spelled the end of the "Bay fleet" monopoly when it became necessary to license American ships and every type of available vessel to carry the flood of gold-hungry immigrants. This marine boom, which started in 1857, reached its peak the following year. Portland and Seattle had been founded in the early 1850s, but most of the mining adventurers came by sea from San Francisco to Victoria — over thirteen thousand of them between April and June 1858. Some astonishing escapes were recorded during the "sea-trek" from California, as well as on the Fraser River. In July 1858, the *Commodore*, overloaded with cargo, had to turn back three days out from San Francisco in a sinking condition, with all 350 passengers bailing to keep her afloat. A ferry service connected many of the newcomers between Victoria and Queensborough (later New Westminster). The pioneering vessel on the river in 1858 was the 220-foot sidewheeler *Surprise*, owned by Wright Bros. and under command of Captain Thomas Huntington. She carried between five and six hundred prospectors on some thirty trips between Victoria and Hope. A similar type, the *Sea Bird*, under Captain Conner, had several mishaps, including grounding below Hope. Later she was destroyed by fire while en route from Victoria, but fortunately she carried only a few passengers and there was no loss of life. These events occurred only forty years after Simon Fraser first descended the river that bears his name.

Captain William Irving sold out his Columbia River interests and joined with Alexander Murray to build the first steamer at Victoria in 1858 — the stern-wheeler *Governor Douglas* and later a sister ship, the 145-foot *Colonel Moody*. New Westminster had now been named the sole port of entry for the new Province of British Columbia, and two new measures aided the early mariners: a pilotage service at Victoria

5

in 1865, and a lightship the following year at the mouth of the Fraser River.

There were thirteen canneries on the lower Fraser by 1882 and, with more settlers arriving, new canneries were established in Rivers Inlet and on the Skeena and Nass rivers. More American ships were employed in Puget Sound, too, following decline of the Columbia River traffic after 1883 when the Northern Pacific Railway came through to the coast.

Captain John Irving, who succeeded his father as the leading personality in the river trade, obtained additional ships, including the *Reliance* and the *Wilson G. Hunt*, to ferry between New Westminster and Victoria, and on Puget Sound. Irving's fleet and the Hudson's Bay fleets were amalgamated in 1883 to form the Canadian Pacific Navigation Company under Commodore Irving. The combined fleet of ten steamers, with the addition of the *Yosemite* several months later, was one of the largest on the Pacific Coast and entered into keen competition with the American flag vessels for the Puget Sound trade. In 1901, the Canadian Pacific Railway bought Irving's fleet for $350,000 and began operating their own B. C. coastal service under Captain J. W. Troup, who had been in charge of the Railway's "inland fleet" on the Kootenay Lakes.

As early as the 1850s, in the quiet backwaters of Burrard Inlet, a few settlers had made their homes on the south shore. Their numbers increased rapidly following construction in the early sixties of Moody's sawmill on the north shore, and Stamp's Mill, later called Hastings Mill, on the south side. A few deep-sea "sails" from Australia and China now entered Burrard Inlet to load lumber at the mill wharves, and this meant harbour work for tugs and movement across the inlet. Captain James Van Bramer, born in New York in 1832, started his steamboating on the Fraser River in 1866, and brought the small vessel *Sea Foam* from New Westminster around to Burrard Inlet. For two years she served as a ferry across the inlet to Moodyville before sinking in November 1868 alongside the Hastings Mill wharf after an explosion. Later, Van Bramer obtained a tiny craft called the *Chinaman*, so named because it "came from the Orient stowed in a sailing vessel." Then he constructed the *Lillie* for the cross-inlet ferry, installing the *Sea Foam*'s engines. In 1876 he launched the *Leonora*, wood-built at Victoria and named after his daughter. This steam-propeller tug was 57 feet in length with a narrow beam of 9 feet. One of her early masters for four years was Captain William Holmes.

With the growing ferry demands, Captain Van Bramer had the

wooden vessel *Senator* built at Moodyville by Henry Maloney in 1880. Named after Senator Hugh Nelson, one of the mill partners and a later lieutenant governor, she was 51 feet in length, with a breadth of 12 feet, and was a steam-propeller vessel with an enclosed cabin for twelve passengers, although many more rode outside at all seasons.

At this time, the mail was rowed from the end of the road at Hastings across the inlet to Moodyville and, before the *Senator* was built, to Gastown, as the first Vancouver settlement was called. One of the mail rowers was "Hans the Boatman," the Norwegian-born Hans Hansen, who worked for George Black's store and hotel. Hansen accomplished his rowing with the aid of an iron hook buckled onto his left arm, having lost a hand in an accident. He looked after the post office and accepted the mail at Port Moody from the first CPR train.

The trial run of the *Senator* on April 15, 1881 was quite an event in the small settlement life. It cost a ferry passenger 10 cents to cross the inlet while cattle were transported on deck for 50 cents a head and even wagons were towed behind on a scow when required.

It was this equipment — two tugs and attendant scows — that was bought in January 1886 by Captain Donald McPhaiden, a Scotsman who had sailed between Melbourne and Puget Sound for twenty-five years, to form the Burrard Inlet Towing Company. His associates in the venture were Alfred King, Captain Hugh Stalker and John Morton, the last named being one of the "Three Greenhorns," the original pre-emptors of Vancouver. With the influx of new settlers, Captain McPhaiden's idea was to branch out to meet the needs of both the inlet mills and the loggers working along the Gulf of Georgia. In early 1889 he acquired the *Skidegate*, 76 feet in length, 12-foot beam, to expand his towing business. A staunchly built tug, she was launched on April 7, 1879 in Victoria, as a cannery tender for use in the Queen Charlotte Islands.

The old Bodega Saloon and the Alexandra Hotel at the corner of Water and Carrall Streets in Vancouver were the favourite meeting places of the steamboat men, where prospects were discussed and yarns swapped. They talked about the growth in towing contracts as hand loggers steadily moved out to start falling operations at points accessible to salt water for over a hundred miles up coast on Lewis Channel and beyond Cape Mudge and Seymour Narrows along Johnstone Straits, where rich virgin timber often reached almost to the shoreline. Parties of settlers, coming mostly direct by sea to Victoria from San Francisco, or arriving on sailing ships after several months voyaging round Cape Horn, also began to push up-coast by way of any craft available, to take up land they had obtained or heard was available. Their means of transport was often of the crudest variety. Sometimes they were constrained to a passage of the narrower channels by rowboat or even by canoe, frequently with all their belongings towed by scow. The pioneers entering the territory between Campbell River and Rivers Inlet, a very sparsely settled region save for several Indian settlements, and largely unexplored beyond the main channels, were frequently forced to charter their own transportation. Vessels operating out of the ports of Seattle or Victoria — before any Vancouver existed — made scarcely any calls en route to Alaska or the Skeena and Nass River fishing grounds. Occasionally a government ship from Victoria helped, and even the old *Beaver*, which now had some passenger cabins installed, is recorded as having carried "several bands of settlers" to Valdez Island in 1887.

Even along Burrard Inlet, except for the Moodyville ferry and an outrageous little craft called *Union*, nicknamed "Sudden Jerk" because of its unpredictable engine, there was no passenger transportation in existence. There is a poem, written by Nora M. Duncan in 1936, entitled *The Heroine of Moodyville*, based on the true story of Mrs. John P. Patterson. On a stormy night in 1883 Mrs. Patterson, with an Indian boatman, paddled in a dugout canoe to bring aid to the sick wife of the Point Atkinson lightkeeper. Burrard Inlet's north shore was then described as "a rocky terrain of trail-less forest and unfordable streams."

Two events hastened the organization of the Union Steamship Company — the arrival of the first Canadian Pacific transcontinental train on May 23, 1887, and a visit to Vancouver the following year by John Darling, a director and retired general superintendent of the Union Steamship Company of New Zealand, in company with Mr. (later Sir William) Van Horne. Mr. Darling sensed the urgent need for staunch and handy vessels to provide safe and regular service in all weathers for passengers and supplies to the new communities springing up along the coast. At his instigation a local group purchased the equipment of the Burrard Inlet Towing Company as the nucleus of a Vancouver coast shipping line. Captain McPhaiden, who needed more capital, also agreed to participate in the new company.

Following two productive meetings in September 1889 at the law offices of Alfred St. George Hamersley, a provisional prospectus of the UNION STEAM SHIP COMPANY OF BRITISH COLUMBIA (LIMITED) was issued to cover the taking over "as going concern," as of July 1, 1889, of the assets of Burrard Inlet Towing. This included

8

the Moodyville Ferry Company with its three-year postal agreement for mail carriage. The equipment comprised the three steam tugs *Skidegate*, *Leonora* and *Senator*, and eight scows including a water lighter; the total value of the floating stock being assessed at $20,000. Initial capital was $100,000, in four thousand shares of $25 each. Provisional directors, with power to add to their number, were given as: C. D. Rand, A. St. G. Hamersley, W. D. Creighton, Captain W. H. Soule, Captain D. McPhaiden, F. Carter-Cotton, Captain William Webster (secretary pro tem), Chas. E. Hope and Ed Penzer. The prospectus noted the "rapidly increasing demand for water carriage of passengers and cargo," and "the trebling of Vancouver's population in two years." It asserted that there was not "a tug owned in Vancouver sufficiently powerful to tow a vessel of 500 tons to or from the sea." Port figures were adduced to show that the tonnage of foreign-going vessels had doubled in a year, and in the coastwise section that steam vessels outnumbered sailing ships ten to one.

The Vancouver *World* of September 4, 1889 commented on the prospectus: "It is not unlikely that Vancouver is to have a steamship company of its own, which in time may grow to important dimensions in keeping with the extent and importance of the city." Everyone was not so convinced of the profitability of the venture. A "disappointed one" wrote a letter to the *World* on October 7, citing the heavy expenses to be expected and quoting the cost of wages alone — $250 per month for five crew including the captain and engineer of the *Skidegate*; $185 for four on the *Leonora*; and $120 for the captain and engineer of the *Senator*.

And what did these prospects amount to, especially the early lumbering business, the growth of which was almost ecstatically described for the benefit of the Union Company's prospective shareholders?

A factual answer is conveniently provided in a Victoria *Daily Colonist* article on September 13, 1889, quoting in part from the *Columbian*:

Logging operations, always an important industry in British Columbia, have obtained greater proportions than before. . . . Some twenty large camps are hard at work along the coast between the Fraser River and Port Neville, sixty miles above Yuclataw rapids. The camps are widely separated. On Howe Sound there are two, namely McPherson's and Gillis. On Jervis Inlet, Mr. Dineen is working a camp for the Moodyville Sawmill Co., and at Grief Point is Wm.

McKay's large camp. Ireland and Leatherdale are getting out an immense number of logs on Lewis Channel. Some nine miles above Yuclataw rapids is situated the Hastings Sawmills' Camp and store. This is the most important establishment on the coast, it being a point of supply for all the company's camps, timber cruisers and also for the numerous hand-loggers working in the neighbourhood. Seven miles from the last named camp is Mathieson & Gillespie's camp, where a very large cut has been made during the last four months. Taylor Bros. camp is in the same vicinity, and hand loggers are working in every bay between the rapids and Port Neville. On Vancouver Island, King & Casey's establishment near Campbell River is getting an immense cut this season, and ten miles above Angus McCallums' is Sayward's camp. Last year (1888) the cut of logs was estimated at 100 million feet. . . . The connection with these camps is placed at 600 (men) which, with the hand-loggers will probably make a grand total of 700 men who are cutting logs for the various lumber manufacturing companies.

At this time, eight or ten "sail" were often tied up discharging their cargoes and loading lumber at the Hastings Mill wharf, and John Hendry had become president and general manager of the new B. C. Mills, Timber and Trading Company, which in 1889 combined the Hastings and Royal City Mills.

A general meeting of the first shareholders of the Union Company was held on November 16, 1889 when the following new provisional directors, superceding the earlier slate, were appointed: C. D. Rand (real estate agent), Captain D. McPhaiden (manager, Burrard Inlet Ferry Company), Captain H. Stalker, Captain W. Webster, James Orr, M.P.P., D. Cartmel (retired fleet engineer R.N.), A. St. G. Hamersley (barrister), W. D. Creighton (merchant), F. Carter-Cotton (president, San Juan Lime Co. Ltd.), J. D. Townley, Page Ponsford (merchant) and E. Penzer (coal merchant). It was resolved that the Company be registered with a capital of $500,000, in shares of $5. In the final prospectus issued afterwards, the European agent was listed as E. G. Buchanan, Leith, Scotland, and W. Cargill (accountant) named as the secretary pro tem. After estimating "there are at present between two and three thousand people employed in logging, mining and various pursuits . . . to the north of Vancouver," this new prospectus concluded significantly: "The tourist travel, which is now very considerable, must rapidly increase. The want of a steamer adapted for this purpose, and excursions amongst the grand scenery of the North, is felt during the summer months."

At the next general shareholders' meeting on February 18, 1890, seven permanent directors were elected: A. St. G. Hamersley (chairman), with Captain William Webster, Captain D. McPhaiden, I. Oppenheimer, W. F. Salsbury, E. E. Rand and I. Wolffson. The Company's first chairman, a former London barrister of the Middle Temple, was regarded as a man of sound business judgment. A member of a well-known Oxfordshire family, Mr. Hamersley had captained England's rugby team and had much to do with the introduction of the game to New Zealand, where he spent eleven years before settling in Vancouver. An old register of the Sunnyside Hotel served as the Union's first minute book.

John Darling was empowered to try to raise additional funds in Great Britain to supplement the local subscription, and to arrange for the ordering and laying down of suitable ships for the British Columbia coastal trade. He was responsible for the well-known red and black funnels being chosen for the Union fleet — the colours of his New Zealand company's vessels.

Captain Webster, who had been appointed managing director, left for Great Britain in October 1889. He had been instructed to arrange the purchase, at a maximum cost of £8,000 (approximately $39,000). of a suitable steamer wherever one could be obtained to go into immediate service. On November 8, 1889, the Vancouver *World* reported that Mr. Hamersley had received a cable from Captain Webster stating that the remaining unsold Company's stock had been subscribed for in Glasgow.

Vancouver city's newspapers were preoccupied with covering the visit of Governor General (Lord) Stanley in late October 1889, so that only limited interest was shown locally in coastal developments. It says much for the foresight of the founders that their plans for the Union Steamship Company were made at a time when anywhere beyond Cape Mudge and Seymour Narrows was considered the North, and communication to the interior was limited to only two sailings a week up the Fraser River from New Westminster to Chilliwack.

In contrast, twenty new steamers had entered service in 1889 at Seattle, Tacoma and other Puget Sound ports. On July 12, the Pacific Navigation Company launched the sternwheeler *State of Washington* at Tacoma for the Seattle-Bellingham Bay route. The Puget Sound and Alaska Steamship Company started up on September 17 with the fine steamers *City of Kingston* and *City of Seattle* so that while the seaways and fjords of British Columbia's northern coast remained relatively silent and unexplored, the whole area 150 miles south of Burrard Inlet was humming with life and water traffic. More than two thousand passengers were being ferried daily between various Puget Sound ports in 1889. Over four hundred lumber cargoes and grain ships were loaded that year at various Puget Sound mill docks, including Port Gamble, Port Ludlow, Port Blakely, Gig Harbour and Tacoma.

Marine activity in British Columbia still hinged around Victoria and, to a lesser degree, the Fraser. In December 1888, Commander John Irving of the Canadian Pacific Navigation Company had welcomed to Victoria the ill-fated *Islander*, a splendid 240-foot twin screw steamer, built at Glasgow for over $200,000, the finest passenger vessel of her day in the Northwest. Her chief officer was Captain John T. Walbran, later to become distinguished for his compilation of British Columbia coast names. The *Islander* commenced service in 1889 across to Vancouver and to Alaska. Irving's line also scheduled two sailings a month from Victoria to Port Simpson via intermediate ports, and would call at the Queen Charlotte Islands "if inducements offered." The 120-foot *Barbara Boscowitz* was running regularly during the season out of Victoria to the northern canneries; and, although the Skeena salmon run was not as heavy as had been expected for 1889, a big run on Rivers Inlet was reported in the Victoria *Colonist* of July 19. Shotbolt and Draney's cannery had put up 3,500 cases of salmon, with enough fish on hand for another 1,000.

With their new Empress ships still under construction at Barrow-in-Furness, the Canadian Pacific had brought on charter several old Cunard liners — the *Abyssinia, Parthia* and *Batavia* — to connect with their new rail terminus at Vancouver and to ply their Orient route. They had also been awarded the Trans-Pacific mail subsidy by the British government. It was April 28, 1891, that the stately *Empress of India*, first of the three original "white Empresses," steamed past an excited knot of spectators in Stanley Park and entered Burrard Inlet with her load of round-the-world tourists.

Such was the marine backdrop when the Union Steamship Company was founded to connect the B. C. coast with the new Port of Vancouver.

On the night of July 26, 1888, the old *Beaver*, outward-bound from Vancouver under Captain George Marchant, was swung by a strong current onto a rock off Stanley Park's Prospect Point. During the next four years she slowly disintegrated until she was dislodged by the backwash of the sidewheeler *Yosemite* and sank. The *Beaver*'s work was done; the Union Steamship Company's was just beginning. Together, their service to the coast spanned 123 years from 1836 to 1959 with only one year intervening.

CHAPTER 2

1890-1896

The Building of a Fleet
The Coquitlam Incident and the Cutch Affair
Early Logging Service of the Comox

> The knowledge we have now obtained of the coast
> of America and of the periodical winds and seasons
> gives us an advantage over all our competitors.
> JOHN MEARES (1790)

The vessel secured in England as a stopgap by Captain Webster was the *Cutch*, built to order in 1884 by J. Bremner & Co. at Hull as a pleasure craft for the Maharaja of Cutch, one of the princely Indian states of Gujerat. This iron-screw yacht (as it was technically described) of 324 gross tons was 180 feet in length with 20-foot beam. The Rajah died soon after taking delivery and the vessel came into the hands of a group of wealthy native East Indian merchants who ran her to the Gulf of Cutch in the Indian coastal trade for twelve months. She was then purchased and used by the German government in the East African trade before being laid up at Bombay and listed for sale in London. Captain Webster travelled to India to take delivery from Hajeebhoy Lalljee and sailed from Bombay on March 23, 1890. It was an odyssey of over ten thousand miles from the Malibar coast via Singapore, where he stopped for fifteen days and then called at Nagasaki and Yokohama, before sailing for Vancouver on May 14.

Captain Webster brought the *Cutch* safely via Victoria into English Bay at 10:30 a.m. on June 2, but as no arrangements had been made for customs' entry, it was 6 a.m., June 3 before she finally came alongside the Union wharf. According to the *News-Advertiser* of June 4, "All day yesterday crowds flocked to the wharf to inspect and admire her."

The *Cutch* was described as a "taut, smart, handsome vessel,

13

having a resemblance to the *Danube* [one of Captain Irving's Pacific Navigation vessels]." Having been designed as a cruising yacht, she indeed had graceful lines, with an enclosed passenger lounge amidships, and two rakish funnels. Her aft cabins were "handsomely furnished and well ventilated, having been built for tropical climates." She was licensed for 150 passengers on the B. C. coast, and had space for over 150 tons of general cargo in two capacious 'tween-deck holds. Her compound condensing engines carried a guarantee of 14 knots, but she was generally operated at around 13 knots.

After refitting following her long voyage, the *Cutch* was intended to be the first Union vessel to serve the new up-coast settlements. As it turned out, her starting assignment was to fill a contract made with the Canadian Pacific Railway Company to meet the arrival of their Pacific Express daily, except Saturdays, and take passengers, mail and cargo across to Nanaimo, connecting with the Esquimalt & Nanaimo Railway departure for Victoria. It was advertised that "On and after July 3, 1890 the *S. S. Cutch* will leave U. S. S. Co.'s wharf at 2 p.m. and the CPR wharf at 2:30 p.m. (or after arrival of train) daily for Nanaimo. Returning from Nanaimo to Vancouver daily at 7 a.m. Single Fare $2.00. Return Fare $3.50." Many Orient-bound passengers crossed the Gulf of Georgia in this manner aboard the "fast and powerful *Cutch*" before the Empresses made Vancouver a regular port of call. Her first master was Captain Peter Johnson, of Swedish birth, who had sailed round the Horn to Vancouver in 1882 to become a skipper of the company's tugs. Before the *Cutch* arrived, the CPR brought the steamer *Robert Dunsmuir* around from New Westminster and chartered her under Captain Rodgers to carry rail passengers to and from Nanaimo.

On Monday, July 7, 1890, the *Cutch* made a special trip to Nanaimo at 10:30 a.m. when the Union hosted a party of over fifty city notables and friends to inaugurate the new service. Guests included Aldermen Fox and McLeod; D. E. Brown and W. Downie, of the Canadian Pacific Railway; Board of Trade representatives and merchants, as well as stockholders and company officials. The *News-Advertiser* reported: "*Cutch* showed herself a most comfortable vessel, while the fact she is able to make the passage in three hours or under places the communication between the two cities in a more favourable condition than has been the case before . . . The majority of those on board had never visited Nanaimo before, and they were surprised at the fine site the place occupies, possessing as it does every qualification necessary for an important seaport."

The Nanaimo city band struck up a lively air as the vessel

approached at 1:30 p.m., and later played selections on the deck of the *Cutch* during the official luncheon. Mayor John Hilbert and members of Nanaimo's city council welcomed the ship and joined the visitors for lunch presided over by the Union chairman, A. St. G. Hamersley. Mr. Hamersley asked for generous support of the new service, and D. E. Brown observed that the ". . . Canadian Pacific Railway had watched with interest the inception of the Union Steamship Company and the Railway Company would be ready to do what it could to assist it." It was more than ten years later before the CPR had coastal vessels of its own in service.

That summer, publicity was given to a Union proposal, which they subsequently dropped, for a city subsidy of $250 a month towards maintaining the *Cutch* in Vancouver-Nanaimo service. The Vancouver *World* on August 9 was friendly but cautious:

> We approve of all enterprises that are calculated to build up the trade of this city . . . The desirability of running such a steamer as the *Cutch* to Nanaimo is unquestioned, and our citizens must see to it that she remains on that route . . . We are sure every good citizen would take stock in the concern rather than see it fail, and so far as the *World* is concerned it will always be ready to give its mite. Instead of a subsidy by-law we would ask the people, not the city, to take stock in the company . . . and so continue in operation the pioneer of a daily line of steamships, which we hope to see yet bringing to Vancouver such a volume of trade as will indeed make it the commercial metropolis of British Columbia.

The public encouragement evidently did more good than any subsidy.

On April 18, 1890, in preparation for the new fleet, and six weeks before the arrival of the *Cutch*, the directors purchased the City Wharf at the foot of Vancouver's Carrall Street for $10,000. The approach was largely mud flats, only partly filled, on the north side of the railway tracks. It was assumed at the time that the purchase brought full ownership, as "a parcel of the township" area of Vancouver, but subsequently the Company was drawn into litigation with the Canadian Pacific Railway, who claimed foreshore rights under the terms of their original grant from the Dominion government. The drawn-out controversy was eventually resolved in favour of the CPR who retained ownership with their right of way and access, while the Union company got in effect a permanent lease of its wharf premises. Despite this compromise there remained for years a feeling that the Union had been "robbed of its birthright" and had forfeited some of its independence. After all, one cannot be too obdurate about rates with a competitive landlord parked on one's doorstep!

On December 3, 1890, a meeting of the Union Company's English shareholders was held in London. Reporting it on December 30, the Vancouver *World* said: "There was a considerable attendance, Mr. John Darling occupying the chair. Captain Webster of this city, managing director, was present and detailed the work and progress of the Company, with which the shareholders expressed themselves as highly pleased." An encouraging report from the Vancouver chairman stated that the Company was paying a dividend for the first half-year of 6 per cent per annum, and a further dividend would be paid for the second half. Mr. Hamersley said that the Company had a current arrangement to carry mails and passengers for the CPR with an agreement almost reached with the new line of steamers between Vancouver, Japan and China. "Vancouver," he added, "had experienced a wonderful development and the work connected with the canneries and lumber trades would tax the carrying powers of the Company to the utmost." John Darling said that, with the extra capital raised in Glasgow, Edinburgh and London to build three steel ships, construction was already underway for quick delivery, two of the steamers being of 300 tons each. "These three vessels," he announced, "were the forerunners of several of a similar type for employment between Vancouver and the adjacent ports in British Columbia."

Under a pre-fab plan with distinct modern overtones, John Darling arranged for the three steel hulls to be fabricated in sections, convenient for shipment to Vancouver by J. McArthur & Co. of Glasgow. The engines, with all the latest improvements, were to be supplied by Bow McLachlan & Co. of Paisley — a company experienced in constructing light craft and small coasters.

While the engines and components were being built in Scotland, Captain Webster was making the best use he could out of the small tugs, as well as the *Cutch*, to develop business during the waiting period. He also had two smaller vessels on charter from the Union wharf — the *Mystery* and another tug with the fearsome name of *Dreadnought*. The latter is recorded as having brought down a boom of logs from Howe Sound to repair the CPR wharf. Then the Company had the *Skidegate* entirely rebuilt with extended passenger accommodations, and new Bow McLachlan engines and boilers, installed by D. Doyorouk, former engineer of the *Senator* ferry. "A party of ladies and gentlemen" was invited to make a trial run in the re-built *Skidegate* on Saturday, April 18, 1891, over the measured mile, where she exceeded 11 knots. The *News-Advertiser* commented that "the additional accommodation made was tastefully decorated under the supervision of Captain McPhaiden."

16

The *Skidegate* then re-entered service on April 21 under Captain Holmes Newcombe, and on two occasions actually relieved the *Cutch* on the Vancouver-Nanaimo run while that vessel was busy conveying 300 tons of railway rails for the new Vancouver Coal Company at Nanaimo. The *Skidegate* was indeed a busy little ship; on another day she sailed from Union wharf with freight for the logging camp at Point Gray (the spelling used in the advertisements of the day).

Contrary to the general belief that the Union Steamship Company came "later in the day" to serve Howe Sound, it provided the first scheduled service to Squamish River nearly ten years before Captain Cates's vessels started in the area. On July 5, 1891, the Vancouver *News-Advertiser* reported: "Another progressive step has been taken by the Union S. S. Company. This enterprising Company has decided to enter into the Howe Sound trade and for the present *S. S. Skidegate* will be put on this route." Commencing July 12, *Skidegate* began an advertised service "To Howe Sound and Squamish River, leaving on Mondays, Wednesdays and Fridays at 8 a.m. for all points on Howe Sound (Squamish River on Mondays only). Cargo received at Company's wharf must be paid for in advance!" It was intimated that the *Skidegate*, which continued through the year, would be replaced by one of the new vessels building at Glasgow.

On many summer Saturdays after her arrival, the *Cutch* was booked to take hundreds of the city's early residents on picnics to nearby sandy beaches that had float landings. So it was that the Union developed an appetite for the excursion business. This was a rare treat for Vancouver's early pioneers and their families. One of them, George H. Fry, recalled how, before the arrival of the *Cutch*, he had rowed a 14-foot boat on many occasions to Bowen Island to fish in Honeymoon Lake and hunt grouse and deer. On August 16, 1890, the *Cutch* was chartered for the CPR employees' picnic to Victoria. The notice cautioned: "No person will be allowed on board without a ticket. The *Cutch* leaves at 6 a.m. sharp and no one will be waited for!"

In the following year, the *Cutch*, filled on most days to capacity with passengers and many train-car loads of freight for Nanaimo, still found time to handle some interesting excursions. On Saturday, July 18, 1891, she made the first recorded Union excursion to Pender Harbour with 250 passengers. The notice read: "*Cutch* to Pender Harbour off Jervis Inlet — that little bay is noted for its scenery. While on the way the vessel will pass Bowen Island, Howe Sound, Sechelt Indian Village, Trail Bay, Welcome Pass, Texada Island and other places of interest." The following day the *News-Advertiser* editorialized:

"Scarcely any place could be more naturally adapted for holidaying than this beautiful water which has the distinction of being the first land-locked harbour on the mainland north of Vancouver, deep enough for ocean vessels." Lunch was taken on the Point where the party landed and then "the visitors dispersed to explore the different areas of the harbour, to visit the pretty lake at the eastward of the landing, to fish, bathe and enjoy themselves as their inclinations lead." Mrs. Kingcombe was the first lady to visit the lake, and Mr. A. E. Brown, owner of the property, named it Kingcombe Lake. The party left Pender Harbour at 7 p.m., arriving back at 11:45 p.m.

On Saturday, July 4, the *Cutch* left the U. S. S. wharf at 8:30 a.m. with the Odd Fellows' picnic for Ladner's Landing. The New Westminster Odd Fellows came down the Fraser aboard the *Delaware* to meet and join with the Vancouver group.

Then, on August 1, 1891, the *Cutch* made the first Union excursion to the Squamish Valley under the auspices of the Women's Hospital Society. The proceeds were to assist in the building of a new hospital. The notice referred to the "ridiculously low fare of $1.50, whereas the usual fare on boats that carry passengers is $4.00."

It's a far cry from excursions to Squamish to trans-Pacific voyages to Australia, but in 1891 the Union sold passage to Australia on a four-master. On Tuesday, July 21, the Company's advertisement announced:

UNION S.S. CO., B.C.
SAILING TO AUSTRALIA, MELBOURNE DIRECT
(A.I.) **LEADING WIND**, 1208 TONS, CAPT. S. R. SAVORY
WILL SAIL ABOUT AUGUST 1ST
First Class Accommodation for Passengers

Vancouver's steamship line was a going concern in those pioneer days.

The waiting days were over for the young Company as the sectional hulls and engines of the new steamers were finally completed and stowed in the hold of the steamer *Grandholm* at Glasgow; after calling at Liverpool for additional cargo, she sailed under Captain Masson on May 4, 1891, for Vancouver. The *Grandholm*, built in 1884 by Hall, Russell & Co. at Aberdeen, was an iron vessel, classed 100 A1, of 1,361 gross tons, and, although smaller than expected – 243 feet in length by 32-foot breadth and 14-feet, 4-inches depth – she could carry up to 2,000 tons deadweight. On this voyage the hull sections of the three Union ships with their engines, boilers and auxiliaries filled most of the cargo space; there were only four passengers, one of them a nephew of Captain Webster, the Union manager. The trip was without incident after the *Grandholm* weathered a storm in the South Atlantic, and she had a good passage through the Strait of Magellan. Captain Masson himself brought the ship directly into Vancouver Harbour between 7 and 8 a.m. on August 13, 1891, to end the eighty-three day voyage from Liverpool. It was August 19 before all the steamer sections and the last two boilers were unloaded by special tackle rigged up for the purpose on the Union wharf.

Although the Union directors had been preparing for the arrival of the knocked-down ships since the early summer, it was not until two days before the *Grandholm* arrived that a site was obtained on Coal Harbour, close by Stanley Park, for shipways to be set up. Up to this time there was no shipyard in Burrard Inlet, and these historic vessels were assembled in an area where only sailing ships were careened or where Indians had fashioned their dug-out canoes. On August 12, the *News-Advertiser* reported:

> Yesterday, Captain Webster, the manager of the Union Steamship Company closed the negotiations for the lease of some land to be used as a shipbuilding yard. . . . Considerable difficulty has been experienced in getting a suitable site but he has selected some land on Coal Harbour, on the east side of the floating dock. The land has about 300 feet of water frontage. A number of men are employed in clearing the land, and under the direction of Mr. H. Darling, the Company's Engineer, blocks will be put down on which to lay the keels of the vessels. A Blacksmith's shop will be erected and several other preparations made, so that everything will be in readiness when the *S. S. Grandholm* arrives.

There were further problems to settle. The site chosen for the shipyard had been leased from the Canadian Pacific and there were a number of private homes in the area. Three days later the railway company made it known that "several residents had complained" about the anticipated noise of riveting and hammering that would emanate from the shipyard, and the CPR wanted to reconsider the matter. Captain Webster succeeded in persuading them to let the project go forward, but called a directors' meeting to consider the matter further as there was word of a petition being circulated. The directors decided to go ahead, "as the daily work would not start before 7 a.m., and by that time people ought to be out of bed." It was an important decision, and a fortunate one for Vancouver, as Captain Webster said that over one hundred men had applied for work and it would mean $40,000 in wages alone for the city. Victoria had been pressing strongly for the work to be done there and the directors had received a much lower quotation from a Victoria shipbuilder; so much so that, if the protests had continued, they were prepared to send the *Grandholm* there to be unloaded. The Union, however, wanted to support local industry and won out with the site; as a result an operation unique in the history of Vancouver's waterfront proceeded according to plan.

The project, which became one of the local sensations of the day, was under the personal supervision of Henry Darling, son of John Darling, who came out from Glasgow during the summer specifically for this purpose. Born at Port Chalmers, New Zealand, in 1863, Henry Darling was educated in England and served his engineering apprenticeship in London. Afterwards he sailed in ships of the British India Steam Navigation Company before being appointed assistant superintendent of the Union Steamship Company of New Zealand. One of his principal shipwrights at the little Coal Harbour slipways was Andrew Wallace, who started the Wallace Shipyard at False Creek in 1894. Henry Darling told me that Andy Wallace had wanted him as a partner in setting up his own shipyard. Other key helpers were James Frith, who later became chief engineer of the Union Company, and Jimmy Bogart, his chief carpenter, who continued to work for fifty-two years in the Company's wharf machine shop until his death in 1942.

Three launchings within six months of the first steel ships being built on the Pacific coast north of San Francisco made big news in Vancouver's *News-Advertiser*. The keel of the *Comox* had been laid on August 26, 1891, and hammers clanged incessantly at the busy little shipyard, but the rainy fall in Vancouver delayed the work schedule by several weeks. At last, on the fine Saturday afternoon of October 24, the daughter of CPR General Superintendent H. Abbott, christened the *Comox* in traditional style, as the vessel slid into Burrard Inlet to the loud toots of the whistles of the *Skidegate* and *Leonora*. "I feel very much honoured," Miss Beatrice Abbott said, "at being asked to christen the first steel ship ever built in British Columbia."

The *News-Advertiser* report on October 25 of the launching noted: "Among shareholders present . . . Mr. A. St. G. Hamersley, President of the Company, Messrs. I. Oppenheimer, B. T. Rogers, R. G. Tatlow, W. Cargill, T. Freeman, G. Fuller and Captains McPhaiden and Soule," and commented: "The Union S. S. Company deserve much credit for being pioneers in this industry and have done a great deal of good to Vancouver." Captain William H. Soule, who was closely associated with the Company, had sailed to most quarters of the globe before settling in Vancouver. Since 1871 he had loaded ships around Burrard Inlet and was now manager of the Hastings Mill Stevedoring Company.

With accommodation for two hundred passengers and with a top speed of about 12 knots, the *Comox* originally was planned to go into the Moodyville Ferry service, but instead served as a pioneer trading vessel to the logging camps. She was the smallest of the three vessels, being only 101 feet in length, with a breadth of 18 feet and moulded depth of 6 feet. The *Comox* was staunchly constructed with three watertight bulkheads, and was powered with a pair of single-screw condensing engines. Compactly designed, her accommodations included a dining and social hall, a comfortable smoking room, and eight two-berth handsomely fitted cabins on the upper deck abaft the pilot house. She could handle up to 150 tons cargo when not carrying excursion passengers by making use of the main deck space.

Seven weeks later on the morning of December 19, the *Comox*, in command of Captain Holmes Newcombe, underwent her official trials and on leaving the harbour, received a welcoming toot from the incoming *Cutch*. The new vessel exceeded 12 knots on her test and "behaved splendidly" off Howe Sound in rough seas.

Next to be launched was the *Capilano*, at 10 a.m. on Saturday, December 5, 1891. To quote the *News-Advertiser* of December 6: "As the vessel glided smoothly off the ways, she was christened in a graceful manner by little Miss Flora Oppenheimer, daughter of Mayor D. Oppenheimer. After the launch those present adjourned to one of the workshops where light refreshments were provided." Before inspecting the progress of work on the *Coquitlam*, on the ways alongside, the mayor congratulated the Union Company and dwelt on the start of shipbuilding in Vancouver which "was bound to become one of the chief industries of the future."

Capilano is an Indian family name, the English version of Ky-Ap-Lan-Huh or great chief; Chief Capilano along with many war canoes escorted Captain Vancouver when the explorer first entered Burrard Inlet. *S. S. Capilano*, 120 feet in length with 22-foot beam, was much larger than the *Comox*, grossing 231 tons, compared with the latter's 101 gross tonnage. Built of mild steel throughout, and intended principally for freight carriage, the *Capilano* was classed A1 at Lloyds for twenty years. She was fitted with water ballast tanks and guaranteed by the builder to carry 350 tons of deadweight cargo. She also had a licence and deck space to berth twenty-five passengers. Powerfully engined, with large steel boilers for economic consumption, her estimated speed was 8 to 9 knots fully loaded, and 10 knots travelling light. After the launch, she was taken in tow by the little *Senator* to be completed for service.

The *Capilano* ran her trials successfully in Burrard Inlet on February 4, 1892, and left immediately for Victoria to fetch new boilers for the Moodyville Mill. Her next job was carrying coal from Nanaimo, but her subsequent history was more colourful and full of excitement.

Before the *Coquitlam* was ready, the *Capilano*, which could handle lifts up to 6 tons, had a nasty accident on March 31, 1892 while unloading sandstone brought from Nanaimo for the new Vancouver post office building. Through carelessness, a guy slipped when a 5-ton stone was being hoisted by her derrick onto a wharf wagon, crashing the stone overboard together with her mast and all the rigging. Fortunately, there were no injuries, and a new mast, ready for the *Coquitlam*, was available as a replacement.

Finally the last of the trio, *Coquitlam*, was launched in April 1892, and named by the small daughter of Union Chairman A. St. G. Hamersley. The largest vessel to be launched from the pioneer Coal Harbour shipyard, she was 127 feet in length, with 22-foot beam, 256 gross tons, and a freight capacity of 350 tons including bunkers. Her crew including officers numbered fifteen, and she was a very handy and economical vessel to operate on a coal consumption of thirty miles to the ton.

Henry Darling was appointed superintendent engineer of the Company, and then for six months sailed as chief engineer in the *Cutch*. He was appointed manager in June 1894, but continued to exercise engineering responsibility for the fleet until 1901. The new fleet was now fully listed, and advertised daily with the note, "Small steamers and scows always available for excursion, towing and freighting business."

Within a month of completing her trials, the *Coquitlam* became the centre of an international incident which took thirty years to settle. It involved the young company in a heavy financial loss and upset several of its initial plans. It all had to do with seal hunting, which had been pursued by trading vessels in far northern waters since the early 1800s, and with the Americans who had become very jealous of their territorial rights since taking over Alaska in 1867.

In May 1892, the *Coquitlam* was chartered by the B. C. Sealers to carry supplies to their schooners in the Gulf of Alaska. She sailed from Victoria on June 9 under Captain E. E. McLellan. It was known to be a hazardous voyage as the United States was watching closely for any encroachment on their rights; Captain Milne in Victoria counselled "making all transfers on the high seas," In fact, Commander (later Admiral) Robley D. Evans, aboard the *U. S. Yorktown* and accompanied by a revenue fleet, had been tipped off by an agent and was already on the prowl for the *Coquitlam* which meantime had reached and supplied a Canadian fleet of sealers off McLeod's Bay, and had taken aboard their skins.

On June 22, the *U. S. Corwin* boarded the *Coquitlam* in Port Etches, Prince William Sound, where she had put in for repairs and to restow some shifted cargo. The Americans found a log entry recording that on June 19 off Cape Tonki, the *Coquitlam* had towed some schooners outside the three-mile limit to provision them and receive their sealskins. In Port Etches at the time was Captain A. K. St. Clair in the sealer *Ocean Belle*. Writing later about "old sealing days," he said that the only items taken off the *Coqutilam* before the American revenue cutter arrived were kegs of Jamaica rum: "We got one. While the U. S. officers were coming on board one side, we were taking one out from the window of the steward's room on the other."

A charge was laid that cargo had been illegally transferred – at or near the island of Afognak – in U. S. waters within the collection district of Alaska, as cannon shot was now twelve miles and jurisdiction was claimed for that distance from the coastline. The court at Sitka, where the *Coquitlam*, though still in charge of her own men, was directed by a prize crew, upheld the charge and ordered that the vessel be taken south to Port Townsend pending confiscation of the ship and cargo, including six thousand seal skins.

The arbitrary action of the United States in making the Bering Sea seizure promoted many telegrams between Victoria and Ottawa. On July 14, Prime Minister Sir John Caldwell Abbott said: ". . . the Governor General has transmitted to Lord Salisbury all the facts," which were then in the hands of the Imperial government. The *Coquitlam* was later ordered released on a stiff bond of $600,000, although the case continued in the courts for years with grave concern to the Union directors. Then, in 1897, the U. S. Court of Appeals reversed the decision, ruling that "the seizure was entirely without law" and the bond was returned. The Company claimed damages of $104,709, but it was not until December 1921 – twenty-nine years after the seizure – that Washington advised that "the claim would be paid in part" and settled for $48,000. The U. S. Commission exonerated the crew of the naval cutter but concluded that ". . . their interpretation of the regulations had been at fault." This was meagre compensation for the Union's loss in trade and costs, and for the incredible legal delay.

There is an illuminating postscript to this episode in Admiral

Evans's memoirs, quoted by the Victoria *Colonist* in 1908. "If I took her [the *Coquitlam*] at sea, the Department would disavow my act but the schooners would have to go back to Victoria for provisions." This startling admission shows his intention to seize our vessel by any means to put the Canadian sealers out of action. The subsequent enquiry was a "whitewash."

While ocean shipping between Australia, the Orient and the Pacific coast had doubled since 1887, Vancouver did not reap much direct benefit since the trans-pacific liners sailed on regular schedules only to San Francisco or Portland. The Union even discussed with the Dominion government the possibility of getting a subsidy for a monthly service to Honolulu which would connect with the Australian route to San Francisco.

Later on in 1891 the Union Company contracted with the Canadian Pacific Railway to act as a feeder in ferrying passengers and cargo between Vancouver and Portland, where the CPR Empress liners now made regular calls. Two vessels in turn were chartered: the *Tai Chow* until September 25; and then the *Grandholm*, which had remained on the Pacific Coast, carrying coal from Nanaimo to San Francisco until being engaged by Captain Webster to operate as a ferry to the Columbia River. The *Grandholm* was now advertised as making "Fortnightly trips between Vancouver and Portland via Victoria, Sound Ports and Astoria." The result was nearly disastrous to the Union's hopes. "Owing to competition between the C.P.R. Empress line and the Upton line across the Pacific," said the Company's annual report for 1891, "the freight carried by the chartered steamers between Portland and Vancouver has not come up to expectations." This put it mildly. The rivalry resulted in a heavy loss and an overdraft of $40,000 at the Bank of British Columbia. Captain Webster, who had personally made the arrangements, contended that Mr. Abbott of the Canadian Pacific had given assurance that under no circumstances would the Union Company be allowed to lose on the contract. However, the matter of "working expenses" was not spelled out in the agreement and a poor compromise had to be accepted.

In 1892 the directors again sent Captain William Webster to Great Britain to explain the serious loss to Mr. Buchanan, the Company's agent in Glasgow, and the English shareholders. Although Mr. Buchanan succeeded in getting a little more capital subscribed, the financial resources of the Company were strained to the limit by the unlucky *Coquitlam* and by the Portland Ferry gambits. Its small fleet was subjected to a bank mortgage of $32,000 and a second mortgage to

Dunsmuir & Sons to cover outstanding coal purchases for bunkering the ships. These reverses had one good result — they brought a quick end to the Company's outside ventures and enforced concentration on the local coast. The Klondike days ahead provided a "golden" exception to this rule. The directors decided at their meeting ". . . to work quietly for the next few years and take advantage of the present equipment and opportunities as they occur."

It was the little *Comox*, which sailed on the first logging camp run under Captain Charles Moody on May 2, 1892 with a large number of passengers and a heavy cargo, that provided new hope to offset the disappointments. Her weekly schedule from the Union wharf with passengers, mail and freight to the settlements was set for 11 a.m. on Mondays. It covered nearly forty calls on the round voyage of over four days along the mainland coast via Lewis Channel to Port Neville, a trip of about five hundred miles, allowing for the back-tracking between off channel ports.

From seven in the morning, at the bustling little dock, freight of every variety was steadily unloaded in the small Union shed from a succession of horse-drawn wagons and drays, and handled on boards or with hand trucks through the forward side-doors of the *Comox*. Freight included flats of groceries, sacks of feed and bales of hay, barrels of beer, pipe and household effects, oil drums, and crates of live poultry and pigs. The larger livestock had to be held back for a freighter. The sides of beef and perishables went on last. It was an animated scene when, just before sailing time with most of the passengers already embarked, the mail van arrived and the coast's most welcome item, some forty or fifty mail sacks, would be passed aboard by hand.

When this route was started the schedule was still very flexible. After calling at Gibsons Landing (now simply Gibsons) and Sechelt — whose settlers still got their mail at Welcome Pass post office — the vessel proceeded to Van Anda on Texada Island and then crossed the Strait of Georgia for a stop at Comox before returning to the mainland to tie up overnight alongside the wharf float at Lund. Charles Thulin had built a hotel at the site north of Powell River as well as a store. Mansons on Cortez Island, Read Island (once the site of an iron mine) and Heriot Bay were among the next morning's landings. This was mostly small ranching area and to reach the main lumbering scene, the *Comox* had to navigate a passage through the Euclataw (or Yucalta) Rapids on a favourable tide. These famous rapids lie between Stuart and Thurlow Islands off the mouth of Bute Inlet — and it was dead ahead of them northbound that Captain Vancouver, when exploring these waters, made his camp at a spot which bears the title on our charts of the "Old Village of Vancouver."

Early logging calls of the *Comox*, which continued her route into several uncharted inlets, included Shoal Bay, where Pete McDonald ran a small hotel and store, and stops "in stream" along Cardero Channel where hand-loggers rowed over from sites around Greene Point and Blind Channel. Finally she entered Johnstone Strait to complete her run with deliveries for several sizable camps. Except by special arrangement, only the main stops were made southbound.

Later, the *Comox* calls were divided between two sailings which left Vancouver on Mondays and Thursdays. By this time, in 1894, when Captain J. Cowper was skipper and Percy Chick was purser, her route had been changed and alternated to give fortnightly service through Seymour Narrows — many new logging camps having been located between Campbell River and Rock Bay — and through the "Hole in the Wall" channel to Okis Hollow. To say that the *Comox* service was greatly welcomed by the pioneer communities would be an understatement; to both settlers and loggers, the regularity of the calls bringing mail and weekly groceries, as well as providing safe transportation to and from the city, was the equivalent of a lifeline to the outside world. So it was that the *Comox* found the role that characterized the unique nature of the Union Steamships' operations for several generations to come. The financial success of this route, and the increasing volume of trade over the next three years, stiffened the resolve of the directors to concentrate on coastal shipping.

In October 1892, the Dominion government with some appreciation of the essential service being performed by the *Comox*, together with the northerly trading of the *Capilano*, granted an annual subsidy of $60,000 to the Union Company to carry mails to the north, including all the logging settlements. This in turn encouraged the Company to expand its routes to cater to the new communities. Although described as a postal subsidy, the contract was shrewdly worded to ensure the maintenance of a minimum frequency of calls during the winter and summer periods so that the Union ships were now officially linked to the coast communities. The *News-Advertiser* commented: "The establishment of a weekly service between the city and these settlements . . . has in a large measure induced many to locate in these areas."

For more than two years after the late summer of 1890, the *Cutch* had been maintaining an excellent schedule on the daily ferry run between Vancouver and Nanaimo, connecting with the CPR transcontinental trains. Increased business had developed as a flood of new immigrants and visitors crossed the continent, and the route was showing a profit. The course of the *Cutch*, however, was not to be a smooth one. She collided with the Esquimalt & Nanaimo Railway's steamer *Joan* on November 12, 1892, when both vessels were heading simultaneously for the south channel of Nanaimo harbour, striking the vessel amidships and seriously damaging her. The accident occurred after both ships had left Gordon's Wharf about the same time although it was later ruled that the *Joan* had cast off first. When the *Cutch*, after backing astern to starboard, endeavoured to pass her, the *Joan* — which had the right of way held to her course. Realizing too late that he was on a collision course, the master of the *Cutch* tried to go astern but rammed the other vessel.

Behind this incident was an intense rivalry between the *Cutch* and the new *City of Nanaimo*, which had recently started in direct competition on the Nanaimo-Vancouver run and was already capturing some of the local business. There was speculation, which happened to be correct, that the *Cutch* had been trying to beat the *Joan* to the harbour entrance to catch the *Nanaimo*, which had pulled out several minutes earlier from the other side of the wharf. The case for the *Cutch* was not helped by the fact that her master failed to stop after the accident but continued to chase the *Nanaimo*. Fortunately there was no loss of life or personal injury suffered on either vessel.

The case was something of a "cause célèbre" when it came up in the Exchequer Court in April 1893 before Chief Justice Sir Matthew Begbie and two naval assessors, Lieutenants Masters and Nugent. C. E. Pooley Q.C. acted for the plaintiffs (*S. S. Joan*) and E. V. Bodwell, assisted by Mr. Irving, for the Union Company. In his judgment delivered on April 28, the Chief Justice found ". . . the *Cutch* to be alone at fault," and awarded damages and costs against the Company. A writer for the Victoria *Colonist* on May 9, 1893 was not quite so sure that the *Joan* was entirely innocent, as her captain admitted that " 'a collision might have been avoided had he stopped the starboard engine'. . . . If every ship's captain governed himself . . . by a strict insistence upon his right of way, how many vessels might not have been run down?"

The celebrated Chief Justice Begbie made some pertinent observations in handing down his judgment. He referred to "the unaccountable sympathy that every man feels for the vessel in which he happens to be; to the suddenness and unforeseen nature . . . of all collisions, and of the erroneous views too often taken by masters of vessels of their own rights and of the rights of others." He pointed out that "the evidence taking eleven hours in two days refers . . . entirely to events which in fact from first to last [took] eight minutes of time. It is just possible the *Cutch* had no eyes for anything but her rival the *City of Nanaimo* just disappearing with a few minutes start." Then he added: "Although it was in evidence these vessels never race — that is forbidden by the Pilot Rules — yet it was ingenuously confessed that they never meet without seeing which of them can go faster."

The Chief Justice was objective "as to the very serious consequences of allowing several steamers to leave wharves, especially in narrow channels, at the same hour," and proposed that a fine be laid on any ship which left harbour within five minutes of another vessel. His analogy was a grim one:

> In time of war, when two belligerents are in a neutral harbour, they are never permitted to leave together. . . . In the present case the *Cutch* and *City of Nanaimo* are not in one sense belligerent. They do not fire red hot bullets or shells at each other, but they run the manifest risk of inflicting . . . quite as important damage and loss, both of property and life. Two steamers colliding . . . may settle their differences quite as substantially by going to the bottom with all their cargo and passengers as they could possibly manage it with the most improved projectiles or explosives.

By coincidence the *News-Advertiser* had editorialized on April 29, 1892, six months before the accident: "The rivalry between the crews on the *Cutch* and the *City of Nanaimo* is now very strong, and both vessels usually leave the wharf at the same time. The *City of Nanaimo* has had the advantage on the last two trips, but the *Cutch* is going to be beached and have her hull scraped, and then the crew say she will 'knock the spots' out of her rival." Perhaps the Chief Justice had read this.

Begbie's strictures were not lost and rivalries continued on the coast but in a friendlier and less dangerous manner. Over the next sixty-odd years, the Union and its shipmasters built up an enviable reputation for courtesy and restraint in the sealanes of British Columbia.

Nearly thirty years later when the Union Company bought Captain Cates's fleet, they got both the old *Joan* (the *Ballena*) and the *City of Nanaimo* (the *Bowena*).

While Mr. Hamersley was still Company chairman, Captain Webster, the manager, resigned in 1893 soon after his return to Vancouver, as the directors were not satisfied about the financial loss with the

Portland Ferry. Captain McPhaiden took over as acting manager, and he was succeeded very briefly in the same year by Walter F. Topping, former purser of the *Grandholm* who had been acting as secretary. This was but the prelude to the emergence of what might well be called the "Legg-Darling" administration, one of the happiest combinations of business acumen and technical skill ever to guide the Union Steamship Company's destiny.

With the election of Gordon Tyson Legg as chairman in 1893, and appointment of Henry Darling as manager the next year, the Company entered one of its most exciting periods. Mr. Legg, who joined the board in 1892, came from England in 1889 as agent for the United Trust and Edinburgh Land & Mortgage Company. Not a shipping man, but having a solid business background and an eye for "the main chance," as well as a quiet sense of humour, Gordon Legg successfully steered the Union fortunes through many shoals over the next eighteen years. He had become well known in the community, was fond of sailing and was a founder of the first Vancouver Yacht Club. Despite an outward austerity he was equally well-liked in the fleet and Union office. One of his secretaries, later accountant, James Crookall, who often accompanied him on his up-coast trips, told me of his uncanny ability to handle any situation that arose, whether appeasing an irate logging customer at a way port, or exhibiting a fine knowledge of expletives when counselling old Captain Patterson, the watchman, to have his dog painted white after he had tripped over it at the wharf one dark night.

It was hard going for a while to recover lost ground and keep the firm solvent. With another mortgage executed on the fleet to tide it over a stagnating lumber market, the Company struggled to bring in more revenue to supplement the *Comox* earnings. In the Nanaimo ferry service, the *Cutch* had fended off competition and was paying its way under the command of Captain Newcombe, but the freight markets were poor. In the search for new revenue the *Capilano* and *Coquitlam* were chartered in 1894 to the New England Fish Company and participated in the starting of British Columbia's halibut industry; the *Leonora* tug contracted to haul stone for paving Vancouver's city streets; the *Capilano* was kept going for a spell by transporting stone from Nelson Island quarries and elsewhere for the new Parliament Buildings in Victoria; even extra space in the Company's wharf shed was rented out temporarily to store hay, canned fish and other commodities.

It was now over two years since the *Comox* first opened up the

29

logging camp route and a Vancouver visitor, "W.F.G.," recorded his impressions of a trip in 1894 aboard the vessel cruising "the inlets, bays and rapids of British Columbia." The account was printed for the Company and conveys the atmosphere of those days far better than any business record. The writer was accompanying a friend who had to visit several lumber camps, after first being "assured that the boat, if not of the tonnage of a man of war, was roomy enough for taking exercise, that the meals though plain would be plentiful and well served, the berths clean and our fellow travellers, if destitute of collars and cuffs, perfectly *civil*. All this I found to be true, and the passengers were not only civil, but in some cases interesting."

I took passage on a radiant summer morning and the first breeze of Burrard Inlet soon inspired a feeling of buoyancy and vigour after spending several days in the railway cars.

Leaving Vancouver a lessening mass of business blocks and finally of scattered villas we were soon through the First Narrows . . . at the gateway on the southern side stands a stern and formidable mass of rock known as Beaver Point [now Prospect]. At its foot lie the few remaining traces of the famous little *Beaver*. We are now in the open of English Bay . . . on our North is Point Atkinson, where stands the lonely lighthouse that guides the modern mariner into one of the best harbours in the world. Just east is Skunk Cove where the pilots who bring in the mercantile marine have their moorings.

Our first stopping place is Gibsons Landing, at the west entrance of Howe Sound. On the shore is descried Bowen Island teeming with deer . . . Mr. Gibson at this landing — the tide being low — yanks ashore the cow and calf we have brought by the simple method of persuading them sternly into the water and inducing them to swim to land. Outside lie Paisley and Ragged Islands, sometime the camps of whalers who harpooned these waters profitably . . .

We observe the gay sea dog or seal, who loves to lie a-basking in the sun. . . . We too on deck bask on . . . past occasional shanties and clearances that skirt the shores of Georgia's Gulf, past Trail Bay, until our good ship signals in Seechelt [sic] Village, an Indian settlement where we have to put ashore the Roman Catholic Bishop. Canoes, contending for the honour, are soon alongside and the dignitary is landed to the strains of music furnished by the native band, whose members are shining like the Stars, in gold lace in a firmament of blue cloth. . . . As we sail through Welcome Pass the sun is setting in a wealth of colour over the north end of Texada Island. All about these waters, it should be said, the gentle angler can find captives to his spear or spoonbait. Salmon teem round the shores . . .

We relinquish our comfortable berths, as we enter Evans Bay on Head Island and put ashore to the lonely ranchman his welcome mail. The steamboat shortly enters the Hole-in-the-Wall, not romantically

30

named, but a channel that provides a romantic succession of vistas. No scenic painter could conceive the beautiful effects furnished by such an archipelago of inlets, clad in moss and stately trees, flushed by the dawn. The tide runs fast and the ship needs careful steering. . . . We are soon among the logging camps again delivering huge sides of beef and bales of hay, and letters to the lonely camps of loggers . . . as they shoot out from the shore in their motley crafts and return with their spoil. We sail on, past huge fir-covered mountains where snowy heads rest against the deep blue sky above, through virgin seas and deserted spaces where the steamer's whistle, reverberating through the hills, puts up flocks of wild duck.

The return voyage from Port Neville begins at mid-day. The boat turns opposite the ivory-white strand, formed of powdered clam shells, that fringes the shores of Sayward's lumber camp. And so leaving behind in the boat's track a succession of small settlements and more lumber camps, where teams comprising sixteen or more huge patient oxen haul down the forest giants, whilst big hirsute men with spiked boots and long poles dance over the floating logs as they arrange them into booms, our route is varied somewhat from our upgoing trip. . . .

We sail through Euclataw Rapids and see around us in the cold moonlight the evil-eddying currents which would jeopardise the safety of a small boat. There is an Indian Potlatch in full swing at the settlement of Green Point, and we are amused at the ingenuity of the squaws, who to be rid for a time of their maternal cares, have planted their dusky sucklings in a long trough where, clad in particoloured dresses, the youngsters look in the distance like a row of human flowers. Our little voyage is now nearly ended. We enter the Narrows as the afternoon sun is sinking in the west . . .

One has only to read such an eye-witness account to be conscious of how much a part of coastal life the *Comox* had become.

Business slowly improved, and the logging route was further extended when the Provincial government granted an extra subsidy for a call into Bute Inlet every six weeks. The cost of freighting general supplies to the main ports along the logging routes in 1895 ran from $1 to $1.50 per ton.

An interesting financial report for the year 1895 was issued by Henry Darling as secretary (his operating title was Superintendent Engineer and Manager). It showed a small surplus and that the Company had been able to discharge both its mortgages, although an unsecured note for £500 unaccountably had never been repaid to the Darling family before the Company changed hands. There was one item of good news in the report concerning the *Coquitlam* matter: the Imperial and Dominion governments agreed to undertake all further legal costs of presenting the case. Prospects for 1896 were considered good — "activity in the lumber trade means business for our tugs and the *Comox*." The presence of more sailing ships in port was expected to benefit the ferry, there was more stone lightering to do for the government with the cargo boats after the fishing season, and some coal cargoes for Alaska were in sight. Because of the substantial overseas investment in the Company, a committee of "home shareholders" was appointed. The number of British Columbia directors was reduced to five, three representing the overseas investors and two the local shareholders: Gordon Legg, H. McDowell, D. McPhaiden, D. Oppenheimer and J. C. Keith. The physical assets of the Company, including the wharf and steamers, had increased to $205,000. The two elected auditors of the Company divided a remuneration of $100.

Mr. Alfred St. George Hamersley K. C., who had piloted the Union Company's affairs until 1893, remained in British Columbia until 1905 when he returned to Britain and later became a member of parliament. He was prominent in the development of North Vancouver, and the second ferry steamer *St. George* was named in his honour. He is said to have been fond of riding and to have named his horse "Business." When he took a day off his legal work, the sign on his door read "Out on Business."

CHAPTER 3

1897-1906

Union Ships in the Klondike Gold Rush
The Cassiar *and the* Camosun *Establish Union Routes*

We threaded an interminable labyrinth of watery
lanes and reaches that wound in and out of a network
of islands, promontories and peninsulars for thousands of miles. This wonderful system of navigation
. . . is furnished with innumerable harbours on either
hand. One is lost in admiration at the facilities for
intercommunication which are thus provided for the
future inhabitants of this wonderful region.
LORD DUFFERIN
"Through the Northern Waters of
the Western Coast" — 1894

The Klondike gold rush caught the world by surprise, and no less the young city of Vancouver. There was no fanfare to herald the phenomenon which created so much wealth and excitement, drew so much trade and attention to the northwest coast, and caused so many tragedies and heartbreaks. Through late 1896 and the first half of 1897, coastal shipping moved normally, although early reports were discussed in mining circles and noted in the press concerning rich placer deposits being discovered in the gravels of Klondike Creek, near the junction of the Yukon river and its Klondike tributary.

In January 1897 the tug *Skidegate*, which had been partly rebuilt in 1891, was taken out of service and broken up. Her fine Bow McLachlan engines were put into a 60-foot tug which was built for the Company at the False Creek ways of Colin McAlpine. This vessel, christened *Chehalis*, went into service in 1897 for both harbour and upcoast towing of log booms. She was more suitable for towing and proved useful in various assignments over the next few years.

The *Senator* was retained to carry on the ferry service across the inlet for another three years, this operation being then taken over by the North Vancouver Ferry & Power Company, the first of whose new ferries was launched in 1900. This was the 83-ton steam ferry *North Vancouver (No. 1)*, with dimensions of 73-foot length and 20-foot beam, which was obtained by the municipal council. The Union

33

directors saw their future bound up in the general coastal business; besides, they did not have the capital to invest in a large ferry replacement.

Early in 1897, the *Comox* was extensively renovated with her steel plating being extended to support additional upper-deck cabins for overnight accommodation. She was relieved for this period, while many logging camps were closed down, by the *Coquitlam*. The *Cutch*, which also needed more passenger space and reconditioning, had been withdrawn from the Vancouver-Nanaimo route after nearly seven years' continuous service. This run was taken over by the Dunsmuir-owned *S. S. Joan*. The *Cutch* was laid up for a lengthy period until events intervened to make her rebuilding a very profitable venture.

The Union Company now planned a direct service to the canneries from Vancouver. More passenger accommodation was built in the *Coquitlam* to provide eight staterooms and a licence obtained for carrying fifty passengers. On Monday, May 24, 1897, she sailed on a new twice-monthly northern schedule, and Henry Darling took along several prominent business men for the trip including Frank Douglas, of Kelly Douglas, and A. J. McLennan, of McLennan McFeely. At Alert Bay, S. A. Spencer went aboard, and one of the cannery pioneers, Henry Bell-Irving, joined the ship at Rivers Inlet. She called at the Skeena Canneries, Metlakahtla, Port Simpson and points up the Nass River.

Life was tranquil in the city; on a Sunday in July, two excursions left the Union wharf, one aboard the *Comox* to Steveston, "for a full view of the fishing fleet and canneries in operation," the other on the chartered *S. S. Burt* which advertised to sail at 2 p.m. for the "Point Gray Summer Resort — round trip 50 cents."

Then the news came of fabulous strikes at Klondike's "Bonanza" and "El Dorado," and a horde of more than forty thousand prospectors and speculators poured in. They came from all over the world and especially from the California and Australian goldfields. The small settlement on Skagway Bay (derived from the Indian "Skagua" meaning "House of the North Wind"), close to the head of Lynn Canal, became the main gateway for this gold rush, and was quickly transformed into a rip-roaring town.

The *S. S. Queen* left Seattle July 3, 1897, with six hundred passengers, livestock and pack horses. About half were destined for Dyea, north of Skagway on the canal at the end of salt water navigation and closer to the Chilkoot Pass. Canadian Pacific Navigation readied the vessel *Danube* in Victoria, but the Union Steamship Company stepped in ahead with the *Capilano* which was fitted with temporary berths. She sailed from Vancouver on July 22, 1897, under Captain Ernest A. Powys, who had been a deep-sea master between Sydney, Australia and Puget Sound before coming to local coasters. She carried a full complement of passengers, sixty-nine head of cattle and twenty horses. Deck passage to Skagway cost $30; the cabin rate when available was $40. According to the *News-Advertiser* of August 7, 1897, "The voyage to the North was completed on the seventh day, the weather throughout being exceptionally fine." The cattle and horses were safely landed at Pyramid Harbour near Dyea, the cattle to be driven and the horses to be used as pack animals.

The *Capilano* was the first Canadian steamer to leave from a British Columbia port in the Klondike trade, and also the first to return, tying up at the Union wharf at 9 p.m. on Friday, August 6. On her way south she passed six steamers bound for either Skagway or the Stikine River, one of two alternate routes to Dawson City via Fort Wrangell, Telegraph Creek and Lake Teslin. The Stikine route seems to have been safer but involved thirty-six miles of portage and six hundred miles by river and lake boat. The other more northerly route to the Klondike was via St. Michael's Bay in the Bering sea, open only from June to September. It involved transferring passengers to flat-bottomed boats for an eighteen hundred-mile trip up the Yukon River.

Again the Company sought and got the cordial backing of the Board of Trade. "The Union Steamships," Mr. Gardner Johnson said, "was eager to commence trade with the much-talked-of gold fields . . . the Company was prepared to carry any number of passengers in the spring but they had to look to the merchants of Vancouver for support." The local stores and wholesalers rallied to help the Union line, as well as themselves. The *News-Advertiser* led the way: "Those going to the Klondike will save . . . by buying in Vancouver, the nearest port and cheapest and best." Hudson's Bay advertised "Complete outfits . . . sleeping bags . . . N. B.: We know what a man should take to the North, and will not land him up with a lot of rubbish!" Brackman Ker featured "Klondike Dog Feed — Sweet Corn for Miners"; and La Mont's crystallized egg for Alaska pancakes and custard was demonstrated daily at 12 Cordova Street. "Revolvers for the Klondike" were on sale at Tisdall's, and one realist said: "Be prepared to go . . . with one of our complete medicine chests."

The accommodation of the *Coquitlam* was further rebuilt and extended for the carrying of 157 passengers, with ninety-three first class berths (eleven in cabins) and sixty-four in the steerage. She sailed on Sunday, August 8, 1897, under Captain A. Freeman, who served in all the pioneer Union ships, for Dyea via the Skeena and Nass rivers. "The wharf," reported the *News-Advertiser*, "presented a very busy appearance with several hundred people to bid bon voyage to the Vancouver people who were leaving for the gold fields." Mr. Legg made the round trip with Alderman McPhaiden, and among the passengers were former mayor Cope and Mrs. Cope. Then on Wednesday, August 18, the *Capilano* sailed again with another bumper load. According to the paper, "Every hour scores of people have visited the wharf to observe the preparations . . . her decks were piled high with freight and passengers' outfits and the total accommodation was taken up. She had seventy cattle and forty horses on board. All the cattle and twenty-six of the horses were shipped by P. Burns of Nelson, in charge of W. Perdue of Revelstoke and a party of seven drivers."

Elsewhere it was reported that "Pat Burns, the well known cattle King" had contracted with the Bennett Lake & Klondike Co. to transport freight and one thousand head of cattle. The going rate for packing from Dyea into the Klondike rose in twelve months from $300 to $800 a ton.

But terrible difficulties lay ahead for the miners. By August 24, 1897, the hazardous trail through the White Pass was impassable, and four thousand men were stranded at Skagway, with more at Dyea. Goods could be taken over part of the higher Chilkoot Pass in wagons, but the White Pass was in an appalling state, with horses being killed daily. Reporting later to the Canadian Mining Association, Mr. C. J. Christie said: "We reached Skagway where a trail was being blazed across the White Pass. The jam in the narrow pass was indescribable. Hundreds of frantic men were attempting to carry supplies to Lake Bennett. Horses perished by the thousands and I have seen them sink out of sight in the mire. My contribution was forty." Returning Klondikers were frozen to death on the trail, two of whom carried $100,000 in bills and gold dust. At Dawson City "the stores had gold dust stacked up in their vaults like so much cordwood." The Klondike's creeks yielded nearly $100 million dollars in seven years, but not without a heavy cost in life, unbelievable hardships, and rampant lawlessness.

On his return from a trip in April 1898, Captain Newcombe said, "the *Coquitlam* left before news of a terrible snowstorm in the Chilkoot Pass was received. However, there was talk of Soapy Smith on the trail, giving much trouble by bold hold-ups and desperate gambling, resulting in bloodshed. He keeps on the American side, having a wholesome fear of British justice as administered by the North West Mounted Police."

The *Coquitlam* continued to carry heavy Alaskan cargoes and enormous loads of passengers. The veteran Captain Andy Johnstone, at that time an eleven-year-old schoolboy, told me: "It was one of the city's most exciting pastimes to go down and watch a Union vessel preparing to leave for Alaska, with goods piled as high as the ship's bridge and horses stabled on deck or teams of oxen in spaces between bales of hay." He recalled the "amazing scene of confusion on board; people were making bunks atop bales of hay. So crowded was the ship with passengers, it was an outside passage for most, camped on deck for five or six days with their packs and provisions all around them."

The first section of the narrow gauge railway between Skagway and Lake Bennett, for which the British Yukon Company obtained a charter in 1899, was due to be completed in September 1898. It was February 1899, however, before the rails reached the summit of the White Pass in the face of almost impossible barriers, and July 1900 before the line to Whitehorse was linked up and the trail hazards finally overcome. Several other shipping lines had vessels engaged in the Skagway trade, the Canadian Pacific Navigation contingent of four ships including the *Islander*, but the Union steamers kept heavily booked. The Company was now also advertising the "Stikine River Route to the Goldfields," connecting at Wrangell with scheduled river boats and issuing through-tickets to Glenora for Telegraph Creek.

In order to compete effectively for the Skagway passenger business, the Company finished a major remodelling of the vessel *Cutch* by June 1898. She was refitted with new engines and boilers, her accommodation was entirely reconstructed with much-expanded cabin space at a cost of $40,000, and in the process, one of her smokestacks was eliminated. On her trials on June 11, she registered a speed of 14 knots; she left two days later under Captain Newcombe on her first voyage to Alaska. The *News-Advertiser* said she was "looked upon as one of the speediest and most comfortable vessels on the Skagway run." In July, she set a speed record that remained unbeaten as long as the *Cutch* was in this service. Although no log survives, from contemporary evidence of her performance, this is reckoned to have been about eighty-eight hours for the eleven hundred-mile run from Vancouver, using the outside passage via Cape Decision to avoid Wrangell Narrows. She had serious boiler trouble in December 1899, which experts said was incurable, but Henry Darling ran tests and had it fixed. A Company report of the day commented on the hazards of navigation in Alaskan waters, noting that "the winter nights are long in those high latitudes, the coast is rocky, neither lighted or buoyed and only half surveyed." In spite of this the *Cutch* kept up her fast schedule night and day on an advertised "Skagway Direct Service — No Stops," leaving Union wharf on the first, tenth and twentieth of each month for a quick turn-around in ten days, carrying near-capacity loads. It was human error, and not the Alaskan hazard, that finally caught up with the popular *Cutch* in August 1900.

Under Captain Newcombe, she sailed from Vancouver at 11:30 p.m. on Monday, August 20, with a large passenger list and a full cargo for Skagway. There was no report of the vessel — not surprising in the days before the telegraph appeared on the coast — until the *S. S. Topeka* arrived at Tacoma from the north on August 29 with the news that the *Cutch* had run aground on Horseshoe Reef, twenty-five miles south of Juneau, on August 24. The Union office still had had no direct word when the *News-Advertiser* printed, on August 31, the Topeka's report that "Passengers and crew of the Vancouver steamer were all safe ashore under improvised canvas, and the cargo of the vessel was being jettisoned in the efforts to float her." The stranded passengers came south by other vessels and, leaving the wrecked *Cutch* in charge of the two mates, chief engineer and quartermaster, Captain Newcombe with the rest of his crew were landed by the *S. S. Aberdeen* at Comox, Vancouver Island, on September 2. The Captain said they "had been all over Alaska for six days" on the *Aberdeen* after leaving the stranded *Cutch*.

Captain Newcombe's story of the grounding appeared in the newspaper on September 3. After leaving the Union dock on August 20, he had "experienced dirty weather, wet and thick." This had kept him "on the bridge most of the way up . . . twenty-one hours on the day previous to the mishap." After five hours' rest, while waiting a favourable tide at the mouth of Stephen's Passage, he resumed duty for seventeen hours and then retired to his cabin at 10:25 on August 24. He said that the course he set from Hilda's Point "would if followed have passed the treacherous reef two miles away." With fine weather coming up, he left the second mate in charge with instructions to call him at midnight or earlier if needed. Half an hour later, at 10:50 p.m., with a terrific crash the *Cutch*, travelling 12½ to 13 knots, mounted the reef near Douglas Island. "Half the passengers," Captain Newcombe said, "were asleep in their bunks and were the coolest lot of passengers I have ever travelled with." Seeing his ship settling by the stern, he ordered the passengers to be taken ashore and, in half an hour, five boats were launched and every passenger landed on the beach two-and-a-half miles away. Tents were pitched and, with an ample supply of food and blankets, everyone was made as comfortable as possible to wait for the small vessel that was engaged to take them on to Juneau.

Although first attempts to succour the *Cutch* failed because of a lack of pumps, Captain Newcombe believed that the vessel would be saved by the Union company. A current report said the ship was "on the rocks exposed to the full force of the northern gales but so far, beyond the loss of her housework, is intact. The vessel is a phenomenally strong one, and hardly a vessel afloat could have withstood what the *Cutch* has." But she was abandoned for fear she would break up in bad weather. She was salvaged and towed to Juneau, where she was beached and repaired by American interests for further Alaska service, operating out of Seattle as the *Jessie Banning*. She was soon sold to the government of Columbia as the gunboat *Bogota*, to assist in quelling their periodic revolutions. There she ended her adventurous days.

Captain Newcombe continued a distinguished coast career as captain of the *Kestrel*. This was a survey ship, built in 1903 at a cost of $65,000, which did fine work around Hecate Strait before Prince Rupert was founded. As commander of an armed vessel, Newcombe carried a sword and a three-bar insignia of rank before the Canadian Navy came into existence.

Although the loss of the *Cutch* was a serious blow to the Union Steamship Company, there was some slackening in the southeast Alaska trade after 1900, and this route became more closely linked with Seattle. The *Coquitlam* immediately replaced the *Cutch* on the Skagway run, from which the *Capilano* had already been withdrawn to meet the call of expanding trade in British Columbia northern waters, where a mail contract for the Nass River was approved by the Dominion government. There were two canneries operating at Nass Harbour and Mill Bay, and salmon packs were being put up at eight Skeena canneries, as well as at Lowe Inlet, Namu and Bella Bella, with another six plants working in Rivers Inlet.

During all the Alaskan excitement, as the camps grew in number and a few shifted to more distant inlets, the *Comox* managed to keep the settlements and loggers well supplied. When Mr. B. B. Johnson, a real estate broker, returned to Vancouver from a trip aboard the *Comox* on August 17, 1897, he was quoted: "The citizens have but a shallow idea of what is going on only a few miles north of Vancouver." He marvelled at the quantity of beef unloaded at the different mining and logging camps, but added cheerfully: "There still remained a big supply for all on board the *Comox!*" At Shoal Bay, he said, "One is met by old and familiar faces like Postmaster Neville Smith, and Archibald and John Collum, proprietors of the Hotel Thurlow, which is doing a rushing business."

At weekends the *Comox* still ran excursions, sometimes along with a chartered sternwheeler called the *Rothesay*. This vessel, originally built for the Stikine River trade during the gold rush, was used by the Union Company for one summer, but her shallow draft made her unsuitable for outside waters and she was not "picked up." A favourite Sunday outing was to Granite Falls, fare 50 cents. On July 1, 1898 the *Rothesay* and *Comox* ran every few minutes between the Union pier and Brockton Point for a return fare of 10 cents, and on July 1 and 2 the *Rothesay* was advertised for moonlight trips up the Indian Arm — "Fare for Gents 50 cents, Ladies 25 cents."

In March 1900, Gordon Legg, the Company chairman, took over active management from Henry Darling, who continued as secretary-manager for another year. Mr. Darling had well served the Union through ten eventful years, and still acted occasionally as an engineering consultant. In 1901 he became general manager of the British Yukon Navigation Company, a division of the White Pass & Yukon Railway, and later established his own paint business in Vancouver. For ship surveys he continued to represent the British corporation. Union directors at this time in addition to Mr. Legg were Captain McPhaiden. H. McDowell, H. Burwell and I. Oppenheimer. Later in the year upon Captain McPhaiden's retirement, Francis Carter-Cotton, MLA, joined the Board. At the turn of the century, the urgency of providing more passenger service, particularly for the Johnstone Strait logging operators, was apparent. The *Comox* alterations had been only a stop-gap, and Mr. Legg decided that another vessel must be obtained if the Company's expansion were to be maintained.

Finally, in January 1901, the Company bought the wooden hull of the one-time steam freighter *J. R. McDonald*, which Henry Darling's survey found in excellent condition and readily convertible into an all-purpose passenger and freight vessel for the logging route. This hull was first set afloat from Lake's Yard at Ballard, now part of Seattle, on March 13, 1890, for the Pennington Navigation Company. Then, on February 23, 1893, while en route from Seattle to Vancouver the vessel's upperworks were so extensively damaged by fire that she was beached at James Bay. She was next rigged as a schooner and pressed into service to carry lumber from the Hastings Mill to Skagway in the gold rush days. This was the stout hull that largely built the fortunes of the Union Steamship Company. It was towed to Wallace's Shipyard in False Creek for a conversion job under the eye of Andy Wallace. The new Bow McLachlan engines and boilers were shipped from Scotland by Mr. Legg, who had travelled to Great Britain for this purpose and to attend to insurance matters. The 120-foot vessel, to be named *Cassiar*, with breadth of 29 feet, was reconstructed completely to provide cabins — fitted with electric light — for 42 berths. Her accommodation included a "loggers saloon" with open berths, a smoking room with bar facilities, and lounge space for her licensed carriage of 144 passengers. Of 597 gross tons with a speed of 9 knots, she could steam 17½ miles on a ton of coal, which, on a bunker capacity of 44 tons, provided a useful radius of nearly four hundred miles. Those were the vital statistics of the little vessel that was destined to achieve coastal renown second only to the *Beaver* in her familiar rounds of the logging camps.

The popular *Cassiar* was launched and christened after her rebuilding, on Saturday, September 28, 1901, and brought around from False Creek into Burrard Inlet. The "loggers' palace" got a rousing welcome throughout the tidewater settlements, after starting her route under Captain Charles Moody. A Newfoundlander, who had worked aboard the *Senator* and had skippered the *Skidegate*, Captain Moody had been with the *Cutch* since 1893. He spent twenty-seven years with the Union before going to the Pilotage Service in 1917. The *Cassiar's* first "pilot," as the Company's first officers were called, was well-known George Gaisford, a former Royal Navy man from Chelsea, who had served as mate on all the Union ships before joining the *Cassiar* and becoming her master in 1908. Later skippers included Robert Wilson, John Boden, James Findlay and John Muir, all distinguished names in the coast story. Her Chief Engineer was A. S. de Gruchy, followed by George H. Foster, both destined to become superintendent engineers of the Company. Percy Chick, from the *Comox* was her first purser, followed by Bob Bryce and Charles V. Coldwell, a genial personality and the well-known port steward and purchasing agent at the Union dock of later days.

Completion of the *Cassiar* came not a day too soon, as there was no suitable relief ship when the services of the hard-working *Comox* were lost for two weeks in the spring of 1901 after she ran aground in the Gut, or narrows, beyond the wharf float in Frederick Arm, about 120 miles upcoast off Lewis Channel. Although she sustained only slight damage, this peculiar episode illustrates the tricky nature of the route. All business at most smaller places, including the exchange of mails, was normally undertaken while northbound, and the signal for a southbound passenger pick-up was a lantern displayed at the end of a wharf. As the *Comox* was homeward bound on the night of April 22, what appeared to be such a light was spotted at Frederick Arm by First Mate (later Captain) James Bartlett, who steered towards it. First report of the stranding was brought back by Purser Chick in the *Saga,* a small vessel which also ran in this area for a brief period. His account to the *World* said:

> Usually there is a light on the float, but this time there was no lantern there, although a man was lying asleep on the wharf ostensibly waiting for the steamer. Just beyond the float the current begins to run swiftly and there are times when the tide through the little narrows runs at twelve miles an hour. On this occasion, mistaking a light away up on shore for the one that should have been on the wharf, the *Comox* passed by the end of the float and got in the force of the current . . . The engines were promptly reversed but the propellor struck a rock and was stripped of its blades, and the steamer, with the way she had on, was carried aground in the Gut hard and fast.

The Postmaster, it turned out, had apparently gone to sleep with the light on in his bedroom, and it was quipped that the *Comox* obligingly came ashore right under his window. Union officials went up in the *Chehalis* to investigate; on their recommendation, the basin into which the *Comox* had strayed was sealed off by two scows serving as a breakwater until a new propellor could be fitted. She was refloated on the high tide of May 6, some two weeks later. Little the worse for her mishap, save for some green paint scraped off her hull, the vessel was returned to Vancouver by Captain Moody under her own steam. After a quick inspection she actually resumed her regular logging-camp sailing the following night with a capacity load of passengers and cargo. During the time the *Comox* was being repaired, the freighter *Coquitlam* was pressed into service.

An aftermath of the accident was that the insurance rates for the whole fleet promptly went up 17 per cent.

Suddenly at the end of April 1901, a cut-rate war flared up between the American and Canadian lines running in Puget Sound and along the northern coast, chiefly caused by the increased calls at Vancouver of Seattle-based vessels trading to other coastal ports. The deck fare to Skagway was slashed to $5 and the round trip on the *Islander* to $20. All coastal companies were drawn into the war, and Union cut the Port Neville fare from $5 to $1. The *Coquitlam,* which was relieving the *Comox,* accepted cargo for $1 a ton. Everyone was running at a loss, and an agreement was soon reached which restricted vessels of both flags from intertrading beyond the first port of call in the other's territorial waters. American ships could not enter the B.C. coastal trade by means of a service into Vancouver and Canadian vessels were similarly restricted within the Puget Sound area.

The first schedule of the *Cassiar*, which carried a crew of twenty-nine, was advertised to serve the northern mining and lumber camps with two weekly sailings. Her Tuesday run via Campbell River and Seymour Narrows called at Rock Bay, an old logging centre of the Hastings Mill pioneers having one of the richest timber tracts in the world, and at Salmon River (Sayward), where the Sacht family and Mr. Kelsey (who gave his name to Kelsey Bay) were the first settlers. Terminal of the route was at Port Neville. Her shorter trip left on Fridays for Shoal Bay via Cortez and Valdez Island stops. The *Comox* was now employed as a second ship on the logging routes, and the two vessels served wharves, float landings and "stops in stream" as far as Alert Bay and Port Hardy. There were numerous places between Campbell River and the northeast tip of Vancouver Island where new settlements clustered around small wharves and tiny float landings. Often, especially at night, only the postmaster came down to take the steamer's lines and sign for the mail sacks. The weekly orders from town were left on the floats at the owners' risk, but little went astray. Sometimes a sack of sugar would be taken in error, but the steamer's manifest record was accepted without question; only a case of liquor had to be signed for.

The *Comox*, meanwhile, was still building up goodwill for the Company. She was assigned in 1902 to a route that included Blubber Bay's lime plant on Texada Island and local ports en route to Cortez Island. Joe Simson, son of coast pioneer Calvert Simson, told me that as a two-year-old at his father's summer home at Buccaneer Bay he had crawled into the dog's feed box and was badly bitten. The *Comox* was at the Buccaneer float when the incident occurred, and Flora Grant, daughter of Alexander Grant, who owned one of the small Thormanby Islands, rushed the child on board for treatment. The young captain of the *Comox* was then Barney Johnson, who unhesitatingly dropped his regular route and steamed with Flora and the child straight to Van Anda hospital, before picking up his schedule many hours later at Pender Harbour.

This story has a happy sequel quite apart from the boy's recovery, for Captain Johnson wooed and married Flora Grant.

A number of years ago, A. M. Wastell, who came West in 1894

43

and established a sawmill and his home at Telegraph Cove, alongside Beaver Cove and the later Englewood Camp of Wood & English, recalled the early *Cassiar* days:

> The crews of the Union vessels became a link for the settlers with the outside world and would often look after children going back to school, and safely delivered them on arrival in town. Your whole family could travel that way on a Union Steamship boat . . . The genial captains, pursers and other officers were the messengers for all, and well they did their job!

Fishing, canning and logging were in full swing at Alert Bay, where the first cannery operators had encouraged development of the Indian village. A sawmill built here by a branch of the Church Missionary Society was later sold with the Spencer & Huson Company to the B.C. Packers Association. The Kalewan Kansa Company made a settlement on Malcolm Island to bring out "selected settlers from Finland of many trades." Two years later, this company was replaced by the Sointula Co-operative Association, which exists today. To the south at Campbell River in 1904 Charles Thulin opened the Willows Hotel and his first store, both of which were boons to the many loggers working around Elk Bay, Granite Bay, Blind Channel and Greene Point, where A. P. Allison was operating in the early 1900s.

Stories about the roistering aboard the *Cassiar* were not exaggerated in the days when hand-logging was at its peak. In the open town of Vancouver there were many saloons too conveniently located in the Carrall and Cordova street area close to the Union dock, and sailings early in the day were more desirable. The vessel's bar did a roaring trade, particularly when loggers headed for the city with a season's earnings after the camp was paid off. Frequently the master would have to order the bar closed, and it sometimes took two husky mates to restore order. Two effective "strongarms" were Arthur Jarvis and red-haired William Hodgson, who were given the nicknames of the "Black" and "Red" mates. Captain Charles Cates, one-time Mayor of North Vancouver and a leading towboat operator, once wrote to me: "I was working up the coast and boarded 'the loggers palace' at Rock Bay . . . it used to be a saying on the waterfront that all the loggers saw when they came to town was the CPR, the *Cassiar*, and Tommy Roberts, who ran the Grand Hotel on Water Street."

In the final phase of its southeastern Alaska service, the Company expanded its northern connections to the scheduling of departures of the *Capilano* and the *Coquitlam* every ten days, calling at Rivers Inlet and Skeena River canneries, where the fisheries enjoyed a greatly increased volume.

It was not all plain sailing, and the Union had some really bad days. In 1902, the northern trade declined to such an extent that some cannery calls were temporarily discontinued and it was thought that one or both northern freighters might have to be laid up, but 1903 brought an improvement.

The following year Union sold its two oldest tugs, the original *Leonora* and the *Senator*, which had outlived their usefulness. With the proceeds, the tug *Coutli* was built at McAlpine's ways in False Creek. This 99-ton steam tug was 71 feet in length with a 19-foot beam, and considerably larger than the *Chehalis*. Three years later, she had the misfortune to lose her tow, the CPR coal barge *Robert Kerr*, which was wrecked on Danger Reef en route from Ladysmith. The *Coutli*, the last tug the Union obtained for the local towing business, was sold in the summer of 1909 together with the remaining scows when the Company moved entirely out of the towing business.

In 1904 came the exciting announcement of the Grand Trunk Pacific Railway's plan to come through to a Pacific northern port. This was followed by equally exciting reports of rich gold and silver deposits near Stewart, at the head of the Portland Canal — the sixty-mile fjord which marks the international boundary. Business looked good in the north.

Both Canadian Pacific, with the *Princess Victoria*, and the Boscowitz Steamship Company, with the *Vadso* and their first iron-hulled *Venture*, were successfully running passengers and freight from Victoria directly to this northern area. Gordon Legg felt the time was overdue for a modern Union passenger vessel to compete. Such a move would permit him to assign the *Capilano* and *Coquitlam* entirely to the growing cannery and freighting demands.

With the upturn in trade and new northern prospects, the Company embarked on its most ambitious venture up to that time by ordering its first combination passenger-freighter, the *Camosun*. The vessel was laid down in the spring of 1904 in the Paisley yard of Bow McLachlan. Her dimensions were 192 feet in length with 35-foot beam and an estimated cargo capacity of 300 tons. Passenger accommodation provided 54 first class berths and 120 deck bunks, as well as comfortable fore and aft saloon lounges on the upper deck which contained the main first-class cabins. There was a well-appointed smoking room and additional cabins on the top deck aft of the pilot house and officers' quarters. Her cabins, the equal of crack coastal steamers anywhere in the world, were bedrooms of the Atlantic type, with settees suitable for families. She had a richly panelled dining saloon on the main deck. A strongly built vessel with double bottom fore and aft, her triple-expansion engines — later converted to oil — gave an economical speed of more than 12 knots, with a margin up to 14. She was fitted with a ship's telegraph to the deck personnel as well as to the engine room.

The *Camosun* sailed from Troon, Scotland, on February 19, 1905, under Captain B. L. Johnson, who had joined the *Coquitlam* as early as 1895 and rose rapidly to become a second officer and a master in the Union line's service by the turn of the century. Andrew Beattie came out with the *Camosun* from Scotland as chief engineer. At Kingston, Jamaica, Captain Johnson handed over the ship to Captain C. B. Smith, who brought her on the long trip through the Strait of Magellan into the Pacific. Despite encountering heavy weather on the voyage, the *Camosun* stood the test well but was delayed for a month at San Francisco to have her decks caulked, and did not reach Vancouver harbour until 3:00 p.m. on Tuesday, June 20. The *Camosun* was berthed at Ward's wharf at the foot of Abbott Street, close to the Union dock, where she was welcomed by a large crowd. The ship looked trim in the line's colours with the customary green hull and white upperwork.

With a coast licence for 199 passengers, and carrying a crew of thirty-eight, she was put into service on July 4 under Captain Frank T. Saunders. By coincidence both Barney Johnson, who brought the vessel across the Atlantic, and Frank Saunders, her first master, were fellow apprentices aboard a sailing vessel and jumped ship in Vancouver to join the Union Company in 1894. The first *Camosun* route was via Alert Bay, Bella Coola, Bella Bella, Port Essington, the Skeena River, Port Simpson and Nass River canneries to Stewart. This was before any Prince Rupert settlement existed under that name; and there was no wharf yet built at Stewart, where the vessel dropped anchor off a landing float. Later when the J. W. Stewart and Portland Canal Mining companies were established in this region, the Union vessel brought in many miners with their supplies.

The *Camosun* was the first passenger vessel to call at Prince Rupert in 1906, although several Union ships had stopped off Tuck's Inlet, as the uncharted harbour was previously known. She was welcomed by the first residents as an old friend who had done business with Port Essington before the new port came into regular use. As one of the crew of the survey ship *Kestrel*, which he joined as an apprentice in 1903, Captain Andy Johnstone was there at that time. He recalled that a survey work crew under Mr. Pariseau from Ottawa, who was responsible for so many fine British Columbia coast charts, established a little camp at Fairview Point (or Beacon, as it is now called). The first post office was set up by Mr. & Mrs. McIntosh in a hastily constructed shack close to the beach. In July 1906, before the survey work was completed, the *Camosun* ran over Kestrel Rock, a reef off Lima Point in the uncharted section of Prince Rupert Harbour, tearing out eighteen plates. Only her double bottom saved the *Camosun* from going down. Damage was not too serious, the loss being more in dislocation of the new service than in the cost of dry-docking and repairs at Spratt's ways in Victoria.

Within eighteen months of commencing service, the *Camosun* had the distinction of being the first vessel on the Pacific coast to have Marconi wireless installed. An interesting letter from Mr. W. O'Neill of Smithers, B. C. said:

> The *Camosun* which came in 1905 was my favourite to travel on with Captain Saunders — the 'fog wizard'. It was from her I sent my first wireless message off Egg Island in Queen Charlotte Sound . . . I went to Vancouver aboard her one trip after leaving Port Essington at the mouth of the Skeena in a dense fog. I never remembered seeing land until we went through the Narrows at Brockton Point but I don't think her old whistle ever stopped blowing."

Union's mariners of the day navigated the narrow channels consistently by whistle echo. Captain John Park told me an echo return of eleven seconds placed his vessel unerringly one mile from land, and this was the only way they kept going when fog blanketed the coast for days on end.

In succeeding years, the northern canning industry expanded rapidly, and every spring the *Camosun* carried several hundred Chinese, Japanese and Indian workers to the twenty-five fish plants on Smith's Inlet, Rivers Inlet and the Skeena and Nass rivers. The main packing season from July to October found the vessel loaded down with salmon and frozen fish. On one occasion in October 1907, she brought south six thousand cases of canned salmon, the largest shipment to Vancouver up to that time. The new route gave a solid boost to the northern coast business, as Captain Saunders continued to clip hours off schedules, on one occasion making the southbound run from Prince Rupert in forty-five hours. The *Camosun* became noted for the regularity of her arrivals at up-coast ports, and the early residents of Prince Rupert quipped: "You can set your watch by the time the vessel docks!" Captain Robert Batchelor, a rugged sailing-ship master who spent his life at sea and gained his coast experience in the *Capilano*, succeeded to command of the *Camosun* when Captain Saunders left to go with the new Canadian National ships.

In its long history, the Union Steamship Company, despite the millions of sea miles covered by its red-funnelled ships, suffered only two mishaps involving loss of life, and both occurred in its early period. The first happened on the sunny afternoon of July 12, 1906, when the little steam tug *Chehalis*, under Captain James House, left North Vancouver on a special charter by Robert Bryce and a party of seven and proceeded directly into the First Narrows. At 2:00 p.m., the Canadian Pacific *Princess Victoria*, Captain Thomas Griffen, also left her berth on the south shore of the inlet on her scheduled departure and rounded Brockton Point at a speed of about 15 knots. The heavy flood tide held back the little *Chehalis*, which was endeavouring to get more way, and swung her across the bow of the 300-foot *Princess Victoria*, which was hampered by a small launch ahead to port and which was attempting to pass her too closely on the south side of the channel. The danger was seen too late, and the large vessel of nearly 2,000 gross tonnage sliced into the port quarter of the 60-foot *Chehalis*, capsizing and sinking her within seconds. The fatal collision took place at precisely 2:27 p.m., most of the victims being trapped in the cabin below deck where they were having lunch. Drowned were Mrs. R. E. Bryce; Dr. W. A. B. Hutton of the Rock Bay Hospital; the small son of J. O. Benwell; and P. J. Chick, who had been a purser in the Company's ships; as well as four crewmen — W. H. Crawford, a student acting as assistant engineer; two Japanese firemen; and the Chinese cook. Those saved were the engineer, C. A. Dean, who was picked up by the boat of lightkeeper Jones of Brockton Point; Percy G. Shallcross, who became a well-known insurance executive; R. N. Rich; and Captain James House, who was left badly crippled as a result of the accident. A granite obelisk was erected in Stanley Park opposite the point in the Narrows where the tragedy occurred. A legal wrangle ensued, and on appeal the Supreme Court held the *Princess Victoria* to blame. Although this judgment was reversed by the Privy Council, a Canadian Government Commission under the Minister of Marine subsequently ruled the *Princess Victoria* was responsible, while commending her captain and crew for their rescue efforts. New ordinances governing the speed and prohibiting the overtaking of ships inside the Narrows followed this tragedy.

So far as general conditions were concerned, higher export prices for timber and salmon in 1906 greatly stimulated the coastal trade and encouraged the Company's directors. Gordon Legg was already planning to lay down two more steamers in Great Britain. The ensuing five-year cycle can well be termed a growth period in which the main Union routes gradually took shape, and continued to expand without major change over two decades.

CHAPTER 4

1907-1911

The Growth Years
Completing the Coast Links
Welsford Company in Control

> My ventures are not in one bottom trusted,
> Nor to one place; nor is my whole estate
> Upon the fortunes of this year:
> Therefore, my merchandise makes me not sad.
> WILLIAM SHAKESPEARE
> *Merchant of Venice*

Fresh gold strikes in the Portland Canal area in 1907 and the founding of Stewart, the "port of the mountain of gold," meant a most hectic and successful period for the *Camosun*. In addition to carrying hundreds of passengers to Prince Rupert and Stewart, the *Camosun* in December of that year landed forty railroad workers at Kitimat Indian village wharf to grade a new Grand Trunk branch line planned between Kitimat and the Skeena at Copper River to link up with Hazelton. "This Kitimat line," said a report, "will tap the heart of British Columbia and from its interior terminus will be distributed the material entering into construction on the main line of G.T.P." Shades of Alcan nearly fifty years later.

Good teamwork in the handling of the ships by the Union Company's marine department was evidenced when, on September 19, 1907, at 4:30 a.m., the *Comox*, running in a heavy fog, went aground on Cortez Island reef. All passengers were landed safely in small boats, then picked up by the *Cassiar* and taken to Heriot Bay for transfer to their destination aboard the *Coquitlam*. The *Comox* was pulled from her rocky perch at high water the following day and beached at Mansons, where a three-foot hole between the boiler and starboard bunker was patched. The vessel was towed back to Vancouver on September 22 by the tug *Tartar*.

Captain Alexander (Sandy) Walker had been appointed in the spring by Gordon Legg as wharfinger and shore captain. Walker had

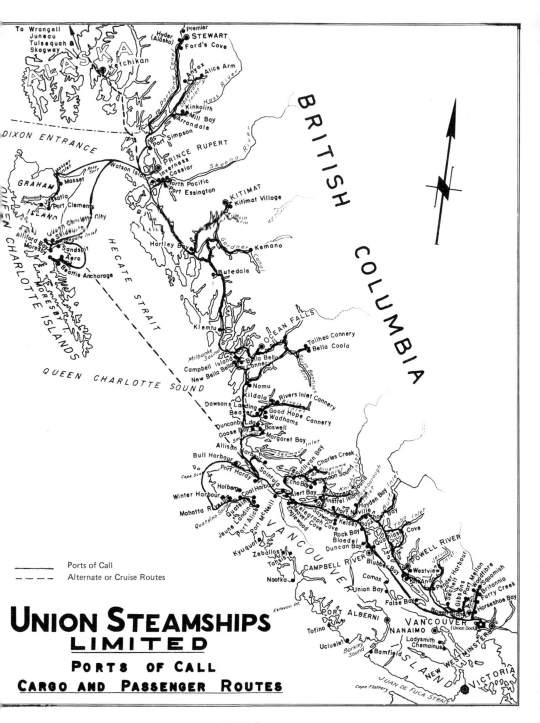

UNION STEAMSHIPS LIMITED

PORTS OF CALL

CARGO AND PASSENGER ROUTES

——— Ports of Call
– – – Alternate or Cruise Routes

1952 Routes

Union Steamship Company of British Columbia,
(Limited).

HEAD OFFICE, - VANCOUVER, B.C.

CAPITAL - - - - $500,000.

IN SHARES OF $5.00,

Payable as follows :—50 cents on application, $1.50 allotment and balance by calls not exceeding $1 per share at intervals of not less than three months.

Bankers—

BANK OF BRITISH COLUMBIA, VANCOUVER, B.C.

Solicitors—

MESSRS. DRAKE, JACKSON & CO., VANCOUVER, B.C.

European Agent—

E. G. BUCHANAN, Leith.

Secretary pro tem—

W. CARGILL, Accountant, Vancouver.

Provisional Directors—

C. D. RAND, Real Estate Agent.
CAPT. McPHAIDEN, Manager Burrard Inlet Ferry Co.
CAPT. H. STALKER, Captain S.S. "Senator."
CAPT. WEBSTER.
JAMES ORR, M.P.P.
D. CARTMEL, Retired Fleet Engineer R. N.

A. St.G. HAMERSLEY, Barrister-at-Law, Middle Temple.
W. D. CREIGHTON, Merchant.
F.-C. COTTON, President San Juan Lime Co., Limited.
J. D. TOWNLEY, Esq.
PAGE PONSFORD, Merchant.
E. PENZER, Coal Merchant.

The above Provisional Directors were appointed at a general meeting of the shareholders held on the 16th of November, 1889.

The Permanent Board of Directors will be elected at a general meeting of shareholders to be held in the City of Vancouver on the 18th day of February, 1890, at a time and place of which due notice will be given, who will have the management of the business of the Company.

THE above Company is formed to acquire, carry on, and extend the business known as the Burrard Inlet Ferry Company, as a going concern, and to own steam ships, lighters and vessels, for mail, passenger and freight traffic, in the waters of British Columbia, or elsewhere.

The Burrard Inlet Ferry Company is the only Steamship Company owned in the City of Vancouver, B. C., which is situated on the shores of Burrard Inlet, being the Terminus of the Canadian Pacific Railway, the Home Port in Canada of the China and Japan Mail Steamers, and shortly probably of the Australian Colonies.

Vancouver, B. C., in 1886, contained less than 1,000 inhabitants. In June, 1889, the population exceeded 10,000. Large business blocks and public buildings are being erected ; land is rapidly increasing in value ; new industries are being started, and the progress of the City is now beyond doubt.

It is estimated there are at present between two and three thousand people employed in Logging, Mining and various pursuits near the shores of the waters of B. C. to the north of Vancouver. They are without regular communication other than occasional steamers that are employed in towing logs from the various logging camps to the different saw mills, and there is no regular communication with the north part of Vancouver Island.

From the geographical position of Vancouver it will be seen people are constantly arriving from the East and West. The tourist travel, which is now very considerable, must rapidly increase. The want of a steamer adapted for this purpose, and excursions amongst the grand scenery of the North, is felt during the summer months. At present the S.S. "SENATOR," now running the Moodyville Ferry, is the only steamer owned in Vancouver employed in any regular passenger route, and carrying the Mails.

As soon as suitable steamers are available it is expected the Postal Department will grant other subsidies for carrying Mails to the newly settled districts. Such steamers will also be in demand for pleasure parties, etc.

The Original Definitive Prospectus of the
Union Steamship Company of British Columbia
(James Crookall collection)

The tug *Skidegate (above)* and the Moodyville ferry *(below)*,
nucleus of the Burrard Towing Company,
taken over by the Union Company in 1889.
(Vancouver Maritime Museum)

The *Capilano (above)* and the *Comox (below)*, two vessels
of the Union fleet assembled and built in Coal Harbour,
Vancouver, 1891-2.
(Vancouver Maritime Museum)

(right) Henry Darling, Manager
1894-1900, set up the first shipways
on Burrard Inlet to assemble and
launch the *Comox*, the *Capilano* and
the *Coquitlam*.
(Misses C. & M. Darling collection)

(above top) The *S. S. Cutch* on a daylight excursion in 1891.
(Union Steamships collection)
(above left) The famous *S. S. Cutch*, wrecked on Horseshoe reef
25 miles south of Juneau, Alaska, August 24, 1900.
(one of the only known records of this event from the James Crookall collection)

The ferry *Senator*, leaving Union wharf on an "official visit" to Moodyville
in the summer of 1893.
(l-r) E. V. Bodwell, Lt. Gov. Edgar Dewdney, Mrs. Dewdney, Mrs. E. V. Bodwell,
Mrs. David Oppenheimer, Mrs. H. J. Cambie (CPR), unidentified,
Mrs. Isaac Oppenheimer, Miss Rose Townley (Mrs. Grange Holt),
Miss Annie Bodwell (Mrs. Sherlock), Mayor David Oppenheimer, James Orr MP,
Capt. Hugh Stalker (with rope).
(standing l-r) Ald. Robt. Clark, unidentified, Ald. Thos. Dunn.
Photograph presented by Mrs. Hirsch, nee Oppenheimer, to the City of Vancouver
(Vancouver Maritime Museum)

The *S. S. Cassiar* at Union wharf, Vancouver; the *Coquitlam* is tied up astern.
(Vancouver Maritime Museum)

The Union Steamship wharf office about 1906.
(l-r) Unidentified, Tom Melton (Cashier), Gordon T. Legg (Managing Director),
unidentified, James Crookall (Secretary)
(James Crookall collection)

James Hugh Welsford,
English shipping magnate and
founder of the Welsford Company
(Union Steamships collection)

The early Prince Rupert settlement in 1906-07.
(above) Building the townsite.
(below) The *Camosun* loading at the end of Center Street;
she carried the mail and provided a mainline service from Vancouver five years
before the GTP Railway steamers were built, nearly a decade before the
northern transcontinental line came through. The shack *(lower right)*
is the first Post Office.
(James Crookall collection)

The *Camosun* alongside the first wharf in Prince Rupert harbour,
part of which was still uncharted about 1907.
(James Crookall collection)

The *S. S. Comox* entering the Narrows, Vancouver, in 1907.
(James Crookall collection)

Vadso and *Venture*, the two Boscowitz cannery steamers
taken over by the Union Company in 1911.
(*above*, Union Steamships collection; *below*, Vancouver Public Library)

The *Melmore*, filled with trippers on a scenic cruise to Granite Falls
on Vancouver's North Arm in 1914.
(James Crookall collection)

The *S. S. Chasina* (formerly the *Selma*), one of two ships purchased with
All Red Line in 1917.
(Lloyd Stadum collection, Seattle, Washington)

The *S. S. Cassiar* was recovered from her only major stranding on
Privett Island reef, near Simoon Sound, August 26, 1917.
(Vancouver Maritime Museum)

The *S. S. Chelohsin* at Wadhams cannery, Rivers Inlet, during a fishing season.
(James Crookall collection)

E. H. Beazley and directors in upcoast group on the *Camosun* about 1918.
(standing l-r) Grange V. Holt (Chairman), A. Beattie (Chief Engineer),
R. Kerr Houlgate, George Seymour (guest), Henry Darling,
Captain Alfred E. Dickson.
(seated l-r) Gentleman & Lady (unidentified), Miss Madge Highmoor
(Priv. Secretary), Miss Cattermole (staff), Miss C. Highmoor.
(front seated on deck) E. H. Beazley.
(Mr. Frank R. Barnsley collection)

Union Steamship dock in 1919, with most of the fleet alongside.
(left, closest) the *Coquitlam*, the *Chelohsin*, the *Cheakamus*;
(end of dock) the *Cowichan*; *(right, farthest)* the *Camosun*;
close in on right are believed to be two of Captain Cates' ships.
(foreground left) wharf machine shops and supt. engineer's office.
(James Crookall collection)

Picnickers came in thousands to Bowen Park in the early 'twenties.
(Vancouver City Archives)

The wood steamer *Capilano*, completed at B. C. Marine ways, Vancouver
began service in May 1920 to Roberts Creek, Selma Park
and the Gulf coast holiday resorts.
(Union Steamships collection)

Indian families travelling aboard the *Venture* for seasonal cannery work, 1923.
(Union Steamships collection)

The *S. S. Lady Evelyn*, purchased 1923 — best known on West Howe Sound.
(Vancouver Maritime Museum)

M. V. Comox II – The Company's Whytecliff-Bowen Island Ferry, 1924.
(Vancouver Maritime Museum)

sailed the world in fourmasters as a master of Andrew Weir's largest sail before settling down with his wife in Vancouver. A dour Scot, slow of speech but shrewd, he demanded a high standard of seamanship. He was an official of the Union Steamship Company for thirty years and was equally respected by his shipmasters and the "country shippers" in the Water Street warehouses, and he contributed a great deal to the Company's success over the next quarter-century.

Gordon Legg's philosophy for the Union was to serve the coast as a whole and to secure a profit from the total fleet movement. There were bound to be one or two losing routes, especially during the winter months, but the all round service and profitable logging and cannery runs paid for looking after the more isolated and unprofitable points. This same policy was adopted by succeeding managers throughout the Union's most successful years.

The Union wharf had become one of the busiest spots on Vancouver's waterfront. October 20, 1907, must have constituted a record for a single day for a local shipping company, with six steamer arrivals and four departures. These included the *Camosun* from Victoria, to load for Prince Rupert the same evening, and the *Iroquois* from Seattle — her owners, Inland Navigation Company, were using the Union dock at this time. Both the *Cassiar* and the *Comox* came in from their logging runs, which combined served over fifty camps, while the Company's two freighters brought in loads of canned salmon from the north. Canneries were now operating at Quathiaski Cove, Charles Creek, Knight and Smith's inlets and Alert Bay, and at about forty more sites on tidal rivers or carved out of mountain sides in isolated inlets.

With all this activity and more promised as reports of contracts being let for construction of the Grand Trunk Pacific Railway came in — the section from Prince Rupert to Copper River was due to begin in May — the first of the new Union steamers was ordered from Ailsa Shipbuilding Company of Troon, Ayrshire. This was a breakaway from Bow McLachlan with whom the Company was in litigation arising from repairs to the *Camosun* after her arrival in the Pacific. To prepare for the latest vessel, which was laid down under the name *Cariboo*, work started in January 1908 on a much needed 250-foot extension to the Union dock, with provision for larger shed space and improved handling facilities. The new ship was carefully designed to serve distant logging camps and had an overall length of 157 feet and a breadth of 32 feet. She was a twin-screw steamer of 962 gross tons, and her handy size permitted easier manoeuvring in the small bays and confined channels around Minstrel Island, Wells Pass and Kingcome Inlet.

She was brought from Scotland around the Horn by Captain Charles Polkinghorne with George Foster as chief engineer, and her performance during moderate gales on the ninety-day voyage proved her seaworthiness. She arrived in Vancouver at the reconstructed wharf on July 21, 1908, and the name *Cariboo* was quickly changed to *Cowichan* when it was found to be duplicated on the Great Lakes. Her first-class accommodation provided fifty-three berths in comfortable staterooms. The cabin area and lounges were finished in white English oak, with the dining saloon being panelled in rich mahogany. There was a smoking-room on the upper deck aft of the pilothouse, and a ladies' lounge near the stern. Her maindeck accommodation included a sizeable loggers' saloon and separate sections with deck berths for Indian and Oriental cannery workers. The purser's office and a card room were located in the forward cabin.

New features of the *Cowichan*, especially valuable when making awkward landings, were the larger size of the wheelhouse and the moving forward of the bridge so that both navigator and quartermaster could see over the bow. The vessel carried a coast licence for 165 passengers and could handle 125 to 150 tons of general cargo. With a crew of thirty-four, she had a speed of about 11 knots.

The *Cowichan* sailed on a trial excursion to Campbell River in command of veteran Captain Moody, calling en route at Van Anda. This was the port for a number of Texada Island's iron ore and copper mines and the site of a coast mission hospital before Powell River was founded. The entire Van Anda settlement welcomed the *Cowichan*. She then relieved the *Cassiar* on the Kingcome Inlet logging route and, on August 20, temporarily replaced the flagship *Camosun* on the crack run to Prince Rupert. The "Cow," as she was affectionately called, started her own route on Mondays and Thursdays to Campbell River and the Rock Bay area and beyond into Loughborough Inlet on the Monday trip. For a time she made a Saturday night sailing over to Vancouver Island, calling at Nanaimo, Denman Island, Union Bay and Comox and returning Sunday midnight from Nanaimo after she had bunkered. At this period, the practice was for a vessel to pick up bunker and galley coal from a pile at the end of the Union wharf unless she was to call at Nanaimo.

The entire coast suffered unexpectedly from a bit of a slump in 1908, which was attributed to "financial stringency" in the United States. This retarded building of the railway in the north, and depressed the export markets for fish and lumber. The following year, however, saw a big improvement in the Union Company's earnings, and the authorized capital was increased to $1,000,000, half in 6 per cent preference shares. A new surge of life and activity seemed to embrace the whole coast. Fred Lindsay, a feature writer, has recalled the sight of "hundreds of husky, cheerful men" heading north from the Union dock. He wrote: "I am still in love with the memory of the gallant little craft that plied the stormy B. C. waters bringing food and equipment and gossip to so many far flung spots of isolated beauty. . . . The old Union boats were part of the warp and woof of British Columbia of long ago."

The northern rail developments brought a new major steamship line into competition with the Union. The Canadian Pacific (B. C. Coast Service) already had the *Princess Beatrice* and the 250-foot *Princess May* on the northern run. Then, in 1909, the Grand Trunk, in preparation for the future extension of the rails to Prince Rupert, bought the old steamer *Bruno*, which was renamed *Prince Albert*, for the Prince Rupert-Queen Charlotte Islands run. A federal subsidy had been obtained to provide this service. With great confidence that the railway would be completed on time, the Grand Trunk ordered two magnificent 310-foot passenger liners — the *Prince Rupert* and *Prince George* — to be built at Wallsend-on-Tyne. The Union also had to fend off competition from Northern Steamships' *Petriana*. John Galt, who had been the Union Company's secretary in 1906, went to the new line for several years until the *Petriana* was withdrawn.

In spite of the rivalry in the northern trade, the *Camosun* remained the favourite. Representations from Prince Rupert merchants, who expressed appreciation in December 1909 for the "regularity of service," were instrumental in getting the mail contract awarded to the Union ship. Her outward cargo frequently included beef on the hoof; for weeks on end in 1909, she carried fifty head of cattle from Vancouver on her maindeck. The stock was put ashore at Port Essington on the south bank of the Skeena, to be slaughtered by George Frizelle for the large gangs working to link up the railroad. The *Camosun* also brought south from the new mill at Swanson Bay the first load of pulp ever carried by a coastal steamer.

Gordon Legg had planned to lay down two passenger vessels in Great Britain, with considerably more accommodation than the *Camosun*. These ideas were modified by the approaching completion of the Grand Trunk ships, each of about 3,380 gross tons with a speed up to 18 knots. The Grand Trunk Pacific Coast Steamship Company was incorporated on May 26, 1910. The *Prince Rupert*, a luxuriously appointed ship, arrived on the coast from the Tyne on June 4, followed

53

on July 12 by the *Prince George*. In July, the former began her run from Seattle to Prince Rupert via Vancouver. In 1911 the Grand Trunk bought an old ship in Scotland, renamed *Prince John*, for the Queen Charlotte Islands connection. Although there were construction crews and railroad materials to be transported, it was April 8, 1914 before the first through train from the east reached Prince Rupert, nearly four years after the arrival of the palatial vessels that were primarily built to connect with it. While they were designed for rail traffic and called only at larger ports where their size permitted safe docking, they siphoned off long-distance passengers and cargo from Union's way-port vessels so that the Union's own expansion program had to be curtailed. Instead of a large steamer, the small *Cheslakee* was prudently ordered from the Dublin Dockyard to supplement and partly replace the *Comox*, which, on June 7, 1910, passed through Vancouver's harbour entrance for the two thousandth time. The *Comox* remained in service for another nine years.

Mr. Legg travelled to England in May, and the steel single-screw *Cheslakee* of 132 foot length overall and 28-foot beam, was launched in Ireland, but only the hull and maindeck with crew's quarters were completed at Dublin Dockyard. She was towed to Belfast, where her triple-expansion engines of 650 h.p., built by MacColl & Company, were installed to give a speed of 11 to 12 knots. Her superstructure and cabins were not built at this time; as a result, the *Cheslakee*, devoid of any deck housing, was described as "looking more like a tug than a passenger vessel" when she arrived on the Pacific coast. She left Belfast on June 29 under Captain J. W. Starkey, a specialist in delivering new ships to their owners. She made the long voyage via St. Vincent, where she took on coal and water and then refuelled at Montevideo before rounding South America. She called at Coronel and San Francisco, which she left on September 20, arriving at Vancouver on Monday morning, September 26, 1910, eighty-nine days after her departure. According to the *News-Advertiser* of September 27, Captain Starkey said of the trip: "Varying kinds of weather were struck but in the worst of the storms the vessel took the seas easily and shipped no water . . . the crew which brought her round the Horn were all impressed by the seaworthiness of the craft."

A contract for completing the vessel's superstructure, including the cabins and general fitting-out, was placed in October with Wallace's Shipyard at North Vancouver. The vessel had been designed by A.T.C. Robertson, a local naval architect who had served with Bow McLachlan. After the addition of the twenty-three first-class cabins to provide fifty-six berths and a small but comfortable lounge, the *Cheslakee* was granted a B. C. coast licence for 148 passengers. Her well-planned dining saloon provided thirty seats, and an estimated freight capacity of 120 tons was adequate for the logging route and settlements up to Kingcome Inlet. Her entry into service two months later under Captain John Cockle, a Whitehaven seaman who had served in the Union fleet since 1896, was a welcome relief to the *Cassiar* and *Comox*. And new tonnage was urgently needed, for within only seventy miles of Vancouver, at Powell River, M. J. Scanlon and associates had acquired fine timber in the area and on Vancouver Island and were establishing the largest pulp and paper company in the West.

The *Cassiar* was always a lucky ship. On the night of January 10, 1910, and under Captain Jack Edwards, she had a narrow escape when she hit a log, while backing out of Surge Narrows in a snowstorm. When Captain Edwards attempted to swing clear, she was carried by the tide against a rock and imprisoned by the reef for several hours. After midnight, she broke clear and proceeded on her way, reaching port in Vancouver unharmed and only a few hours late. For the *Cassiar* with her wooden bulwark of a hull it was just another bump and she did not lose a trip. Little wonder she became a coast legend!

Captain John Park, born at Lonnay, Aberdeenshire in 1880, the oldest living master of the Union Steamship Company, joined the Company in March 1910 as second mate of the *Coquitlam* under Captain Edwards. Park, holding a master's ticket, made several trips to Vancouver as an officer with the Blue Funnel Line before settling down on the coast. He recalled that when the new gold rush was in progress in the Stewart area, the skipper took fifty-six passengers aboard at Prince Rupert despite the fact that the *Coquitlam* was supposed to be a freighter. When they got to Stewart, the tide was so low that the vessel could not get alongside the wharf, so the miners walked ashore over the mud flats. All the Union's smaller ships of the period carried three officers only — the captain and two mates. By this time, Captain A. E. Dickson had taken over from Captain Batchelor on the *Camosun*, Captain Moody had the new *Cowichan*, Captain Gaisford the *Cassiar*, and Captain Brown the *Comox*.

From the *Coquitlam*, John Park went as first mate of the *Capilano* under Captain Cockle, and his second mate was Neil Gray, a silent Argyllshire seaman from the Scottish coast trade. When Captain Cockle went to command the newly arrived *Cheslakee*, a captain who had been released by the CPR was appointed to the *Capilano*. According to John Park, the new man from the 250-foot Princess May "was supremely

55

confident but didn't know anything about the smaller port landings." When the vessel arrived off Salmon River (now Kelsey Bay), Captain Park told the new skipper it was "always a starboard landing" on account of the heavy current. The newcomer assured him, "I can manage a port landing all right," and promptly crashed the vessel against the wharf, shaking every timber. "He shook up a good deal more than the timbers," John Park added. "There were twenty-one tons of dynamite in the bow of the *Capilano* and I was petrified – a miracle the whole place with all of us wasn't blown up!" Soon afterwards, John Park was given command of the *Capilano*, and for six months carried capacity loads of lumber and machinery for the new plants and mines.

A Union ship was involved in the picture as usual, soon after the founding of Ocean Falls in Cousins Inlet, where industrial pioneers landed in 1910 to build a dam and harness the waterfall for the manufacture of paper. They set up a sawmill, groundwood mill and the first fifteen houses for the workers constructing the townsite. The *Coquitlam*, under Captain Jack Edwards, with C. B. Smith as first mate, took in a load of steel plate for the pipeline from the dam to the millsite. The steel lengths were strapped in 5-ton bundles and the tiny wharf, no longer than 50 feet, was so fragile that horse wagons were waiting to drag each load away as it was slung ashore. Several years after this, in 1915, Pacific Mills was incorporated, taking over the original Ocean Falls Company.

The last of the new vessels laid down by the Union Company during Mr. Legg's regime was the *Chelohsin*, also ordered from the Dublin Dockyard Company at the end of 1910. The contract was for £28,850, approximately $140,500. This fine twin-screw vessel of 1,133 gross tons, perhaps the best known after the *Cassiar* ever to operate under the Union flag, was built to a length of 175 feet with breadth of 35 feet. She was designed to furnish sixty-six berths in first class cabins, with ninety-five deck bunks, and was given a coast licence for 191 passengers with provision for a crew of thirty-eight. Great care was taken with the hull design and all four decks were plated with steel. Her two 34-foot derricks provided a lift capacity of over four tons, and a single forward hold had space for 150 tons of general cargo.

While the *Chelohsin* was still building, a change took place in the management of the Union Steamship Company when J. H. Welsford & Company of Liverpool bought control. Further reference will be made to this event that ended Gordon Legg's successful regime. The transfer of ownership brought a new Welsford manager, Ernest Beazley, who, with his bride Elsie, took up residence in Vancouver in August 1911. Born at Birkenhead, Cheshire in 1876, Mr. Beazley was a shipping man of great promise, and had been outside manager of Welsford's cargo operations. His father, in whose firm young Beazley served his apprenticeship, was the principal of Gracie, Beazley & Company, shipowners and charterers, Liverpool. Educated in England and Heidelberg, Ernest Beazley had been a captain in the 1st Cheshire Volunteer Battalion. He was a good-looking man of medium height with a forthright manner. A keen angler and inveterate pipe smoker, he had many interests. It fell to him to welcome the arrival at Vancouver some months later of the new ship that Gordon Legg had laid down in 1910.

The *Chelohsin* was taken to Belfast for the installation of the twin triple-expansion engines built by MacColl & Co. Ltd. She ran her trials on September 25, 1911 over the measured mile at Belfast Lough at a speed of over 14 knots; and in spite of the "boisterous weather," there was no vibration.

Three weeks later, after final outfitting, Captain Starkey took out his second Union vessel from Belfast harbour on October 17, with the cabin windows boarded up fore and aft. He had high praise for the seagoing qualities of the *Chelohsin*: "She was like a racing yacht" was his comment on her trip round the Horn, after calling at Montevideo. The vessel encountered rough weather only on the last leg and loaded more ballast at San Francisco for the run up to Cape Flattery. She reached her Vancouver destination after seventy-two days on Friday evening, December 28. The *News-Advertiser* reported the next day:

Old timers who were at the wharf to welcome the vessel said that she was one of the smartest looking vessels they had ever seen. The *Chelohsin* is very beamy, but with her racing lines and her sheer, loses the appearance of width . . . Her passenger accommodation is the equal of any vessel in the coastwise business. The *Chelohsin* embraces many ideas which will commend her to travellers on this coast.

The *Chelohsin*'s facilities were indeed fine for her day, nearly all passengers being accommodated in two-berth staterooms on her "awning" and "shade" decks. Staterooms, which were finished in oak and had sliding windows, had running water, some with hot and cold. A number of rooms had an extra "cabinet bed" which could be folded into a day settee. The main observation room with its large square windows was sited forward on the top deck, and aft on the same deck was a ladies' saloon. There was a convenient smoking room forward on the upper deck, and the panelling all through the *Chelohsin* was exceptionally fine. A handsome dining saloon on the maindeck seated forty-six passengers.

"Flying the Red Ensign at her bow and the Canadian flag at her stern, resplendent in the spotless white of her paint," as the press described her, the *Chelohsin*, under Captain John Cowper, sailed up Howe Sound on the glorious Saturday afternoon of February 24, 1912, for her official house-warming trip. Many of the city's shipping and business leaders marked the event at a luncheon aboard. They included R. H. Alexander and A. Hendry of Hastings Mill; Andrew Wallace; J. O'Brien of Stillwater; Charles Thulin from Lund; W. B. Brenton of B. C. Packers; T. W. London of Balfour Guthrie; Peter Wallace of Wallace Fisheries; Captain T. H. Worsnop of the Canadian Mexican Line; and Henry Darling. Ernest Beazley, the new manager, and J. H. Wrigley, presided. That same evening, the *Chelohsin* left on her maiden voyage, with George Foster as chief engineer, for the Skeena River, Prince Rupert, Port Simpson, Nass River and Goose Bay (later Anyox).

Captain Cowper, born in 1852, was a Manxman who had been with local steamers since 1889. He was succeeded in 1912 by the bluff seaman, Captain J. T. (Jack) Edwards, who went to sea at sixteen and was with the White Pass Steamship Company before joining the Union Company. He was a fine skipper and was a character "dressed like a buccaneer who had stepped straight out of one of Jack. London's adventure yarns." Arthur Dunn of Powell River once wrote: "I knew big Jack Edwards, a tough old veteran of sailing days, who ended his career as a pilot. When the *Chelohsin* had to lay-over at Powell River, on several occasions he took an axe into the woods and chopped trees just for exercise." Best known of the *Chelohsin* pursers at the logging camps were H. B. Lennard and "Pinky" Hughes, the latter possessing a devilish sense of humour.

When the controlling interest was bought by J. H. Welsford & Company Limited the transaction was conducted personally with Mr. Legg in Vancouver by James Hugh Welsford, J. P., principal owner of Welsford's. It involved the purchase of majority shares amounting to nearly $400,000.

A man of dynamic, and, at times, almost relentless activity, Welsford made his mark early in the shipping world when, by the age of thirty-six, he had acquired a fleet of nine cargo vessels ranging from 4,000 to 8,000 tons. In 1911, he bought control of the famous Leyland Shipping Co. Ltd., and, under the name of Gulf Transport Line, his ships were largely engaged in the cotton trade between Liverpool and

Galveston, Texas, where Welsford's at one time had an American office. Just before Welsford sold it, he doubled the manager's salary "as a going away present." There were many who thought his choice of Mr. Beazley to run the Union Steamship line in Vancouver was the smartest move he ever made.

Mr. Welsford, a great "tariff reformer," set something of a record by standing unsuccessfully three times as the Conservative candidate in England's Crewe riding. He moved in the brilliant London Carlton Club circle of F. E. Smith (later Lord Birkenhead) and the great "F. E." defended him in a civil suit in 1912 over the Union purchase arrangements. Mr. Welsford was an impulsive man — he once gave me five shillings on the spur of the moment, a lot of money for a schoolboy.

Mr. Welsford crossed the Atlantic annually until after 1914, to look over his Union interests. Always impeccably dressed, the new owner had a most engaging presence, and a powerful temper when he did not get what he expected. He could be a regular tartar on occasion, as some local businessmen quickly found to their cost. Once, when Mr. Welsford was losing at cards at his London club with the eloquent F. E. Smith as his partner, he made a cutting remark about one of their opponents, whereupon "F. E." laid down his hand and said: "Do you know, Welsford, who's the most unpopular member here?" Welsford, rather taken aback, said: "I suppose you mean me." "Not at all," Smith blandly replied, "I'm the bugger who introduced you to this club!"

It was announced on September 23, 1911, that the Welsford company had enlarged its holdings in British Columbia by acquisition for $160,000, half cash and the balance in Union Steamship stock, of the Boscowitz Steamship Co. Ltd. of Victoria, which had been officially incorporated on March 18, 1899. The purchase included the steamers *Vadso* and *Venture*, the latter completed at Napier & Miller's Glasgow yard only in 1910 to replace the previous *Venture* which was destroyed by fire at Inverness Cannery. These were sizable vessels, well adapted to the northern trade. The *Vadso*, brought out from Liverpool by Captain B. L. Johnson in 1907, was 908 gross tons and 191 feet in length; she was employed chiefly as a cannery freighter, carrying only fifty passengers. The *Venture*, 1,011 gross tons and 180 feet, was a splendid combination type for the Union's trade. She had a licence for 186 passengers and cargo capacity of 500 tons with sixty-two first class berths, extra loggers' berths and deck space for the canning crews. Her speed was 12 to 13 knots.

Captain J. D. Warren, a Boscowitz principal who had sold out to

Mr. Welsford, was associated with Joseph Boscowitz in the operation of four steel schooners for more than ten years before 1883, when the *Barbara Boscowitz* was built in Victoria. Shortly after the first *Venture* was lost, Captain Warren chartered a small steamer called *St. Dennis*, which Captain B. L. Johnson brought up from San Diego, as a temporary replacement in the cannery trade. At the end of the season, on her return voyage from Victoria to San Diego, the *St. Dennis*, with a crew provided by her owners and loaded with coal, vanished without trace except for a wood deck-cabin which evidently floated loose when she foundered with all hands on or about November 21, 1910. Under the company's sale agreement, John Barnsley, secretary-manager of the Boscowitz Line, joined the Union company and was appointed agent — in effect, northern manager — at Prince Rupert. George McGregor, another major Boscowitz shareholder, became Union's representative in Victoria, the home of J. H. Todd & Sons cannery operations. Such mariners as Captains Walter Moorhouse, James Noel and Andrew Sinclair, and Chief Engineer Clarence Arthur, came over to the Union with the Boscowitz ships.

On September 22, 1911, Mr. Legg resigned as managing director of the company he had controlled since 1894, and retired to England where he died in 1940 at the age of eighty-eight. The day following Legg's retirement, James Hugh Welsford was elected President, Ernest H. Beazley and Secretary J. H. Wrigley were named joint managers.

The Hon. Francis Carter-Cotton, MLA, B.C.'s finance minister from 1898 to 1900 and president of the Council until 1910, was named chairman of the Union's board of directors. He had been a "provisional director" as far back as 1889. He gave up management of the daily *News-Advertiser* in 1910, and in 1912 was elected first chancellor of the University of British Columbia. The following year he became chairman of the Vancouver Harbour Commission and president of the Board of Trade.

Mr. Welsford's first action was to acquire thirty thousand additional Union shares at par to pay for the new *Chelohsin*. Welsford's also took up a further fifteen thousand shares to complete the Company's purchase agreement with the Boscowitz line.

Mr. Welsford's entry into the British Columbia coastal trade was part of a wider ranging plan. He was looking ahead to the completion of the Panama Canal, which was to open on August 15, 1914, and had in mind the linking of a freight service between Vancouver and Panama with his cargo operations which ran from Liverpool into Galveston and the Gulf of Mexico. On December 31, 1911, the *News-Advertiser* carried this shipping note: "The Gulf Transport Line of Liverpool (owned by Welsford's), affiliated with the Leyland Line which operates to Mexico, may come to Vancouver. The *Inkula* has been ordered to load for Vancouver, Puget Sound and California to test business conditions." She was one of the six 5,000-tonners in the Gulf Transport operation.

As the next step in this bold scheme, Mr. Welsford, in equal partnership with B. C. Pearson of London, bought for $100,000 the Canadian Mexican Line, that was managed by Captain T. H. Worsnop and which operated chartered steamers from Vancouver and Victoria. They planned to establish a through cargo service from British Columbia and Pacific coast ports to Europe by means of steamers connecting with Pearson's 125-mile Tehuantepec Railway across the isthmus from Salina Cruz to the Gulf of Mexico.

In July 1912, the Pacific Canadian Steamship Co. Ltd. was formed, with the expectation of starting a fortnightly cargo schedule from Vancouver via San Francisco to the terminal of the railway, with the through steamer service to be maintained on the opening of the Panama Canal. It was intended to be managed by Mr. Beazley, with Captain Worsnop as his assistant. The first of three vessels designated for this new service was the *Lonsdale*, brought from Liverpool on charter, her second officer on the Mexican run, Sydney A. Smith, later becoming Judge Smith. He had earned his master's ticket before studying law and rose to become one of Vancouver's leading experts on marine legal cases. But the Mexican project, anticipating some of the volume of the future Canal trade, was a little ahead of its day and quickly lost money, forcing its discontinuance before the year was out. Still, it was an imaginative "Welsford gambit," as the Holt Line and P. & O. traffic proved in later years on this route. As a wind-up of this episode, the *Lonsdale*, in which Welsford's and the Union shared a mutual interest, went to Japanese buyers for $63,000 in November 1912.

Mr. Welsford returned to Liverpool on October 25, 1911, leaving Mr. Beazley at the helm of Union Steamships' affairs. Before he left, he told the press that the Company planned to add 150 feet to its wharf, saying that "the present pier will not have sufficient accommodation for the two vessels of the Boscowitz line and other vessels being brought out [from Great Britain]." The *News-Advertiser* noted:

October 24 marked the 20th anniversary of steel shipbuilding in British Columbia and of the real beginning of the Union Steamship

61

Company. On that day in 1891 was launched the little steel *Comox*, the first of seven that have been built for the Union Steamship Company which has received such an impetus by the amalgamation of the Boscowitz and Canadian-Mexican lines under the Presidency of J. H. Welsford. . .

The *Comox* has a singular record. She is probably the only vessel her own age which has never been in a serious accident, although she has been sent over a coast notorious for accidents. Apart from her first skipper, Captain Moody, many local mariners have been in charge of her including Captain Bartlett, now in charge of a fishing steamer, Captain Cowper, Captain Cockle and presently Captain C. Brown . . . He who knows more about the steamer than anyone is Mr. Dragalovitch, Homer Street, who put her engines together in Coal Harbour and up to last fall (1910) acted as her chief engineer continuously.

The Boscowitz acquisition greatly strengthened the Union's position on the coast, and helped to combat aggressive moves of the Grand Trunk Pacific Steamships, which had two fast weekly sailings to Prince Rupert. The addition of the vessels *Venture* and *Vadso* gave Mr. Beazley predominance not only in the cannery trade but also in the smaller port business along the entire mainland coast.

CHAPTER 5

1912-1918

Ernest Beazley at the Helm
Coastal Hazards and the War Years
Purchase of All-Red Line and New Planning

> Once upon a time there was a Liverpool man who had
> a dream that he was living in the time of the flood.
> And in his dream he saw the Ark, which had painted
> on its bows its name, and the word LIVERPOOL, the
> port of registry . . . Lloyds had no record of Noah's
> ship being registered, which is not surprising, for that
> shipmaster was probably too busy embarking live
> stock to think of little matters.
>
> H. R. SHAW
> in *Liverpool, the Capital of trade and travel*

One of Mr. Beazley's first tasks was to get the loading and embarking facilities in better shape and in 1912 an extensive renovation was undertaken. The wharf was widened and a larger freight shed built, while rail trackage was switched alongside where rail cars could be spotted for direct loading. Several of the old buildings were torn down and new business offices erected, together with the installation of modern equipment for the engineers' machine shop. Beazley was not so lucky in his attempt to obtain a footbridge over the railway at the Carrall Street end, although meetings took place with the Canadian Pacific Railway and Vancouver city, represented by aldermen Baxter and Woodside.

Next, both the *Chelohsin* and *Cowichan*, and later the *Camosun*, were converted to oil, the high installation cost being more than compensated for by the cleanliness and economy achieved, not to mention the convenience and time saved by obviating coal bunkering. In November 1912, Beazley arranged with Captain Jack Cates of the Terminal Steam Navigation Company for his Bowen Island and Howe Sound steamers to berth at the Union dock.

The new managing director held the reins of a small and competent team ashore. John Galt returned as assistant manager for the next six years, with the dour Northumbrian Tom Melton as cashier and James Crookall as secretary. Mr. Beazley started a stevedoring office on

Hastings Street under the management of E. Cowdell, who came from Liverpool with a background in cargo handling. A most valuable gain from the Boscowitz line was little Billy Vaughan — "One-eyed Billy," as the cannery workers called him — the popular ex-purser of the *Venture*, who joined Captain Walker's marine office as freight agent. Billy had worked for a time out of the Prince Rupert office, and because of his intimate acquaintance with the cannery managers, the bulk of the southbound salmon pack was retained by the Union vessels.

Sitting on the wharf years later, Billy Vaughan told me a strange tale about the precognition of the early Indians in the Nass River. He said that they knew unquestionably to the hour, from the movement of the birds and other natural signs, when the cannery steamer was coming. By the time his vessel hove in sight around the point, they would be milling around the small Kincolith wharf. This was before the days of the telegraph in the north. Some time later I came across an article in a geographic magazine which attributed the same kind of extra perception to the native islanders of Mauritius in sensing the approach of a sailing ship at least a day before the event.

After rehashing the schedules to reap the benefit of the Union-Boscowitz amalgamation, Beazley deployed the *Chelohsin* alongside the *Camosun*, under Captain A. E. Dickson, on the northern route out of Vancouver on Saturdays. This taciturn Nova Scotia mariner, who had served on Union ships since the days of the *Senator*, had no peer as a navigator. I knew the kindly skipper and can appreciate the opinion of his contemporaries that "Dickson was in a league by himself." Two mail boats arriving in Prince Rupert in the early part of the week suited the merchants admirably. The entire fleet was kept busy, and the *Coquitlam* was running in the herring season from Steveston to Seattle. Beazley was disturbed by a grounding of the *Chelohsin*, soon after entering service on the Skeena River, which involved extensive repairs. A strong protest to the marine department at Ottawa called attention to the absence of important aids to navigation in this area. The *Venture* was the principal vessel assigned to look after the Skeena and Nass River canneries, and she performed magnificently.

Captain John Park was sent to Victoria in September 1911, to take over the *Venture* from Captain Moorhouse of the Boscowitz line. Park's chief officer was John Boden, who was river-boating both on the Fraser and in the Yukon around 1900 before joining the Union Company in 1905. On Captain Park's first trip, the *Venture* left Hardy Bay at midnight, and soon afterwards John Boden, who had taken over the night watch as pilot, roused the captain to report a vessel ashore on the rocks in Christie Passage off Noble Island. Fires had been lit on the beach by the crew. Captain Park took the *Venture* close in and found it was the *Princess Beatrice* under Captain Robertson with two hundred passengers aboard, mostly cannery workers returning home after the fishing season. They were taken off in the *Venture*'s life-boats and as there was no means of looking after them at Hardy Bay, they were landed at Alert Bay to be picked up by another Vancouver-bound vessel.

On October 26, 1911, the *Venture* (Captain Park) reached Vancouver with passengers and a full cargo of canned salmon. Reporting the arrival, the *News-Advertiser* said that the officers took part in a potlatch at Bella Coola. The press said.

An Indian, George Robertson, gave a potlatch which all the Indians from miles around attended. Many Indians contributed so that during the ceremony $3,875 in money, 700 boxes of biscuits, 1,000 sacks of flour and 500 bags of sugar passed among other things from the owners of the past to the present owners. A great feast was held at which the captain, purser, pilot, other officers and passengers of the *Venture* attended, during which six whole cattle were eaten. After the feast, presents were given away wholesale, the larger the social rank of the recipient, the larger his gifts, so that while an Indian chief from Alert Bay received over a hundred dollars in money alone . . . the officers received six bits (75 cents) each!

The visitors were asked "not to consider the intrinsic worth of the gifts as indication of the goodwill." Several large coppers of great value which had been hammered out and carved by the Indians in various designs were also given away. The report concluded: "The next Indian potlatch is to be held in Kitimat, where many of the gifts will find their way back to the giver."

The missionaries had tried to stop the potlatches and the custom of "living off one another," but they had not been very successful up to this time. Mr. Gibson, the missionary at Bella Coola, had a large family and two of his daughters travelled south on the *Venture* with J. B. Saint, manager of the Bella Coola cannery, and his wife. Captain Park recalled another occasion when he picked up two hundred Indians with the *Venture* at Kitimat and took them to a potlatch at Bella Bella. The potlatch lasted for three weeks — always at the end of a fishing season — and when it came time to embark them again at Bella Bella, he alerted his crew in case of trouble. While some of the natives were "the worse for wear" after all the feasting, he said they were quite peaceful on the voyage back to their Kitimat settlement.

In 1914, John Park had with him in the *Venture* as chief officer

James Noel, who succeeded him in 1916. His first mate was Andy Johnstone, the second mate (later Captain) being Sinclair. All four officers were eventually to become coast pilots. The quartermaster at this time was Ernest Sheppard, who became mate of the *Venture* in 1916 before joining the Royal Flying Corps. It is difficult to conceive of five more distinguished mariners aboard one Union ship, but it is perhaps not surprising that it was the *Venture*.

There is a 23-foot rise and fall of tide at Inverness Cannery, situated in what is called the Skeena "slough," and skippers exerted the utmost care to avoid being trapped by the tide. On one occasion, the *Venture* saved herself only by running her engines full ahead while holding her bow head on against the wharf. These were the great cannery days with twelve plants operating in the Skeena, including three at Port Essington. Mr. Wallace was at Claxton cannery, Mr. English at Balmoral, Mr. Gilmore at Oceanic, Mr. Lamb at Cassiar and Mr. Johnson at Todd's Inverness cannery. There were four canneries working in the Nass River: Arrandale and Nelson's being looked after by Mr. Walker, Nass Harbour by Mr. Chambers and Mill Bay by Mr. Doyle. On Rivers Inlet there were seven, as well as Mr. Hickey's cannery in Smith's Inlet and canneries at Alert Bay and Quathiaski Cove, the latter owned and managed by Mr. Anderson.

The Draney family was well known in coast cannery circles. Charlie Draney was manager at Kimsquit and later at Namu, where his father built the first cannery and a small sawmill. On one occasion, the *Venture* took Mrs. Draney south to enter hospital in Vancouver for the birth of her son. When the vessel docked at Namu the following trip, Captain Park had all the flags flying, which was the first news Charlie Draney received that he was a father. It was these intimate relations of the Union ships with the little communities that fostered trade and made the Company's name a household word on the B. C. coast.

Captain Park spent some tense moments soon after the *Venture* was changed to fuel oil in 1912 when John Boden reported "Ship's stopped!" It was an alarming situation trying to keep the vessel from grounding on Helmcken Island, but the captain dropped anchor and managed to swing the ship clear. It turned out that the sudden halt had been due to a stoppage of fuel oil from the tank. All that day the *Venture* held on, while Chief Engineer Clarence Arthur went below and bored a hole in the extra tank to get the oil flowing again into the double bottom. In 1916, John Park joined the Pilotage Service, following such Union mariners as Captains Saunders and Batchelor. In 1917-18 he commanded the *Turret Crown* and other big cargo liners running between New York and the Mediterranean during the submarine menace.

Ernest Beazley participated wholeheartedly in the business and social life of young Vancouver, especially with the Board of Trade and transportation committees, and he was president of the Ship Owners Association of B. C. His easy style of expression, along with his expert knowledge of cargo handling in many world ports, made him the doyen of the local steamship operators. His managerial skill was reflected in the high earnings of 1911-12.

News of a disaster first reached Mr. Beazley's desk on January 7, 1913, in a laconic message from Captain Cockle CHESLAKEE SUNK VAN ANDA ALONGSIDE WHARF STOP THREE PASSENGERS AND SECOND COOK DROWNED ALL OTHERS SAVED CAMOSUN STANDING BY. This accident — the only one involving loss of life in a Union passenger ship in the Company's entire history — occurred in the early hours of that day, barely twenty-seven months after the *Cheslakee* entered service. The vessel had sailed from Union dock at 8:45 p.m. on Monday, January 6, with 45 tons of cargo and ninety-seven passengers under command of Captain John Cockle, who joined as a mate in 1905 and, to quote Mr. Beazley, "was in the front rank of coast navigators." At 12:40 a.m. he gave her in charge of the pilot (later captain) Robert Wilson, the mates being John Aspinall and James Dobson, and at 3:25 a.m., the *Cheslakee* arrived at Van Anda, first port of call, where eight passengers got off and several boards of freight were unloaded. Twenty minutes later the vessel left in very stormy weather, with the wind east-by-southeast, on a course to Powell River. Within ten minutes, about a mile and a half across the strait, she was struck on her starboard beam by a heavy southeast squall with a velocity, according to First Officer Wilson's report, of 65 m.p.h. This caused her to list to port at an angle of about 25 degrees, dislodging some cargo when the vessel shipped two heavy seas. The pilot put the helm aport, bringing the gale on to her port side in an endeavour to right the vessel, thus turning her back to Van Anda, and then called Captain Cockle. Although the *Cheslakee* was somewhat more upright, the master had no hesitation about continuing the return to Van Anda wharf. Before reaching shelter, however, she once more listed dangerously to port, and the moment lines were on the dock a gangway was run out on the starboard side. The Captain had told Chief Steward G. J. Booth to call all passengers to disembark immediately, and ordered everybody ashore.

According to to a passenger's account in the *News-Advertiser* of January 8, conditions were nightmarish since

> lights were out almost as soon as the vessel reached the wharf, as water had drowned out the fires and there was barely [any] steam . . . the officers acted with cool precision and there was practically no panic among the passengers . . . [the officers] did not tell the passengers what had happened but ordered them to get off as quickly as possible . . . The boat was sinking rapidly, in fact one could feel the deck falling beneath one's feet and the lower she sank the further away from the wharf she tilted.

Finally, the gangway became too short to bridge the gap and a longer common plank was pressed into use. Over this the stream of thinly clad passengers continued to pour. Captain Cockle himself rescued three men from the forward smoking room, because they were unable to climb the now steeply inclined deck. The gallant skipper, reported the *News-Advertiser*, "lowered himself down the sloping deck, hanging on by his arms to the brass capped entrance. Extended at full length, he placed his foot within their reach, and one by one they scrambled over the Captain's body to safety." Four years later, John Cockle was to give his life for Canada in World War I.

Despite the perilous situation, there would have been just time enough for all to get off the ship. It was tragic, therefore, that several who apparently delayed briefly to dress got trapped in two aft cabins when the vessel, within five minutes of coming alongside the dock, suddenly lurched, snapping the forward line, and sank. At daylight, only part of the funnel and deckhouse were visible. Two school teachers, Mrs. Simpson and Miss M. Pepper, were drowned, as was Samuel Courtney, a logger who had returned to a cabin which he shared with John Hartlin. The two men shook hands. Then Mr. Hartlin miraculously escaped by smashing the glass in the cabin window, which was only twenty inches wide, and swimming ashore, badly cut. When everyone had been accounted for, the death toll was seven, including Miss C. Nesbitt and a small child, a logger named Johnson and Sun Ling, the Chinese cook. Two Japanese firemen, who were also trapped below, struggled clear and clutched the wharf piling in the icy waters until they were pulled up by ropes. The discomfort of the survivors was soon relieved in the shelter of Van Anda's hotel, only a quarter-mile away. Hot meals were served and clothing was provided from the general store. Most of them were re-embarked by launch aboard the waiting *Camosun* and returned to Vancouver.

The marine court of enquiry which assembled on January 20, 1913, and comprised Captain George E. Robertson, Captain Charles

Eddy and F. F. Pickard, found that there was "no lack of discipline and the serious and critical nature of the ship's position was not realized at the time." But it was critical of the addition of the ship's superstructure two years earlier which was "heavier than allowed for by the designer" and of other alterations made after the *Cheslakee* first arrived on the coast without a further survey having been taken. While not determining a positive cause of the maindeck's flooding, the court of enquiry found that "It was the general practice to keep the 'midship gangway ports open for the purpose of ventillating the 'tween decks in moderate weather . . . it is possible and probable these [freight] doors were open or not properly secured at the time of the list." The court considered that the seamanship exhibited by the Master and Pilot at the time of the disaster was commendable and was the means of avoiding what might have been a much serious and lamentable catastrophe."

Immediately following the sinking, Beazley arranged with the B. C. Salvage Company to send up *S. S. Salvor* to attempt recovery of the *Cheslakee* on the basis of "no cure, no pay." Weeks later, the stricken vessel was raised, pumped out and towed back to Vancouver. After docking, Beazley had the ship replanned and lengthened 20 feet, by slicing the hull in two — the first time this method was used on the B.C. coast — to give a greater margin of stability. To overcome nautical superstitions, with special sanction from Ottawa for a name change, she was returned to service in June 1913 as the *Cheakamus* and ran successfully for another thirty years.

In the spring of 1913, the services performed by the Union fleet and those of other passenger lines were as follows: the *Chelohsin*, *Cowichan* and *Cassiar* made five weekly logging sailings along Johnstone Strait and to Kingcome Inlet while the *Comox* looked after the Jervis Inlet, Texada and local area. The *Camosun* made a weekly trip to Rivers Inlet, Ocean Falls and Bella Coola, while the *Venture* sailed weekly to the canneries and to Prince Rupert and Granby Bay. The Grand Trunk Pacific had bi-weekly sailings with the *Prince Rupert* and *Prince George* to the north, and the *Prince John* connecting for the Queen Charlotte Islands. Canadian Pacific had one northern sailing a week with the *Princess Beatrice* to Prince Rupert, in addition to a west coast of Vancouver Island service. It had four Princesses including the *Sophia*, on the triangle route, the *Patricia* daily to Nanaimo, a service to the Gulf Islands with the *Joan*, and another to Union Bay and Comox with the *Charmer*. Terminal Steam ran to Howe Sound, and the All Red Line had the *Selma* running three times weekly to Powell River. From this it is apparent that, excluding the local runs, the Union provided seven out of twelve up-coast services, and almost exclusively looked after the region from Powell River north to Bella Coola, which contained over a hundred ports and small landings. For the summer of 1913, Mr. Beazley also operated the 90-foot *Tartar* on West Howe Sound under Captain W. L. Yates who had just received his master's certificate.

Years later in the *Powell River News*, Arthur C. Dunn, a wharfinger who had tied up the *Comox* and *Cassiar* at Powell River during this period, summed up Union's role:

> They pioneered transportation of people and freight, and serviced the most isolated and remote settlements . . . It seems uncanny how they located some of the places during foggy weather. The ships were designed for the type of work they were engaged in. None were glamorous in any way as they never catered to the tourist trade to any extent. Big ships could never have served the holes and corners the smaller ones were quite able to.

After pioneering in the cannery trade under the Boscowitz flag the thirty-year-old *Vadso*, one of the two vessels taken over by the Union Company in 1911, met with disaster early on the morning of February 3, 1914. Northbound from Prince Rupert under command of Captain J. Richardson on a freight run with cannery supplies, including a deck-load of oil drums, she grounded heavily on an uncharted rock at the entrance of Observatory Inlet near the mouth of the Nass River. In a raging snowstorm and with the ship foundering, Chief Officer (later Captain) Larry Thompson immediately ordered two lifeboats lowered. While the ship was being abandoned, the gasoline drums broke loose on the up-ended vessel which quickly became an inferno as flames from the engine room enveloped the oil drenched decks. Somehow the men, some only partly dressed, got clear of the burning wreck without injury. After rowing through the storm safely, they reached the Arrandale cannery wharf. Only nine months earlier, the *Vadso*, running in thick weather, had been heavily damaged in a grounding on Reef Point, Baynes Sound, en route to Union Bay. After repairs at the Wallace Shipyard, she was put into a separate Vadso Company and capitalized at $30,000, with the shipyard accepting a half share for the repair bill — an example of friendly co-operation between two pioneer companies.

Soon after taking over the management of the Union Steamship Company, Mr. Beazley suggested a program for progressive development of the fleet and urged immediate construction of a new day-steamer for the Powell River route. But Mr. Welsford thought that the 1912 prices for ships were too high and that this would prevent competitors from taking the field. In one sense perhaps he was right, but a specially designed ship might have been better than picking up old ships of another line, as occurred four years later. Welsford evidently had a change of heart, because in 1914 he purchased in England the vessel *Melmore*, which had been built at Port Glasgow in 1892 by D. J. Dunlop & Co. and as the *Wolfhound*, had run as a Londonderry-to-Liverpool mail packet along with the former *Deerhound* (*Lady Evelyn*), before being engaged on the Fleetwood run of the Isle of Man freight service. This vessel, of 424 gross tons, 156 feet in length and 26-foot beam, was converted to carry 200 passengers and 100 tons of cargo, and was put into service by Beazley in July 1914 just before the outbreak of war. She ran to Sechelt and other local routes, including those to West Howe Sound and Burrard Inlet's North Arm. Probably due to the experimental nature of this operation as well as war conditions, her name was not changed to the Union's traditional Indian style. She was not successful, being too big for the times and in competition with Mr. Whitaker's boat to Sechelt. The *Melmore* was sold at a profit in 1916 by Welsford to C. W. Brown of London and went south to Peru as the *Santa Elena*.

General business on the B. C. coast had been depressed since early 1914, with many logging camps being shut down. The outbreak of war caused a further sharp drop in Pacific coast trade, affecting all shipping companies alike. Two ships launched in Scotland during that time for the Canadian Pacific, the "Ghost Princesses" *Margaret* and *Irene*, passed directly into war service and never did ply B. C. coastal waters.

A total of sixty-five ship, wharf and office employees of the Company left for active service during the first two war years. Several masters offered their services to the British Admiralty, Captain John Cockle and Captain Alfred E. Dickson being accepted into Water Transport. Captain Dickson left the *Camosun* to spend eighteen months carrying munitions and dodging minefields in the English Channel. Captain Cockle died overseas from illness in 1917. Captain Francis Bannerman lost an arm serving with the 7th Battalion, but returned to the Company's service for several years after the war. Nine Union engineers went to the Royal Navy; and R. M. Logan, later Company superintendent engineer, served in the flagship *H. M. S. New Zealand*.

Captain B. L. (Barney) Johnson, who left Union for the Boscowitz line and later went to command the Grand Trunk's *Prince Rupert*, was given command of one of Canada's two submarines purchased from Chile. He crossed the Atlantic in charge of *Submarine H 8*, and in 1916 received the D.S.O. After his submarine struck a mine in the North Sea, he navigated astern for one hundred miles back to the Harwich base. Six other Union men, including mates E. Emerson, J. D. McPhee and J. W. (Chips) Williams, went overseas with Vancouver's 29th Battalion (Tobin's Tigers). Andy Johnstone, mate of the *Venture*, a vessel he was later to command, went overseas with the Royal Canadian Artillery and was away for nearly four years. The wharf freight agent, O. Fyson, was killed serving with the 16th Battalion (Canadian Scottish); and three employees, including ticket agent J. Douglas Dingwall, served overseas with the 72nd (Seaforths). From head office, Secretary James Crookall was away two years with the Canadian Forces.

In August 1915, Mr. Beazley concluded new mail contracts with the Federal Trade and Commerce Department, covering both northern B. C. ports and the Queen Charlotte Islands. But fate finally caught up with the *Capilano*, one of the original "pre-fab" ships, when, under command of Irishman Captain Sam Nelson, she found a reef in Malaspina Strait. Northbound from Vancouver on September 30, 1915, she scraped heavily on a rock off Texada Island. The skipper thought that she could make Campbell River, but her hull was badly punctured. The fine little ship foundered in deep water between Baker Passage and Cape Mudge, after Captain Nelson had safely transferred the crew ashore at Indian Point on Savary Island. A letter from Frances Keefer, daughter of the Savary Island postmaster, to Mr. McInnis, which is preserved in Vancouver's Maritime Museum, provides this eyewitness account of the wreck:

On the morning of October 1st, 1915, I was having breakfast with my parents, when two officers from a U. S. S. Co. vessel came to our door to inquire if we had a telephone, as they were shipwrecked at Indian Point and wanted to notify headquarters and have them send a vessel to pick up the crew who were all safe on shore at Indian Point, after the *Capilano* had sunk some distance off the point. The officers had walked along the beach to the east end and located our house. They gave us a vivid description of the sinking of the *Capilano* from the time it struck an object off Texada Island and later on started to leak and finally sank, somewhere off Savary. They said it was an awful sight to see the ship with her lights still glowing headed for the bottom and at the last moment, just before she submerged, the whistle gave a final blast as something fell against the cord. It was dark and they wondered what land they were near and they rowed for some time in an easterly direction, until they finally landed on the west end of Savary Island. The vessel sank so quickly that the men had very little time to gather some food supplies, but they managed to do so and get away in a large life-boat. Fortunately there was a vacated miners' shack on the point that the crew was able to occupy while they waited to be rescued . . . A vessel was sent for the crew and my father, who knew these waters very well, was invited on board by the Captain and he asked father to pilot them up to Indian Point, which he did and they picked up the crew.

In a spirit of wartime co-operation, Mr. Beazley completed arrangements early in March 1916 with Captain Nicholson, manager of Grand Trunk Pacific Steamships, for an interlocking schedule by the two lines to look after the northern ports. To supplement the Union ships, Beazley took over the operation of Grand Trunk's *Prince Albert* to serve the Queen Charlotte Islands on a fortnightly route, calling at Ocean Falls, Surf Inlet gold mines, Kitimat Indian village, Anyox and Prince Rupert, where she connected CTP rail passengers north and also southbound to Vancouver. The larger Grand Trunk vessels sailed from Seattle twice weekly via Victoria and Vancouver to connect rail passengers at the Prince Rupert terminal.

At 2 a.m. on March 7, 1916 the crack *Camosun* under Captain Dickson was proceeding at quarter-speed in a heavy snowstorm when she went ashore on Lucy Island, near Digby Island, outside Prince Rupert harbour. She was en route to Masset, and there was no danger to the seventeen passengers who were taken off in launches summoned from Prince Rupert. At low tide the vessel was "high and dry" and 100 tons of coal and other wartime supplies for the Queen Charlottes were lightered off. Luckily the *Camosun*'s strong hull was not punctured. She was pulled free at high tide on March 17 and proceeded south for repairs under her own steam, being replaced by the *Prince Albert*. A sigh of relief went up in the northern communities when it was learned that the popular Union "flagship" had been recovered with only minor damage.

The reputation of the Union Steamship Company never stood higher in Vancouver than at this time, despite wartime conditions. Fleet replacements had come at an opportune time. In 1916, the authorized capital was again increased, this time to $2,000,000 with the issuance of 100,000 preference shares and 100,000 ordinary shares at $5 par. Under a new charter, the Company was empowered to invest in land development and more plans got under way. Then on May 1, 1917, president James Hugh Welsford died suddenly at his London residence at the age of only fifty-three. His deep-sea cargo line had suffered grievously from the loss of five ships by seizure in German ports and by torpedoes. Before his meteoric career abruptly ended, his shipping interests, although halted by the war, extended to several other parts of the world besides British Columbia. To fill the vacancy,

Grange V. Holt, manager of the Canadian Bank of Commerce, who had a particularly wide acquaintanceship with trade on the Pacific coast, was invited to join the Union board. Following the retirement of Mr. Carter-Cotton who had been with the Company since its founding, R. Kerr Houlgate, a real estate executive and former manager of the Yorkshire & Canadian Trust Company, also became a director.

Soon after Mr. Welsford's death, Ernest Beazley met with the Liverpool managers and trustees concerning future development of the Union Steamship Company. At Welsford's new offices in the Cunard building, co-directors were now G. S. Page and Arnold Rushton, my father. Mr. Page, a well-known shipping man, died in December 1920. One of his sons, Dudley Page, later became head of the Cunard Line in Canada. The secretary of the Welsford companies was J. G. Cowman, a kindly man with a liking for matte (Argentine tea) and a wizard on the chessboard. I served under him for several months after being demobilized from the Rhine Army in 1919. I had given up my classical studies to enlist in October 1915, and, at the end of the war, joined the staff of J. H. Welsford Company before being transferred to their Union Company subsidiary.

The entry of the United States into the war in 1917 gave a tremendous fillip to shipbuilding and to the lumber market, with the local B. C. coastal trade undergoing a great expansion in the ensuing twelve months. Ernest Beazley had seen the potential of trade on the seventy miles of mainland coast since the opening of the Powell River Company's pulp and paper plant in 1912 and the growth of the local settlements over the past five years. The Company now entered the day steamer business, a step which Beazley had recommended earlier, with the purchase for $117,500 in October 1917 of the All Red Line with its two small steamers *Selma* and *Santa Maria*, together with seven acres of land owned by the line south of Sechelt known as Selma Park. This acquisition of day boats and property, even though the acreage was small, had a dynamic effect on the direction of the Union's expansion over the next quarter-century.

The All Red Line ships were luxuriously built as private yachts by John Elder & Company of Glasgow — the *Selma* as the *Santa Cecilia* in 1881 for the Marquis of Anglesea, and the *Santa Maria* two years later for John A. Rolls. Each had a clipper bow and a speed of 13 knots, the *Santa Maria* of 154 feet having a 10-foot advantage over her sister yacht. Stories have been passed down about lavish parties and highjinks aboard the yacht *Santa Cecilia*, whose owner was known as "the Mad Marquis." Among the noted guests were King Edward VII and the celebrated actress Lillian Langtry — the "Jersey Lily." Charles Polking-horne skippered the yacht to the South Pacific and finally to Vancouver in 1910. Lord Hartswell once owned the *Santa Maria* which left England under a Captain Sauter in 1914 for Vancouver where she was bought by the All Red Line.

From an office on the Johnston wharf, adjoining Union dock to the east, Captain Polkinghorne, who had delivered the *Cowichan* to this coast for the Company, had been managing the two All Red Line ships on a daily route between Vancouver and Powell River. They called en route at Roberts Creek, Sechelt, Pender Harbour, Stillwater, Myrtle Point and other small landings. The name of the line was a misnomer, as the *Selma* and the *Santa Maria* sported yellow and black funnels. One of the joint owners with Captain Polkinghorne was Captain Sam Mortimer, who came to Vancouver in 1890 in the *Batavia* and served on the CP "Empresses." After coming ashore from deep-sea, he was in the government service and was also associated with Herbert Whitaker, owner of the hotel and other property at Sechelt. He had run several vessels for Bert Whitaker, including the little *Tartar* and the *Sechelt* from Ward's wharf at the foot of Abbott Street. The *Selma* and the *Santa Maria* each left Vancouver and Powell River respectively at 9:30 a.m. on weekdays and usually passed each other at Sechelt, though frequently they were tied up together on the wharf. Especially on weekends, they carried near-capacity loads of passengers and freight, and it was only the lack of capital for needed expansion that prompted their sale to Union.

The two vessels soon acquired the familiar red stacks and black tops, and continued in the same schedule. Following the custom of giving vessels an Indian (and later a Spanish) name of regional signifi-cance starting with "C," within two months the *Selma* became the *Chasina*, and the *Santa Maria* the *Chilco*.

Among the fine mariners who came to the Union with these ships was Captain H. E. Lawrey, a Cornishman who was born at sea and sailed in schooners at the age of fifteen to Labrador and Iceland. After commanding railway steamers in the English Channel, he came to Vancouver in the spring of 1911 and joined the All Red Line's *Selma* as mate under Captain Mortimer. He stayed to become one of Union's most popular excursion vessel captains for a period of twenty-eight years. Together with Captain Townsend, until after the sale, both Sam Mortimer and Charles Polkinghorne relieved as masters aboard these vessels. Captain Harry Roach, Union skipper and once a seaman on the *Santa Maria*, tells a story about the veteran sailor Polkinghorne, who had the appearance of a pirate but who was a very mild man, trying to make a landing at Pender Harbour. When his third docking attempt appeared to be failing, Bob Donnelly, who ran the store and usually took the lines despite having only one hand, looked up at the bridge and shouted: "Hey, Captain, why don't you hire a tug?" The truth was that Polkinghorne had a terrible time with his landings, proving that a fine navigator who had sailed many times round the Horn, was not always a good small-ship handler. The pursers who came from the "yellow and black" funnels were George Read, who served many years on the logging camp vessels, and the bearded J. G. Fletcher, who also had a master's ticket.

One of the Union's busiest sea horses, assigned to every conceivable freighting job, was the *Coquitlam*. She did a thriving trade at this time, and the story is told how she was lying athwart the end of the Union dock just before sailing one midnight, when Billy Vaughan came hurrying down, shouting to the second mate: "We must get one more car aboard." As he spoke, Billy stepped down a short ladder to the ship's deck and went straight to his trouser legs in water. The *Coquitlam* was truly loaded to the gunwales and awash — no more was heard about Billy's last-minute automobile.

The *Coquitlam*'s master was Captain Neil Gray; C. B. Smith was chief officer; and her first mate was John Muir, who, as the later marine superintendent, recalled two amazing experiences. The first of these occurred in April 1917. After delivering freight to the Indian settlement at Kitimat, she was proceeding south on Douglas Channel, carrying supplies for the new Drumlummon mine, with second mate Jock Robertson on watch. As John Muir told it,

> Our freighter, half loaded with coal, was lined up for the landing when it was suddenly caught and swung by a strong current towards the cliffs and bumped heavily several times against the rocks. I was assigned, with the chief engineer, to investigate the damage below deck, and a hurried check disclosed she was taking in some water. The hull was clearly punctured where some rivets had been knocked out. With his vessel in grave danger and with the pumps set to work, Captain Gray decided to make a three hour run for it up Grenville Channel to Lowe Inlet, where there was a shelving beach. During these critical hours I had to keep a constant watch on everything down below where the engineers were striving to control the water. If this condition had worsened we could well have sunk outside in the channel. But we made it into Lowe Inlet, and the Captain ran the *Coquitlam* straight up ashore at the head of the bay alongside the old cannery. He had implicit faith in the skill and resource of our engineers to tackle the job of making the vessel seaworthy again in these unusual surroundings.

According to another informant, Fred Smith, the chief engineer, the Captain tried to take her in 'sidearm' but did not strand the ship quite high enough on the beach. It was nearly low tide and the crew shovelled a sandbank around the stern quarters to keep the vessel dry enough for us to get into the hold. The deck crew then dug through the coal before Second Engineer John Hogan and I could get working on the repairs. One of the deckhands had been a logger and, although we only had a blunt axe on board, he chopped through the wood sheathing which enabled us to put a patch inside and tighten the seams of the careened hull with iron bolts. We just had to make shift with no means of communication on board or ashore, and get home the best way we could.

Finally, at high tide the next day, the *Coquitlam* was refloated, and Captain Gray succeeded in completing his route deliveries before returning the vessel to Vancouver none the worse except for a necessary drydocking and the replacing of several plates later on, as the emergency patch held up for some time.

Perhaps the most hair-raising episode of the *Coquitlam* took place in the spring of 1918, according to Jock Muir.

She hit a deadhead in the middle of Queen Charlotte Sound and 'lost her wheel,' slipping off the propeller and lying helpless with no means of propulsion. We just had to wait, without any ship-to-shore telephone, until it happened that the *Venture* came steaming by southbound, a most welcome sight. She took us in tow and some said the *Coquitlam*, which was only making over eight knots loaded, had never travelled so fast before! But the work of repair had only just started. While still in Johnstone Strait, Chief Officer Charles B. Smith slipped overside the *Coquitlam* in his bathing suit to check the propeller shaft. As a result of this inspection it was decided to strand the vessel on the beach at Alert Bay below the school. The *Camosun* brought up a new propeller — spares were always kept in Vancouver. When the tide was low enough and with the help of chain blocks, Chief Engineer Fred Smith safely put on a new propeller as she lay. The vessel was refloated and continued right on her voyage north, as the bulk of her cargo was non-perishable.

Earlier in January 1917, the *Venture* was in a minor collision with *S. S. Wakena*, which apparently changed course while entering Vancouver's First Narrows in fog. The Union vessel was acquitted of blame and recovered her damages from the Exchequer Court.

The *Cassiar* suffered her only major accident when she hit a reef off Privett Island, near Simoon Sound, en route into Kingcome Inlet at about 2:30 a.m. on Sunday, August 26, 1917. She was nearing the end of her run under Captain Robert Wilson, the pilot on duty being Jack Robinson, and the second officer, L. Godfrey. Fortunately she had only fifty-eight on board, including twenty-eight crew. One of the officers told his story to the Vancouver *World*, which published it on August 30:

"The vessel was proceeding as usual when suddenly she was brought up with a crash which quickly told us what had taken place. There was no panic at any stage. We had one woman aboard going to Charles Creek cannery." The officer said that after the boats were lowered, while the *Cassiar* was fast sinking and with perfect discipline, everyone held back until Mrs. Johnstone stepped into a lifeboat. "Then the loggers piled into the boats. We rowed away reaching shore in a few minutes. How long it took for the vessel to find bottom I don't know. We couldn't see very well in the darkness and I don't know whether she was completely submerged when she settled. A good many of the passengers were able to save their valuables but others lost most of their baggage. Most of the crew lost everything."

When daylight came the *Cassiar* was found to be completely submerged by the stern at high tide with 25 feet of water over her upper deck aft. J. W. Dunseith, the postmaster at Simoon Sound, looked after everyone in fine style, there being plenty of food and the ship's cook helping.

Some loggers went on to their destinations or to Alert Bay in small boats, but the remainder and the crew were picked up by the *Cowichan* on August 29 on her regular call. Purser Clarence Williams did good work in retrieving the valuables and ship's papers from the safe and in helping the passengers with their effects. The *Cheakamus* took over the run in the meantime. Mr. Beazley sent up the tug *Salvor*, and the salvage company figured it might cost at least $30,000 to recover the vessel; on the other hand, a new ship would cost $150,000. Ultimately, through a fine salvage job by Captain Logan, the *Cassiar* was pulled off the reef and beached, then refloated after temporary patching on the shore. Captain Wilson and Chief Engineer P. J. V. Farina stood by the *Cassiar* until she was towed back to Vancouver ten days later. The ship's keel and stern were terribly torn, but Wallace's yard did an excellent repair and reconditioning of the vessel, which was accepted back by the Company under an arrangement with the underwriters. This was the narrowest squeak the *Cassiar* had in all her service, and she lived to steam for another six years under the Union flag.

On June 23, 1918, before hostilities ended, the *Venture*, under Captain Dickson, went to the aid of *S. S. Ravalli*, afire at Lowe Inlet and, for four hours, lashed alongside the stricken vessel at great risk, pumped in water before having to abandon the hopeless battle.

After the war, in January 1919, manager Beazley brought John

Barnsley down from Prince Rupert to be his assistant, replacing John Galt who had resigned to enter his own business. Then he cleared the decks by disposing of the historic *Comox*, now past her day for Union service, to Vancouver Machinery Depot to be broken up. This, as it turned out, was not the end of the *Comox*. She was resold to Captain Alexander Woodside of San Diego, and, after the Bow McLachlan engines were removed, was rebuilt as the motorship *Alejandro*, at a cost of $60,000, for the Mexican coastal trade. The Vancouver *Sun* on May 30, 1920, quipped: "The Master of Ceremonies at her [new] launching should say — Ladies and Gentlemen, meet the motorship *Alejandro*, otherwise the *Comox*, dearly beloved of loggers and cannery hands on the British Columbia coast for thirty years!"

To strengthen the Union's cargo tramp service, the *Chilliwack* was purchased in January 1919 for $112,500. This sturdy vessel, originally built as the *Onyx* in 1903, was 170 feet in length, with an estimated cargo capacity of 700 tons, and proved an immediate success.

About this time in 1919, the late Canon Alan D. Greene, highly regarded throughout the settlements as superintendent of the Columbia Coast Mission, travelled to Whaletown with his bride. He recalled this incident aboard the *Camosun*: "My wife unwittingly sat on the steam capstan forward as the ship was docking, and experienced a rare merry-go-round on it when the crew turned on the steam from 'tween decks, but luckily she was unharmed." Canon Greene, who came to the coast in 1911 and knew all the captains and most of the officers, performed an invaluable service with the Anglican Mission boat. When hospital sites were few and only water transportation was available, his little craft was indeed a vital link.

The expanding coast now saw the effect of increased output from the busy pulp mills at Powell River, Ocean Falls and Swanson Bay, and from the growth of Granby's copper activities at Anyox. Together with Surf Inlet mines, new cannery plants and a vastly higher scale of lumber production for the world markets, it meant more travel, increased supplies and southbound cargoes. Ernest Beazley was already planning new ships to gradually replace the older vessels with more economical steamers better adapted to the trade and to modern ideas of comfort.

This policy was backed by Welsford's whose late president had been succeeded by the chairman, Major George Bahr Haddock, Member of Parliament, who became a minority shareholder and took a lively interest in the affairs of the Union Steamship Company in the succeeding years. From being regarded by Welsford's as a thriving subsidiary, Union became a mainline operation and their brightest prospect.

CHAPTER 6

1919-1924

Two New Ships Built in B. C.
Bowen Island Resort Taken Over
The Coming of the Cardena *and the* Lady Alexandra
Close Navigation in Coastal Channels

Transportation, to be ideal, must have certain aids
such as comfort, ease, attendance, a touch of preten-
sion and a good culinary department.
AITKEN TWEEDALE
North by West in the Sunlight

The two new ships planned by Beazley were a small day-steamer, specifically designated for the Selma Park-Gulf coast excursion run, and a larger modern freighter for the northern trade. In August 1919, a contract to build the *Capilano*, a 135-foot wood vessel, was awarded to Innes Hopkins of the B. C. Marine Limited. Her triple expansion engines were taken out of the steamer *Washington*, which the Company had bought in February 1918 through W. R. Isted of Seattle for $45,000 and which, after a short trial, was found unsuitable for the Sechelt route. Cost of the *Capilano*'s hull construction was $70,000. Built of seasoned Douglas fir, she had a large enclosed lounge, dining saloon and clear upper deck seating for excursionists; and with a gross tonnage of 374 and a speed of 13 knots, she was a handy type of vessel to service the new resort the Company was developing on the Selma Park property.

The Selma program included a new wharf store, a dozen water-front cottages and a splendid 60-foot dance hall, with a verandah restaurant overlooking Georgia Strait. A large picnic ground with covered tables and catering facilities was prepared later in 1922 for organized and private party outings. Designed by Henry Darling, the *Capilano* qualified for a day licence of 350 passengers from May to September, and 150 passengers during the remaining months, and could handle about 50 tons of general cargo. She was, of course, intended to serve all the other resorts springing up along the coast between Gibson's, Gower Point and Buccaneer Bay.

It was a happy occasion, shortly after 2 p.m. on Saturday, December 20, 1919, when at last *Capilano II* was safely launched. The *World* reported that "The little craft slipped down the ways in perfect style," being christened by the wife of the general manager, Mrs. E. H. Beazley. Captain George Whalen took the new passenger ship out for her trial run on May 1, 1920, with several hundred guests. Her chief engineer was "Paddy" Farina who kept her engine-room the best polished in the fleet for the next thirty years.

The keel of the second new vessel, the *Chilkoot*, a splendid 172-foot freighter with breadth of 30 feet and cargo capacity of up to 800 tons, was laid down in November 1919 at Wallace's shipyards in North Vancouver at a cost of $225,000. She had one passenger cabin on the upper deck and carried a licence for twelve deck passengers. Her new engines from Builders Iron Foundry of Providence gave a speed of 12 knots, making her the fastest local cargo carrier in the business. The *Chilkoot* had two cargo hatches and five derricks, including a heavy one for 18 tons lift capacity. She was planned for a crew of twenty-one, including officers, and her fuel capacity gave a range of 2,500 miles, making her an excellent operational type.

The *Chilkoot* was launched on December 26, 1919, by Miss Constance Darling, elder daughter of Henry Darling, the designer.

On the same date, Captain C. B. Smith of the recently acquired *Chilliwack* running southbound from Surf Inlet mines on the west side of Princess Royal Island, experienced a perilous cargo mishap. After stowage of 700 tons of ore for the Tacoma smelter had been completed on Christmas Day by the first mate, Lorne Godfrey, the wet concentrates froze solid in the sub-zero temperature. Captain Smith elected to take the direct "outside passage," where heavy seas caught the vessel broadside in the open Pacific before she entered Milbanke Sound. According to the master's report, by the time he reached a point about eighty miles south, to the west of Price Island, the concentrates had thawed and the cargo — now a floating mass of ore with no division boards — shifted dangerously, giving the *Chilliwack* a list of 30 degrees. Fred Smith, the chief engineer, described the frightful conditions below when

a large amount of water was admitted through the starboard entrance on deck into the engine room and the pumps couldn't keep it down. The situation got steadily worse and the engineers working with the men, up to their knees in water, were unable to stand up and oil her.

81

It was 'touch and go' and we were reduced to pouring cans of sea water over the bearings to cool them.

Unable to right his vessel and with the list increasing, the master finally decided to beach her. By great luck, and having fifteen years' familiarity with this stretch of coast in Union ships, Captain Smith remembered a tiny sand cove around the east tip of Price Island, used only by the odd fisherman and sheltered from the weather, where he would have a fair chance of stranding safely. After rounding Day Point he steered the *Chilliwack* for a mile and a half inside the Sound to this small haven, barely a hundred yards across (named Muir Cove on later charts). Although the lifeboats were swung out, there was no thought of abandonment and the crew worked with the skipper to run aground on a fairly even keel.

The vessel lay there for almost three days while the water was pumped out, and as Fred Smith recounted, "they hauled logs on board from the beach with the ship's winches to use as barricades before restowage of the ore was possible." During this extraordinary stopover, the engines also had to be partly taken down and overhauled. The ship was refloated on a high tide with only a minor scraping before continuing to her Tacoma destination.

After the crisis was over, "Charlie" Smith singled out his engineers for special praise. To his namesake, the chief engineer, he said, "I thought all the time of you poor buggers sticking it out in the flood below, while I was standing on a wing of the bridge with my lifejacket on ready to jump off when she rolled over."

The captain was a bluff and modest sailor from Weston-Super-Mare in Somerset who served his apprenticeship the hard way in square-riggers. He was a powerful man with a broken nose, which he always claimed had been kicked by a mule, but it was said that he had been in a waterfront fight in Sydney as a youth. For his outstanding seamanship, Captain Smith was highly commended with recognition from Lloyds of London. It was typical of the man that he shared his purse with the entire crew.

In encouraging passenger trade, Ernest Beazley was not unmindful of the great attraction of the Union routes for tourists who were coming to the west coast seeking an adventurous type of cruise, even if it meant roughing it a bit. One writer who sampled a number of trips was Aitken Tweedale, who wrote the Company's first pamphlet *Fin, Feather and Fur*, which was descriptive not only of the superb scenery along the channels but also of the easy accessibility to splendid fishing streams and big-game centres. Mr. Tweedale's English was extravagantly colourful: "Travellers therefore look to transportation . . . and seek the means to ensure in perfection these delights their ally can provide, and they enjoy to the full a visit to that Eighth Wonder of the World, the northern coast of British Columbia." About a more southerly route he wrote:

> An Indian village, quaint 'old worldish' with grotesque tribal and family totems, slides past the port bow while to starboard tower the white plumes of a logging 'donkey' blowing and puffing steam over the task of wresting great logs that only a short time before were the greater trees of British Columbia's forest kingdom . . . Through straits and channels westward is seen the never-to-be-forgotten glory of a Pacific sunset as a flaming ball of fire dips near the ocean's rim.

One of the most scenic shorter cruises was the weekend trip on the *Cowichan* to Savary Island, Toba Inlet and Cortez Island. Meals and a cabin berth were included in the unbelievable fare of $12 — a 360-mile round trip from Saturday afternoon to Monday's breakfast!

Before seasonal operations of 1920 got under way a personal tragedy dealt a severe blow to the fortunes of the Company which was just getting set for a postwar expansion.

A seamen's strike on Canadian Pacific coast ships in June 1917 spread to the Union vessels and tied up part of the fleet for a week, even though the Company was not directly involved. Labour troubles again cancelled sailings for a brief period in 1919, and a third strike, originating with the firemen, spread to the seamen of both lines in May 1920. Manager Beazley had agreed to negotiate with the labour committee and believed, on the night of May 23 that a settlement was imminent. Meantime, all the ships were tied up at the Union pier over the holiday weekend.

On the hot Monday afternoon of May 24, Mr. & Mrs. Beazley drove out with Mr. C. S. Meek to Minoru Park in nearby Richmond to watch a flying exhibition. Mr. Beazley was president of the aviation club but had no thought that day of participating himself. Mrs. Beazley, however, accepted an invitation for a short flight with Major Albert C. Baker, a barnstorming pilot who had done considerable wartime flying. Mr. Beazley then accepted a flight.

The pilot, who was not too familiar with this particular type of machine, got the plane into a spin and was unable to regain control. To the horror of several thousand spectators, the plane crashed at a nearby farm, killing Mr. Beazley and seriously injuring the pilot. Besides his wife, he left three small children. The fatality saddened the entire community and stunned Vancouver's waterfront.

One of the most impressive funerals in the city's history was held at Christ Church Cathedral on May 27. Ernest Beazley was borne to rest by his captains, attended by his staff and the crews of all the Union ships in port. Robert Kenmuir wrote in the *Province*: "The flags of the vessels in the harbour may well be half-masted, for one who loved ships and the men who man them has gone out with the tide."

In a similar accident on August 10, 1920, another official, Captain Hibbert B. Brenton, was killed when a flying boat which he was piloting crashed into English Bay. He had joined the Company in 1919 from the Royal Air Force as an uptown purchasing and insurance representative. Union officials were "grounded until further notice."

Following the loss of the Union's managing director, my father, accompanied by my stepmother and R. A. H. Welsford, son of the late president, came out from Liverpool to reorganize the Company's affairs. John Barnsley was confirmed as the new general manager, and young Richard Welsford became managing director and would reside in Vancouver for several months each year. Mr. Barnsley had a wealth of experience in the cannery trade, and was a shrewd operator though lacking the outgoing personality of his predecessor. Strict economy was his watchword. Born in Birmingham, most of his business life had been spent in Victoria with the Boscowitz Company. He was a small man so that when seated behind his huge roll-top desk it was sometimes difficult to see if he was in. His elder son, Jack, succeeded him as Prince Rupert agent.

The shipping strike ended quickly, and on June 16, 1920, the *Capilano II* began a tri-weekly trip to the Selma resort, calling at the Roberts Creek and Wilson Creek camping centres. On Sundays, the trip was extended to Halfmoon Bay (Redroofs) and the Buccaneer Bay resort on Thormanby Island, close to the old site of the telephone employees' camp which was later developed as Vaucroft. This schedule drew many visitors to the growing string of holiday spots.

The Union had no better freighter than the *Chilkoot* when she sailed on her maiden voyage on June 20 under Captain James Findlay. Born in Banffshire in 1873, he worked on Allan Line vessels, earned his master's ticket in clipper ships round the Horn, commanded two of Andrew Weir's big ones, the *Elleric* and the *Osteric*, and finally settled in Vancouver in 1911. He started as third made in the *Chelohsin* before getting his command on coastal ships. James Findlay always said his hardest task was learning to keep moving along the coast inlets in fog without fear. John Hogan, of Liverpool, was the first engineer on the

Chilkoot, "Chips" Williams was the pilot, and Sydney Anfield the purser.

I made my first northern trip on this voyage as "supercargo" to absorb some coastal atmosphere. I had arrived in Vancouver from the Welsford Company in May 1920. It was intended that I should spend several years gaining experience of the Union's Canadian operation under the sponsorship of Mr. Beazley, but his tragic death within ten days of my arrival upset any previous plans. My father believed in "learning from the bottom up," and my B. C. coastal education was to last almost a lifetime.

Life is always more free and easy in a freighter, and I met some real characters. For the benefit of the Liverpool greenhorn, "Chips" turned the air blue with his nautical obscenities, though always in good part. *Chilkoot* was hailed with a cheery greeting at every port and small landing on our freighting intinerary, and it was rare that the captain or the pilot was not invited to visit ashore. The grandeur of the fjord-like waterways and the variety of cargo discharged were equally amazing to a newcomer. After mentally picturing for so long what a Union coaster might be like, it was a real thrill to spend ten days aboard the new *Chilkoot* and hear her whistle sound up the inlets. The whistle signal was the Morse alphabet letter X, sounding one long, two short, and one long blast, which I believe originated with the first Union ships. The Company house flag was also a blue cross (or letter X) on a red ground with U. S. S. Co. distributed on the four segments of the cross.

Another vivid impression I brought back from that ship was the immense ramification of the salmon-canning industry, with the fish-cutting and canning being performed by scores of workers in the cannery buildings, in almost every case alongside the up-coast wharves, where huge catches were unloaded straight from the nets. With a favourable tide, the *Chilkoot* delivered her supplies for the Skeena River canners before entering Prince Rupert's sheltered harbourage, fourteen miles in length and the centre of the north coast's fishing industry. She continued her voyage as far as Wales Island, poking in at several Nass River canneries nestling beneath a seemingly unbroken mountainous wall. It was hard to conceive of the vastness of the territory comprising these scattered landings that relied for its subsistence on the little Union vessels.

In December 1920, the Company bought the business and Bowen Island property of the Terminal Steam Navigation Company, including the steamers *Ballena* and *Bowena*, from Captain Jack Cates — pioneer in both the Howe Sound trade and in the towboat industry. He had engaged in passenger and freight service to the upper end of Howe Sound since 1899 with the little *Defiance*, augmented later by the *Britannia* and the *Barramba*. From this small beginning he had built up a growing trade with Britannia Mines, the Woodfibre pulp plant and the town of Squamish. Simultaneously, he had developed since 1900 the picnic, summer camping and hotel resort centre at Bowen Island, on the site of the old Manion ranch. Part of this area at one time was a brickyard, and the *News-Advertiser* of September 7, 1889 carried this advertisement: "To builders and contractors – For Sale – A Kiln of Mannion's Bowen Island Brick." The Terminal Company latterly used the Union wharf for their sailings with organized picnics and excursions, and their ticket agent and bookkeeper, John Larnie, had a ticket office on the dock. Negotiations had been proceeding privately for some time with the Union officials who saw both the opportunity to expand their entry into the day-trip field, and the potential of the Bowen Island resort for future development. This purchase brought with it the growing and profitable East Howe Sound route to Squamish, which Captain Cates gave up with the Bowen Island business.

The deal involved about $250,000; but, before it was consummated, the *Ballena* was destroyed overnight by fire with the loss of a fireman while alongside the Union dock. This left only the *Bowena*, which also sustained upperworks damage to the extent of $15,000. She was our old friend the former *City of Nanaimo*, built, by R. P. Rithet in Victoria in 1891, and renamed *Cheam*. Her master was Captain F. W. Gilbert, who came over from the Terminal company. This veteran wood vessel of 159 feet and speed, at this date, of 10 knots, could carry 500 passengers and about 200 tons cargo. It was Mr. Barnsley's plan to make use of her until a large excursion vessel could be built. "We hope to make Bowen Island a continental resort," he said, and an expansion program was ready before the spring of 1921. With the fire putting both Captain Cates's vessels out of commission in November 1920, the *Capilano* was given the route to Bowen Island and Squamish until the *Cheam* had been reconditioned to enter service the following May.

By early summer, good progress had been made in bringing the Bowen resort up to date, with construction begun on a hundred attractively designed cottage bungalows, as well as smaller camp cottages. The old shacks and ramshackle "tent-camps" which had been rented seasonally were gradually torn down or replaced. The estate acquired a model farm, with some fine imported Ayrshire stock for fresh dairy products, and the old store was rebuilt to suit the environs. For entertainment, a splendid dance pavilion, the largest at the time in British Columbia, with a spring hardwood floor and space for eight hundred couples, was finished for a grand opening on May 24, 1921. Designed on octagonal lines, with a central dais for the band, it was built in a charming woodland setting near the point in Snug Cove. These developments also included extensive renovation of the hotel, which was renamed Mount Strahan Lodge from an opposite peak above Howe Sound.

The main beaches were tidied and a salt-water swimming pool of regulation size, with graded sand bottom, was built alongside the lagoon. New rustic trails soon threaded the cottage areas and beyond to Bridal Falls and Lake Killarney, but the winding paths were purposely kept narrow to preserve the rural scene. For three decades the estate, open to day visitors and residents, was off-limits to dogs and motor cars. The island resort was fortunate in its fresh water supply from Trout Lake. Over the next two years, summer service was maintained with little margin of passenger space to the growing Bowen resort by the *Cheam* and the *Capilano*, both of which sometimes "double headed" on extra sailings at weekends when most picnic groups travelled.

Long before any passable North Shore road reached to Fisherman's Cove or Whytecliff, but with the early prospect of the Pacific Great Eastern line from North Vancouver coming into Horseshoe Bay, J. Hilton Brown seized the opportunity to start the first *Sannie* launch in 1920 on a ferry crossing from Horseshoe Bay to Snug Cove. An Australian, he chose the *Sannie* name, it was said, from a racehorse that had brought him luck. He sold out the following year to Thomas D. White, one of his backers, but stayed on as manager for a while. On May 16, 1921, Sannie Transportation announced that it would run the launches, *Sannie* I, II and III, on summer schedule between Horseshoe Bay and Bowen Island. The timing was right, as the PGE Railway began local service that year to the west shore points up to Horseshoe Bay, bringing thousands of holiday-makers, a large number of whom boarded the *Sannies* for the trip across to Snug Cove. In 1928, when the main road was built through to Horseshoe Bay, the railway discontinued this service. Tommy White, who got a provincial franchise for the summer ferry route in 1925, ran independently but always in friendly concert with the Union's direct steamers.

In 1921, the Union Steamship Company entered into an agreement with the PGE Railway to carry rail passengers and express between Vancouver and Squamish, providing an essential connection with the railway's first scheduled trains from Squamish to Quesnel, a section of line opened that year. The railway had its own barge service for freight between North Vancouver and Squamish. In 1922, a special rail steamer was allotted, but it was later agreed that twice-weekly train connections would be made by the regular Howe Sound steamer which called at Bowen Island, Britannia and Woodfibre. Britannia Beach was the site of a company town, headquarters of one of the continent's largest copper producers, while on Mill Creek at Woodfibre was the extensive plant of the Whalen Pulp and Paper Company. This railway opening and projected extension to the north, with the growing attraction for tourists of the beautiful day sea-trip through Howe Sound, influenced the speeding up of the Union's program to obtain more local tonnage quickly.

In early 1922, I engaged on a trip aboard the *Chelohsin* to Loughborough Inlet, and recorded in my journal:

Campbell River was the first call — a distributing centre for the region, and an unbeatable spot for the angler. An interesting way point opposite on Valdez Island at Quathiaski Cove is the site of a busy cannery. The anchored floats and log booms at Duncan Bay and Menzies Bay depict well this end of their operation. Immediately afterwards the steamer undertakes the thrilling passage of Seymour Narrows. Granite Bay has a seemingly impossible entrance and our navigator had to thread between rocky shores barely the steamer's length apart.

The master on this trip was dapper Captain Stacey and the pilot, whose afternoon watches I shared, was Captain Parker. The *Chelohsin* made her principal stop at Rock Bay, site of Merrill Ring & Wilson's vast logging operations. Nearly fifty miles of narrow-gauge railway connected the dispersed logging grounds, which shifted constantly, and the dockside settlement with its hospital and roughly finished hotel.

On an earlier visit to Rock Bay with Mr. Welsford, I had experienced a hair-raising ride for an office man, standing up and clutching a stanchion on one of several flat cars that bumped and swayed dizzily behind a small, puffing locomotive. We had been invited to an enormous loggers' breakfast of steaks and eggs at one of Phil Wilson's main camps.

From Rock Bay, the ship ploughed through a labyrinth of channels before reaching Blind Channel, an apparent cul de sac until the vessel "opens up" the cannery wharf. In beautiful Loughborough Inlet, the bustle and hum of operations around Grassey Bay, and later in Reid Bay, contrasted rudely with the unruffled charm of the inland waterways. At the end of the route, the *Chelohsin* served the Andersons' large camp, Salmon River Logging, based on Sayward. Old "P. B." Anderson and his sons Dewey, a giant of a man, and Clay, the local manager, were among the most prominent lumbering owners who used the Union ships as a second home over the next twenty years, and knew by first name most of the officers. Such stalwarts as these, or the outspoken Phil Wilson, brooked no criticism of the Union line within their hearing by outsiders. They reserved this luxury for themselves on warranted occasions, when the Company got both barrels direct!

The most profitable northern run — the key Skeena and Nass Rivers cannery route — was maintained at this time by the *Venture,* one of Mr. Barnsley's old Boscowitz ships. Her master was Andrew Johnstone, best-known of the cannery skippers of this period and one of the Company's greatest mariners. He was born at Dalton, Dumfrie- shire — a Solway man like the famous American admiral and (according to the Scots) pirate Paul Jones — and came of a seafaring family. His maternal grandfather built racing brigs to run contraband during the Civil War. Andy was brought to Vancouver as a child by his family in 1890. He first went to sea as an apprentice in the survey and fisheries patrol ship *Kestrel,* serving three years under Captain Holmes New- combe. Later, he got valuable deep-sea experience as quartermaster with the Blue Funnel and Cunard lines, before coming back around the Horn to the B. C. coast in the "delivery crew" of the Canadian Pacific *Princess Charlotte.* Then, in 1909, he gained his mate's ticket under Captain Saunders in the *Camosun.* His familiarity with the coast and his professional skills never stood him a greater stead than on September 16, 1922.

At 5 a.m. that day the *Venture* had just finished loading salmon at the North Pacific cannery in the Skeena River slough. According to Andy Johnstone, "There was a thick fog and a strong ebb tide running in this tricky sector of the river, when 'Sparks' came hurrying to the bridge. 'There's an S. O. S. — something I've waited for all my life — from the Seattle ship *Queen.* She's on the rocks at Whitecliff Island, full of passengers from Alaska.' " It was twelve miles away by the chart; and, casting off from the cannery wharf immediately, the captain wirelessed the wrecked Admiral liner: VENTURE WILL PROCEED OUT TOWARDS YOU FROM SKEENA. ANSWER EACH OF MY FOG SIGNALS SO I CAN LOCATE YOU ALONGSIDE. Andy recalled the tense moments:

> We couldn't see fifty yards ahead, but soon the *Queen* started answering my foghorn, which gave me the distance and direction, and about 7 a.m. my ship slid right alongside the grounded vessel, with its bow up on the reef and the stern now in the water. There

were 238 passengers on board and most were already gathered with their belongings near the stern. I ordered a gangway out from our forward deck over her stern, and the American passengers trooped across and were taken aboard without delay and given all the accommodation possible on the *Venture*. All the mail and some valuables and the rest of the baggage was transferred over to us as well, before we backed away and headed to Prince Rupert — still in thick fog. The stranded passengers had to disembark at Prince Rupert to go through customs but quite a number came back aboard the *Venture* — they were pleased with their reception on our ship and many took passage back with us to Vancouver.

The *Venture* was remarkably well-suited to the northern coast, and it was her seagoing qualities that led to the choice of Napier & Millers' Old Kilpatrick yard on the Clyde for the building of the next northern steamer, the *Cardena*. Before the close of 1922, the contract was placed by Barnsley for this ship, a larger and finer vessel than any operated by the Union Steamship Company to this time. The Company departed from its Indian naming custom by picking a Spanish "C" name, given by an early Spanish explorer to Cardena Bay on Kennedy Island at the mouth of the Skeena River. This was Admiral Cardena, said to have been the first white man to see the Grand Canyon of the Colorado River.

No one was more dedicated to the husbanding of Union's affairs than John Barnsley, who was appointed managing director in October, 1922. He proved to be an excellent choice in tackling the postwar problems, which included a heavy rise in fuel costs. His business manner was dry and somewhat sharp, and little escaped his notice; but away from the office he was a kindly man, and I had the privilege of his private hospitality on many occasions.

I happened to be on leave in England while the *Cardena* was still partly on the drawing board. Early in the New Year of 1923, I accompanied my father and Richard Welsford when they visited Glasgow to inspect progress on the new ship, and went aboard the vessel "on the stocks" at Old Kilpatrick, wearing the shipyard tin hat. Afterwards, Welsford and Ian Napier spent considerable time together poring over the old plans of the *Venture* spread out on a drafting table alongside blueprints of the *Cardena*. Allowing for the extra 50-foot length of the ship under construction, all the best features of the older vessel were retained.

The Union Steamship captains were unanimous in their opinion that the *Cardena* was the most graceful and best sea-boat of any line ever to sail the coastal waters of British Columbia. After her launching on the Clyde on March 22, and final fitting out and trials, the new steamer left for Vancouver on May 3 under Captain A. E. Dickson, known as the "Commodore." One of his junior officers was W. (Billy) McCombe, later skipper of both Union and Alaska line ships. George H. Foster, one of the Company's senior engineers, who stood-by at the shipyard during the engine fitting and trials of the *Cardena*, returned as chief engineer aboard her. Shortly afterwards, he was appointed Company superintendent engineer, replacing Mr. De. Gruchy. Unlike early crossings by new ships of the Company, the *Cardena* came directly via the Azores and Panama Canal, arriving at Vancouver the afternoon of June 11, to a rousing welcome from the Union vessels in port as well as from ships at the adjoining piers.

The coming of the *Cardena*, 1,558 gross tons, 235 feet overall, with breadth of 37 feet, which was a far cry from the first ships, marked the start of a new era for the Union line, which now had fourteen vessels of 10,588 gross tonnage. She was a modern ship for her day, not luxurious but comfortably fitted out, with hot and cold water through forty-two cabins, two suites with private bath, and four outside rooms on the top deck with extra facilities. With a large observation room forward, an attractive main lounge and dining saloon seating sixty-eight persons, she favourably impressed the visitors on her trial run up Howe Sound on June 27, 1923. The *Cardena* had 132 cabin berths, with deck berths for sixty on her maindeck and had a licence for 250 passengers. With a top speed of over 14 knots, (she averaged around 13 on the route) she was well adapted to the trade. She had two hatches and could carry 350 tons general freight, a special feature for the first time on a Union ship being a refrigerator compartment which could handle 30 tons of boxed fish.

Captain Dickson took the *Cardena* out on June 20 on her first voyage north to Prince Rupert, where she was given a fitting welcome, and was met by young Jack Barnsley, whose prowess as a wireless buff won international attention for picking up the MacMillan Arctic expedition. Chief officer on the ship was W. Mounce, who became master of several vessels before going to the Pilotage Authority. Mates were Ernest Sheppard, who survived a plane crash overseas to continue a notable career with the Company, and L. Mercer. Russell Smith, who later became Prince Rupert agent, was the purser and Mr. Ebden the chief steward.

In the spring of 1923, having by this time completed a round of all the northern routes, I wrote (under the Company's name) a 32-page booklet about the delights of these cruises entitled "Our Coastal Trips."

It included a page about the Union's early history. I felt a bit elated over the resulting business when requests for the folder continued for years afterwards, until a Seattle school teacher "let the cat out."

"Please send me your 'Coastal trips' book," she wrote, "which is recommended reading by the Washington School Board on the geography of British Columbia."

Following the addition of the *Cardena*, the *Camosun* was now more generally employed on the intermediate Bella Coola route. This vessel had a brush with the *Princess Beatrice* earlier in the year, but with no injury to passengers or serious damage. The two vessels collided in the early morning of January 23 when the *Camosun*, southbound from Prince Rupert, was off Kingcome Point in Grenville Channel. Both ships continued their voyages, the *Camosun* with some dented plates and minor damage.

That same winter, the *Camosun* came practically the entire 340 miles from Bella Coola to Vancouver's First Narrows in intermittent fog, under Captain Edward Georgeson, one of the Company's ablest navigators. On entering the harbour, still in dense fog, she got briefly ashore in the "Bight of Brockton Point," where the bowpiece of the *Empress of Japan* stands as a tourist attraction. The Vancouver Fire Department was summoned to bring their big ladder into Stanley Park and the passengers were disembarked over it. The *Camosun* was an extremely powerful vessel, and a South American republic had offered $300,000 for her during World War I to use as a tug. In fact, it was said that her keel was first intended for a tug on India's Hooghly River; but when this order fell through, she was completed to fill the Union Steamship contract. She had to be slowed down well ahead of landings. Soon after returning from the war, Francis Bannerman who became her chief officer, had loaded 14,000 cases of salmon before approaching Rivers Inlet cannery. Not knowing the ship too well, he signalled the engine room too late and she ploughed clean through the dock into the cannery sheds.

It became possible in 1923, with the new tonnage, at last to retire the veteran *Cassiar*. In her twenty-three years' service, the ship completed 1,700 voyages and logged nearly a million sea miles without losing a passenger. Like all ships, she had her own pattern of behaviour in bad weather. Probably on account of her stiff wooden hull, whenever she encountered rough water the pilothouse started shaking as if to remind her master that she did not approve. Soon after her retirement, she was sold to a Puget Sound fisheries company and, curiously enough, resumed her old name of *J. R. McDonald*. Some years later, while located in Lake Washington, she was reported to have been used as a movie background for a set in Charlie Chaplin's *The Gold Rush*. The late Captain John Boden, her master in 1919, once remarked, "She charted the lower coast," and certainly few of the out-of-the-way channels were properly charted, if at all, in the pioneer days. The master usually kept his own notebook in the wheelhouse with rough sketches for his officers to learn the safest approach to a wharf landing, and where the known rocks were located.

During her last year of service, I made a round trip on the *Cassiar* to Minstrel Island and Kingcome Inlet, and coming south, we had to pass through the tricky Hole-in-the-Wall Channel. The pilot (later Captain) was my friend Jock Muir, who first joined the *Cassiar* as quartermaster in 1913 after coming to Vancouver via Magellan Strait in the *Orontes*. I got up at daybreak to join him on the bridge and to watch him navigate through Okis Hollow in the early-morning light. To my astonishment, after traversing a stretch of water so narrow that it seemed the trees on either bank were actually touching, he stopped the vessel in slack water and lowered a boat with a couple of seamen and the mate, who had a large can of luminous paint. They rowed alongside a rock standing out of the water directly ahead, and repainted a particular mark on a large boulder, upon which the *Cassiar*'s course depended. "See it better next time," said Jock. By keeping the rock well painted, the crew had turned this hazard into a friendly sea-mark. To my surprise, I learned that at one time Jimmy Bogart made two- or three-foot squares of wood in the wharf machine shop, painting them with special white paint, to be set up as beacons in certain hazardous channels. These markers were easily picked up, even by the old carbon searchlights of the early ships. This long preceded the profusion of government aids. One can almost say that the pioneer ships carried their own do-it-yourself kits!

In a Merchant Service Guild annual, "L. C. R." had this to say about *Navigating Coastwise* along our Kingcome Inlet route: "In carrying out this devious and dangerous run, the incredible number of 449 distinct courses are given the quartermaster each week at an average interval of 13½ minutes . . . every one of them exacting attention and absolute knowledge of course, in fog and snow, fine weather and foul, and at every stage of tide and tidal current."

The story was told about George Gaisford, many years master of the *Cowichan*, of his chief officer one misty morning sounding the whistle to summon him to check his bearings. Pulling on his jacket, the captain hurried from his cabin under the bridge, halted briefly before ascending the ladder, took one sniff of the breeze and yelled: "Hard a-port!" His sense of bearing to close land and his reaction were instantaneous.

Another pilot, who kept the midnight to 6 a.m. watch always swore that Captain Dickson woke up immediately if the rhythm of his bunk indicated the ship was a point off course. This was the natural instinct which came to the aid of many Union mariners who learned the hard way before science, with radar and other modern aids, blunted these precious gifts. There was also the matter of natural phenomena which unexpectedly helped the mariners. More than one captain has reminded me that the bark of a dog was often valuable in locating a wharf, especially in misty weather. At Surf Inlet, on the inhospitable west coast of Princess Royal Island, the wharfinger had a big black retriever that gave continuous blasts of welcome to an approaching ship. At Menzies Bay there were two small dogs and a bulldog that pulled in the heaving line without fail, and a barking dog at Roberts Creek wharf was very helpful when the weather was particularly foul. This was the radar of the oldtimers.

There was an unbelievable camaraderie between the ships' officers and the postmasters, the storekeepers and the logging and mining bosses at the different stops. Nearly everyone was greeted by first name while the slings or boards of freight came overside to the wharf or float. For the settlers it was their weekly contact with the outside world. If the ship had a newsstand open, half the local population would visit the "travelling drug store," and if there was a moonlighting bootlegger among the crew the locals found it out long before the office. It was seldom that a favour within reason was refused. It might be an urgent letter or telegram they wanted to send. Wrote "L. C. R.":

> They toss it aboard knowing the matter will be attended to . . . They ask the master to leave a commissary order at some nearby port, or to send out another hand, or give orders for a towboat . . . They want a message to an employment agency in Vancouver to send a gang of men north on the next boat. The master and his officers are called upon, from point to point, to do those little errands, and they perform them willingly and dependably.

I remember once being aboard the *Cheakamus* with Captain Bob Wilson. As we pulled away from Reid Bay wharf, my new Stetson, which cost $7, blew off from the corner of the bridge where I was standing. A minute later, after he had set his course, I told Bob Wilson. Without hesitation he reached for the engine room telegraph. "We'll go back," he said, "and fish it out." Of course I tried to persuade him against doing this, but he remarked with that genial grin the settlers

94

loved: "We'd go in to pick up a goddam letter, why not your hat?"

On May 1923, Richard Welsford, new president of the Union Steamship Company, announced that a large new vessel would be laid down for the Bowen Island and Howe Sound excursion trade, where more tonnage and better transportation were urgently needed. Both the *Coquitlam* and the *Chasina* were sold to clear the decks for the new equipment. It turned out, though, to be a mistake to sell a thirty-year-old freighter without the certainty of her being broken up or permanently removed from the scene, for the hardy *Coquitlam* (under the name *Bervin*) came back to haunt us for another fifteen years in competitive areas. The *Chasina* was bought by local interests and was subsequently engaged in rum-running on Puget Sound. Still later, after being sold by the liquor interests, she sailed for the port of Macao. The *Chasina* became another mystery of the sea, as neither she nor her crew, which left Vancouver under Captain S. Kitchen, was ever heard of again.

On September 8, 1923, after a busy summer, a new and engaging personality, Harold Brown, was appointed assistant manager to Mr. Barnsley, whose health had deteriorated. With a large steamer expansion program ahead, apart from development of the new estates, top management needed experienced support without delay. Mr. Brown had been twenty years in transportation, with a special knowledge of the excursion trade. A Manxman, he went directly from King William College to the Isle of Man Steam Packet Company with its fine fleet, which moved a host of holiday seekers between Liverpool and Douglas. Such was his promise that at the age of twenty-seven, he was made manager of the Manx Electric Railway and did the initial promotion of the Snaefell resort until, after a personal loss, he decided to move to Canada. After serving briefly as secretary to Sir George Bury of the CPR, he joined the Grand Trunk Pacific's steamship staff at Prince Rupert, later becoming in turn their general dock agent in Victoria and Vancouver. During World War I, he served in Italy as a major in the Engineers on the transportation staff of Sir Auckland Geddes, worked for General Sheridan from the Indian Railways, and was decorated for his organizational work when the Italian front cracked after the Caporetto disaster. Returning to Vancouver, he became traffic manager for the Whalen Pulp Company before accepting the post with the Union Company. Tall and striking in appearance, he had great charm and a command of the English language that became almost a legend. Such was the man who came to bolster Union's fortunes and to spark the excursion trade to an extent never seen before in British Columbia.

While the Vancouver waterfront was tied up by a strike for four weeks in October, Harold Brown used the respite to streamline the Company's public information program and to take a first-hand look at the potentials of the Bowen Island resort. As a precursor of things to come, he had a lot to do with the laying down in May 1924 of the small motor vessel *Comox* at Wallace's for a cost of $20,000. She was planned for auxiliary ferry service between Bowen and Whytecliff where a small float landing was constructed. This craft, which went into service later that summer, was 54 feet in length and could carry 25 passengers and 20 tons of cargo at a speed of 8 knots. For two seasons she took some four thousand passengers via the Whytecliff crossing, but unfortunately this useful service was withdrawn after the *Comox* had a winter mishap on Jervis Inlet.

On October 23, 1923, the Company purchased from the Howe Sound Navigation Company the *Lady Evelyn*, which was built at Birkenhead in 1901 and, as the *Deerhound*, plied the St. Lawrence River mail run before being brought to Vancouver by Captain Thompson in 1922. She made headlines in 1914 for rescue work in the *Empress of Ireland* disaster which claimed 1,024 lives. Company officials had been impressed by the weekend crowds the vessel had been packing in West Howe Sound, and wanted the 189-foot vessel, which could carry 480 day passengers, as a stop-gap until new ships were completed. John Barnsley told the press that she would probably be used on the Powell River run. He tried out the *Lady Evelyn* the next summer on a daily trip to Pender Harbour, scheduled back about 11 p.m., until he caught sight of her huge fuel bill. "Good heavens, slow her down! Put the brakes on!" he cracked to the chief engineer. The ship was pulled off the run after she got back between one and two o'clock in the morning on several trips. She was the first Union vessel to have the "Lady" prefix, and this style was followed in the naming of their future steamers built for local day routes.

In retrospect, while the tonnage need was most urgent, $180,000 seems an expensive buy for an old vessel that never made money in year-round operation. It also had the side effect of saddling the Company with the general West Howe Sound route, for which a small ship would have been adequate except in July and August. An operating profit of nearly a million dollars in three years clearly pointed to the need for securing only the latest and most economical vessels for the excursion boom, which came almost too rapidly for the Company to take advantage of.

The purchase of the *Lady Evelyn* had one happy result since it brought back to the fold Captain W. L. (Billy) Yates, as her master. He had left Union in 1914 to become captain of the *Marine Express*, and then master of the *Britannia* on West Howe Sound in 1919. The little skipper first came into Vancouver harbour by way of Japan on a Blue Funnel ship, after training at the age of eleven in *H. M. S. Indefatigable* and shipping out of Liverpool on various Canadian Pacific and White Star liners. From the deck of the *S. S. Cyclops* on the morning of April 1, 1907, he saw a red-funnelled Union ship, which "he liked the look of," heading into an adjoining wharf. Later, he tackled the mate on the small .Union wharf for a job and, as Billy recounted it, "His name was Mr. Jones, and of all the luck he was an old Blue Funnel officer." Thus Billy Yates sailed north the same night on the *Camosun* via Nanaimo for bunker coal. His progress was rapid as quartermaster and winchman; he went to school for his mate's paper two years later and was subsequently promoted to second mate on the *Cassiar*. He recalled, "I was not thrilled when I finally got aboard the old *Cassiar*, but the three years I spent in her will live in my memory as the best ones of my life as far as steamboating is concerned."

In the late summer of 1923, a new excursion vessel, to be named *Lady Alexandra* was ordered from the Coaster Construction Company at Montrose, Scotland, whose managing director was W. D. McLaren. This was the first of four Union vessels to be constructed under his supervision, followed by two conversions in British Columbia. The keel of the *Lady Alexandra* was laid in October 1923, and a large crowd of spectators at the Rossie Island yard and along the quays on the opposite side of the South Esk witnessed her launching on February 21, 1924. The christening was performed by my step-mother, then the Lady Mayoress of Liverpool, in the presence of Provost Foreman of Montrose and a distinguished company. After running her trials in the North Sea, *Lady Alexandra* left Scotland on May 7 under Captain Charles B. Smith, who was bringing out his second new ship for the Company, and Chief Engineer George Foster, who had stood by at Montrose during the building. A fast trip brought her to Vancouver on June 21, where she was welcomed by both President Richard Welsford and W. D. McLaren, who came out to Vancouver for her arrival and to discuss further plans. Mr. McLaren later settled with his family in Vancouver and was a founder of West Coast Shipbuilders.

The "Alex," as two generations of Vancouverites affectionately called her, was a grand day-boat for this period. With a length of 225 feet, 40-foot breadth and maximum speed of 14 knots, she had three spacious decks including a large enclosed saloon aft on her upper deck, while her forward accommodation included a refreshment counter and six staterooms. She boasted a magnificent open promenade deck stretching three parts the length of the ship. Below, the finest dining saloon of any coastal steamer, seating eighty-six, had a splendid hardwood dance floor extending the breadth of the ship, complete with orchestra stand, and was convertible for cruise dancing on short notice. The *Lady Alexandra*, with a daylight licence for 1,400 passengers, was an ideal day-trip steamer and transported the largest organized picnics to Bowen Island. She was the biggest excursion carrier north of San Francisco, but her 300-ton cargo capacity was rarely used for more than 100 tons of general freight and express on Howe Sound.

Four days after her arrival, she made her first trip, with eight hundred passengers, to the Strait of Georgia to salute Britain's largest warship, *H. M. S. Hood*, which was on an official visit to Vancouver. Under the veteran Captain George Gaisford, she then began a regular daily run to Bowen Island, and a series of popular dance cruises from Union pier every Wednesday and Saturday evening. During the stopover at Bowen, the orchestra transferred to the pavilion, where summer campers joined in the dancing.

For her last season, before being scrapped, the *Cheam* was put on a daily summer run to West Howe Sound under Billy Yates. Captain Yates was an old hand at harbour trips, and under his command the *Cheam* also made a number of ferry trips, taking 2,000 children out to see the *Hood* in Burrard Inlet on July 2.

When the *Lady Alexandra* was first planned, it was intended that the extra cargo space could be used if required for bringing canned salmon from the northern canneries in the fall, after the excursions were over for the season. This was only tried on one occasion when she was sent on her longest voyage as a freighter with a load of cans for the Skeena River, but it did not work out as anticipated by the designer. On the southbound voyage, loaded with salmon, the huge swells of the open Queen Charlotte Sound affected her dangerously, with rolls of 35 degrees being recorded. Doubtless some necessary changes could have been made in the vessel's trim for her use in outside waters, but the Company had other ships in the regular cannery trade and the experiment was not repeated.

Barely two months after the arrival of the *Lady Alexandra*, John Barnsley died suddenly on August 19. His death shocked the business community and the Company's Liverpool owners. Described by the press as "an honest business man with a kind heart towards all," he had, by careful administration, obtained excellent results in the short

98

space of four years. There were perhaps more brilliant but no sounder managers of the Union Steamship Company than John Barnsley. Following his death, J. K. Macrae, a prominent lawyer and later K. C. who was currently president of the Vancouver Board of Trade, filled the vacancy on the Union's directorate.

CHAPTER 7

1925-1929

The Catala *and New Day Ships Arrive*
Harold Brown Develops an Excursion Bonanza
A Thrilling Rescue and a Near Disaster

Night and day throughout the year go the little ships
that serve up and down the far inlets, when the dark
forest pockets in the looking-glass waters, and smoke
curls upwards from lone chimneys.
HAROLD BROWN, 1927

When Harold Brown took over as general manager, he said: "It is the general desire of the Company to give improved public accommodation, the feeling being that the British Columbia coast is as beautiful and interesting a section as there is in the world and it deserves the best of provision for tourists and for general public service. The policy of the Company is to maintain a fleet of coastal ships second to none." This policy was fulfilled over the next five years, which was the period of the Company's greatest expansion, not only on the northern routes but also in the area of local resorts, which the new excursion program opened up for Vancouver's growing throng of holiday-makers.

Well ahead of the completion of the *Lady Alexandra*, I worked closely with Mr. Brown in promoting the Bowen resort. Splendid coloured posters were made which carried the advertisement "BOWEN ISLAND – One Hour's Sail to Vancouver's Seaside Playground," with a pictorial map impression of a ship en route to the resort. Harold Brown's "Festival of Fitness" folder, which proclaimed the creative value of fresh air and sunshine, helped open up the local coast to half a million visitors by 1930.

Union's second new northern vessel, the *Catala*, was now building at Mr. McLaren's Montrose yard in Scotland. For the second time, the Company chose a Spanish name, this one given to Catala Island at the entrance of Esperanza Inlet on the west coast of Vancouver Island. It commemorates the work of a missionary, Father Magin Catala, who came from Mexico to the Spanish settlement of Santa Cruz de Nootka in 1793 and spent several years among the Indians of the west coast.

The *Catala*, of 1,475 gross tons, was similar to the *Cardena*, except for a promenade encircling the entire top deck which also had a fine forward observation lounge. With an overall length of 229 feet and 37-foot breadth, her comfortable accommodation of forty-six staterooms, including two suites, provided 120 cabin berths and steerage bunks for forty-eight persons, with a licence to carry 267 passengers. She had one main hatch and capacity for 300 tons of general cargo including a refrigeration chamber for 40 tons of boxed fish. Navigation aids included a radio direction finder, and her twin funnels and upper deck profile suggested a much larger vessel — almost a miniature liner!

With all this the *Catala* turned out to be a stiffer sea-boat than the graceful *Cardena*. She was launched on February 25, 1925, being christened by Mrs. Richard Welsford, wife of the Company president, at the Rossie Island yard. Captain Andy Johnstone, well-known skipper of the *Venture*, who acted in an advisory role during the fitting out of the *Catala*, was her first master. Despite a "snorting gale" en route, she made a good passage out from Scotland under Captain James Findlay, who had ferried out several other new vessels for the Company. She left Vancouver for her maiden voyage on July 28, 1925 under Captain Johnstone to Prince Rupert and the Skeena and Nass rivers.

Several hours earlier on the same day of *Catala*'s launching, another ceremony took place aboard the *Lady Cecilia*, one of two day-steamers under conversion in another section of the Coaster Construction Company, when this vessel was christened by Lady Rushton. These former Navy minesweepers, originally of 19 knots, and purchased by Welsford's in 1924, were the sister ships *Swindon* and *Barnstaple*, launched in 1919 at the Ardrossan Shipbuilders' yard. Both vessels were reconstructed at the Montrose yard, with the addition of an upper deck to obtain the necessary excursion capacity. Sponsons were built on to the hulls amidships, which reduced the speed but provided the margins of stability for the extra deck. At first there was some comment about the "side blister" appearance, but later it was hardly noticed. The vessels were each rebuilt with two funnels, but the aft one was a dummy. The twin vessels — *Lady Cecilia*, 944 gross tons and *Lady Cynthia*, 950 tons — were 235 feet overall with a breadth of 29 feet. They were primarily excursion vessels with a day licence in summer for 900 passengers, and space for about 75 tons of general freight. The main saloon was comfortably furnished, and the spacious top deck had a forward observation lounge and three staterooms. Triple-expansion engines, with Yarrows water-tube boilers, gave a maximum speed of 15½ knots, but their usual operating speed on one boiler was about 13 knots. The extra speed provided by the second boiler was most valuable on special runs.

The *Lady Cecilia*, with her saloon boarded up for the ocean voyage, reached Vancouver via the Panama Canal under Captain Charles B. Smith on April 12, 1925. She was placed on the Howe Sound daily run to Squamish under Captain Neil Gray, who retained command with only occasional relief until 1937.

The *Lady Cynthia* followed four months later, entering Vancouver harbour on August 22, and was assigned to the Powell River route under Captain Dickson, the Company's senior master, for her maiden voyage, and then to Captain John Boden. Before the second day-steamer arrived in port, the Union's Vancouver operation was again visited by Sir Arnold Rushton and President Richard Welsford. After inspection of the new fleet in action — the *Cardena*, the *Catala* and the three excursion vessels — plans were laid for the expansion of the Bowen Island resort. The original Union Steamship Company of British Columbia would become, it was announced by Chairman Grange V. Holt, a holding company for two operating subsidiaries: Union Steamships for the ships, and Union Estates for the Bowen and Selma properties. With terminal operations now a major concern, Archie L. Clements was brought in as assistant general manager and remained with the Union until 1937. He had been wharf manager at the Evans Coleman Dock since 1911, after service with the Canadian Pacific Railway as yard superintendent.

The scenic attractions of the daylight route to Squamish were now specially publicized, being described by the PGE Railway Company as the "Gateway to the North." It was a wonderful seventy-mile round-trip sail that was featured in the Union's map folder as "The Magical Day Sea-Trip on Howe Sound." The railway officials were also alive to the tourist value, and together, the two companies in 1925 innovated a "Sea and Rail" excursion on Sundays, which combined the marine beauty of the fjord with a scenic rail trip on sightseeing cars to Brandywine Falls and Alta Lake, where the genial host of Rainbow Lodge, Alex Philip, served tea. This remarkable outing — "a day in a thousand" — from 9:30 a.m. to 8:30 p.m. was a bargain price even in the twenties, costing only $2.50. It attracted capacity passenger loads for many summers, and for both companies was a very successful promotion.

Meanwhile, change had gradually taken place in the logging camp business to more centralized production, and by 1925 many of the scattered smaller camps employing hand-loggers had been eliminated. The bigger companies expanded operations, sometimes in three or four different areas perhaps fifteen or twenty miles from the coast, all controlled from a central headquarters and commissariat. Apart from their own singletrack railways, as at Rock Bay and Englewood, they had constructed company truck roads at Campbell River, Sayward and Port Hardy, where leased truck carriers connected with boat tenders through Quatsino Sound to Port Alice. And a similar trend began taking shape in the cannery and mining business, as several leading oil companies started sending their own fuel barges up coast and the first of the fishing companies' own supply vessels began shuttling to their own depots, cutting into the revenue of the tramp freighters.

With an increasing number of hospital cases to be moved from the work camps and settlements, the Union's overnight passenger ships were fitted out with a special "hospital cabin." The day vessels were also equipped with an emergency bed, although the solid one fitted in a corner of the *Capilano* lounge looked good for a lifetime. Much suffering was eased and many lives saved by the care of the Union crews while the sick and injured were en route to the nearest hospital long before planes could be called for such emergencies. An old quartermaster, Augustus Pearson of the first *Comox*, once wrote of the days in the early 1900s before the advent of navigational aids when Captain Moody was in charge and George Gaisford was the pilot:

At Rock Bay we took aboard a badly injured logger and when in Granite Bay [it] started snowing as it can do up there. I was steering for George Gaisford and the Captain said, 'We will try it — I would like to get that poor devil to Van Anda and the doctor,' and we hit around Granite Point into Okis Hollow and down to the Hole-in-the-Wall. The master himself took the bow look-out and it was snowing so heavy it was only at times I could see him. But we made it and I was glad — we reached Van Anda all right, but the logger passed on before.

A magnificent service was performed through the years by Doctor George E. Darby, of the R. W. Large Memorial Hospital at Bella Bella. On one occasion he made a perilous landing from a Union vessel to succour a stricken lightkeeper.

A most welcome development was the overhead passenger bridge and ramp which was built from Carrall Street across the CPR tracks to the Union wharf. Delays for the general public, especially in the mornings and close to the sailing hours, resulting from the shunting of freight cars, had been an irritation for many years. The new overhead, which was officially opened by Mayor L. D. Taylor on June 30, 1925, was vital to the easy movement of crowds of trippers embarking daily or returning from numerous sailings. Its cost was shared between the City, the property owners and the Union Company.

Near the end of 1925, the Company lost the key logging vessel *Cowichan* in a collision with another Union ship. A Christmas excursion had been put on from Powell River with the *Lady Cecilia*, chiefly for the mill workers, and a return sailing was advertised to leave Vancouver at 7 p.m. Sunday, December 27. In view of the large number who had come down from Powell River by other sailings, a precautionary "steam up" was ordered on the *Lady Cynthia*, as a standby vessel. I was acting as traffic assistant to Mr. Brown, and we had supper together before seeing the embarkation at the Union Pier. There was a light mist, and with such a crowd waiting on the pier — long before our loading gates were installed — I carefully noted the number being embarked. When the purser's tally passed the four-hundred mark, and there appeared to be another two hundred still on the wharf, Mr. Brown ordered the *Lady Cecilia* away with her full complement of five hundred, and another seventy-five boarded *Lady Cynthia*, which left under Captain John Boden thirty minutes behind her sister ship.

Fate now took a hand with a blanket of fog off Roberts Creek bank, where Captain Bob Wilson was cautiously picking his way south with the *Cowichan* after a light Christmas trip. He sounded his whistle constantly, as he was expecting the *Lady Cecilia* to pass northbound, and duly heard Captain Neil Gray's ship go by safely. Then, as he said later, it was only fifteen minutes afterwards that he heard another whistle close at hand — from the *Lady Cynthia* — and, without any chance to clear her, the sharp bow of the former minesweeper sliced into his vessel amidships. Captain Boden shouted from his bridge that he was going to hold the *Cynthia* pinned into the *Cowichan*, and Bob Wilson safely guided forty-five persons, including thirty-one crew, overside to the forward deck of the other vessel which was not seriously damaged. No sooner had the *Lady Cynthia* backed off than the *Cowichan* went down like a stone within nine minutes of the first impact.

It was a bad blow, forcing the Company to use the *Lady Cecilia* and the *Lady Evelyn* on overnight runs for which they were never intended. I sometimes blame myself for not putting a few more aboard the *Lady Cecilia* and cancelling the second ship's sailing. On the other hand, it could have been tragic if the *Cowichan* had struck an over-

104

loaded vessel, and one cannot dwell on the "ifs." The subsequent inquiry praised the seamanship of both masters involved in this regrettable episode.

In 1926, the Sechelt Hotel and about 240 acres were added to the Union's growing Estates in the pursuit of more travel business for the excursion vessels. The property, quickly made over into spacious picnic grounds and resort facilities, was bought from the estate of the late Herbert Whitaker, who built the hotel in 1899 and had an interest in several small vessels running from Vancouver in the 1900s. Earlier still, the land had been owned by Lieutenant Governor Hugh Nelson when there were very few white settlers on the Sechelt peninsula. George Anian was the first store manager and agent at Sechlet, followed by R. S. Hackett, both of whom were greatly respected by the Indian community, the local residents and summer visitors. In addition to providing larger and alternative picnic grounds to Selma Park, the Sechelt Hotel acquisition gave the Union Company a firm hold on the mainland local trade until after World War II. But the picnic resorts had to extend an attractive "invitation" which would capture the public imagination, and it came by way of the happy phrase "Gulf Coast Riviera," coined by Harold Brown. The present-day slogan "Sunshine Coast" also comes from our illustrated folder entitled "Sunshine and Sea-charm along Holiday Shores on the Gulf Coast." It contained a fine map in colour showing in detail all "the enchanting sea-nooks" along the route between Vancouver and Powell River, and at Savary Island. This folder was rushed out for the 1925 season, and the simultaneous promotion of holiday resorts and ships proved an ideal combination.

The summer haunts fed the steamers with a growing volume of passengers and freight, including Saturday's grocery supplies that were sometimes carried aboard under the friendly eye of the purser who often overlooked the rule that everything except hand baggage was supposed to be shipped as freight. The next four years saw the peak of the day-steamer crowds, with a daily choice of trips: "Sunny Hours and where to get them," "Sunny Spots and where to find them," were the headings on the list of illustrated outings. As many as six vessels left the Union pier on summer weekends for Bowen Island and local resorts. On Friday nights, three "Daddy's Boats" sailed between six and seven o'clock for Bowen, Gibsons, Granthams, Hopkins, with local stops to Sechelt. From five to six thousand people embarked between Friday night and Sunday morning, and a host of suntanned holiday-makers flocked across the Carrall Street overhead on Sunday nights.

The atmosphere around the Union dock on Saturday afternoons in the late 1920s and for a decade afterwards, with four or five steamers embarking resort-bound passengers, can hardly be recaptured. Despite the bustle with line-ups at five or six ticket wickets and an unending stream of passengers along the wharf to the designated ships, there was an informality to it all which old-timers will remember, such as Captain Lawrey leaning over the bridge of the *Lady Cecilia* and asking "Where's Mr. ----? He should be here by now. I'll give him another five minutes!" And they will recall, too, after the vessel had cast off and cruised for nearly two hours, her approaching gingerly the tiny float off Gower Point to let off the cottage weekenders, including old Mr. Sinclair . . . the exodus twenty minutes later over the solid Roberts Creek wharf . . . the excited laughing group of Brownies encumbered with camp kits disembarking at Wilson Creek. Then, in glistening Trail Bay, there would be landed a hundred or more cottagers, who would be greeted with shouts of delight from their families who were holidaying at Selma Park and Sechelt where the Burley family, the Flecks and others had sizable homes. Nearby a dozen little boats would be trolling in the bay. The weekend fare to Sechelt was $2, but with a family book of campers' tickets it worked out to 90¢ each way. Watching nearly every departure from Union pier for Sechelt or Buccaneer Bay would be Bryce Fleck and Calvert Simson, of Simson Balkwill, our perennial "dockside superintendents." As a commuter service, it was almost unbelievable; and for the storekeepers at this chain of summer haunts, it was irreplaceable.

Passenger travel to Bowen Island, where the estate's rental cottages shortly exceeded 150, more than trebled with the coming of the *Lady Alexandra*. The publicity for what was now Vancouver's metropolitan resort called it a "Ferry Steamer Service," and a familiar panel on the front of many city street cars showed a picnic family with a small boy carrying a toy "Lady Alex" under his arm, with the slogan, "TAKE A BOAT TO BOWEN ISLAND."

There were now four, and later six, picnic grounds at Bowen Park, but all were booked at the weekends. Each summer large organized groups from leading Vancouver firms and trades sailed from the Union pier on special charters. Once a year the Shipping Federation closed the Port of Vancouver for the occasion of the Longshoremen's Union picnic, when all three big excursion vessels embarked more than three thousand for picnic sports at the island resort. Other large picnics included employees of The Bay, Woodwards, Spencer's Remnants, B. C. Telephone, B. C. Electric, Kelly Douglas, and the "Grain Trade." It was

106

a colourful and accepted part of community life. The large groups took along so much pop, ice cream and food that it was rumoured the Bowen campers did not need to feed their children on those banner days. There are but few oldtime residents of Greater Vancouver today who missed the fun of a basket picnic on the popular "Alex" under Captain Boden, a jovial figure on the bridge for seven successive summers. During this same period, Captain Billy Yates relieved on various day-boats and looked after the night traffic in the summer as assistant to Captain Walker.

In the north, the *Cardena* and the *Catala* had firmly established themselves in service to Prince Rupert and the canneries. Also served by these steamers were Anyox (formerly Goose Bay) in Observatory Inlet with its copper mine and smelter, which ranked as one of the world's greatest mining centres, and Alice Arm where the silver ores made the Dolly Varden Mine famous. At Stewart, the gold ore was being transported from Premier by aerial tram to the dock. In most northern communities, there was an outstanding personality who was generally in the forefront of any new development. Such a man at Stewart was big W. J. (Bill) Crawford, agent for Imperial Oil and other suppliers. The Crawford Transfer Company, later managed by his son-in-law Bill Esselmont, represented the Union in that area for several decades.

Much goodwill was built up by the friendly and informal atmosphere aboard the ships, and word soon spread about the generous meals. The "night lunch," a late evening snack, often at the master's table, was a prodigious affair with varieties of cold meats, cheese and cake. As a traveller remarked to me: "What your vessels lack in deluxe accommodation they sure make up in the dining saloon. Of course you have to keep the loggers happy!" My father, a Yorkshireman who loved his food, always contended that the deep-dish apple pie aboard Union ships was the "best in the world." Seekers after unusual adventure cruises began to arrive from all parts of the continent. I found that we were listed in Harlan's "Vagabond Trips." Where else could anyone cruise the fjords for six days with thirty to forty stops and informal visits ashore at Indian settlements, canneries, and coastal towns with plank sidewalks for an all-inclusive fare of fifty to sixty dollars? Hundreds of British Columbians and visitors embarked each summer on these "voyages of discovery" through the 700 miles of the Inside Passage, a stretch of inland waterways that writer Tweedale once described as "Canada's Norway, but a Norway many times repeated." Most visitors came from Pacific coast states, chiefly California; and perhaps a third of them from Vancouver, Victoria and the prairies. The response was so great that it soon became necessary to limit the number of tourists on each sailing to leave space for the regular travellers and settlers.

The old *Chilliwack* was retired in 1926 and sold to the Gosse Packing Company for use as a floating cannery. It was planned to acquire a second modern freighter which could run in tandem with the *Chilkoot* in the increasing heavy and bulk cargo tramping. It was averaging twelve days to "turn around" the *Chilkoot*, and another vessel of similar type could ensure a weekly cargo sailing to the north. *S. S. Ardgarvel*, the vessel chosen for this purpose, was on berth in the Clyde at Ferguson Bros., Port Glasgow, where she was built in 1917. Of 833 gross tons, she was 200 feet in length with 30-foot breadth, and had a cargo capacity of 1,100 tons. Her operating speed of 10 knots was better than the old *Chilliwack*.

I was in Liverpool at Christmas in 1926 and was called to London to lunch with Major Haddock, the Welsford chairman. While not vetoing the Vancouver ideas, I remember the major's concern and his searching questions as to the need for more tonnage. Subsequently, on March 10, 1927, I took the night express to Glasgow to see the *Ardgavel* being fitted out for Union service as the *Chilliwack II*. There was no question about her staunchness. She had been carrying iron from northern Spain, trading off the British Isles in all weather, and was built 20 per cent stronger than Lloyd's requirements on this account. Her huge hold could take the longest steel girders or pipes and timbers, with a forward hatch of 60 feet. In European waters she had carried a crew of thirteen, but her forward accommodation was increased to nineteen for the B. C. coast. The "ferry captain," James Findlay, arrived from Vancouver and sailed her back later in March to reach the Union dock on May 5, 1927. One of his ship's officers, coming out to Canada, was dapper Angus McNeill, from the Isle of Skye, who was to earn a reputation as one of the Union's best northern skippers. The vessel's first sailing under Captain J. D. McPhee on May 31 began a quarter-century of safe cargo carrying. This fine freighter, which could move 28,000 cases of salmon, was later fitted at Wallace's with fish oil tanks.

In the early morning of Monday, August 22, 1927, Captain Andy Johnstone engaged the *Cardena* in one of the most skilful actions ever recorded in coming to the assistance of another stranded passenger vessel. The *Cardena*, after leaving Rock Bay, was headed for Seymour Narrows southbound. Chief Officer Jock Muir had just come off night watch when, from the deck below, he heard the sharp blasts of a distress signal. "There had been persistent fog in patches," Jock said, "and at this moment, shortly after 6 a.m., visibility was limited to within a hundred yards. Captain Johnstone immediately proceeded through the mist to render aid, and soon perceived the shape of the Canadian National's crack *Prince Rupert* caught fast on Ripple Rock, the bogey of the Narrows." As Jock told it: "Manoevring with superb seamanship, Captain Johnstone brought the *Cardena* in close, and, as he approached the scene, saw that the vessel was completely immobilised with one of her propellers going around in mid-air. The *Prince Rupert* could easily have foundered or been flung against the cliffs."

Andy Johnstone, who was once quartermaster on the old Cunarder *Umbria*, filled in the rest of the story.

The *Prince Rupert* had passed us farther up the straits on her way south, and there was a strong ebbtide running in Seymour Narrows. Apparently she had struck Ripple Rock head-on and passed clear over it. However, with her engines stopped, the force of the ebbtide had swept the *Prince Rupert* astern so that she struck a second time and pinned herself on the rock. The ship's rudder had been driven into and become interlocked with the starboard propeller. Her position, with a capacity passenger load, was extremely hazardous and precariously near the starboard side cliffs. As my ship drew close, I shouted to Mr. Mercer, our first mate, to cast the *Cardena*'s steel towing line aboard from our after reel, which he did and made fast to the *Prince Rupert*'s stern. It was a superb feat of heaving-line throwing by big John Mercer who was an oldtime halibut schooner man with huge hands. The fog was then clearing sufficiently for the *Cardena* to come alongside the *Prince Rupert*'s port side and make fast.

I looked up and called to her bridge and there was my old chief officer of the *Camosun* when I was second mate, now Captain Dan Donald; but in the excitement he didn't seem to recognize me. Then, working the *Cardena* in the manner of a tug moving a liner, we pulled the vessel off the rock pinnacle. I could have towed her all the way to Vancouver if we'd been the other side of the Narrows or if her rudder could have been brought amidships. As it was, we first got her into mid-channel and safe from the threatening cliffs, thus preventing a possible major disaster. Then we towed her back to a safe anchorage in Deep Cove, just a mile from the Narrows entrance, towing being difficult owing to the *Rupert*'s rudder being jammed hard a-starboard. The decision to leave her safely anchored in Deep Cove proved a sound one, as two powerful tugs later had plenty of trouble sharing the task of bringing her the hundred and ten miles to the Burrard Dry Dock in Vancouver.

Once in Deep Cove, Captain Johnstone transferred as many passengers to the *Cardena* as he could accommodate, with all the mail, valuable cargo and express. Then, Andy concluded, "The *Princess Beatrice* hove in sight and was signalled to come alongside and pick up the remainder of the passengers.

Unquestionably it was the speedy action and handling of the *Cardena* that saved the *Prince Rupert* from almost certain disaster. The Union Company elected to waive all claims for salvage, and this "broadminded spirit of co-operation" was warmly acknowledged by the Canadian National. "We regard this," wrote D. E. Galloway, assistant vice-president of the CNR, "as an extremely friendly action . . . Needless to say, should any similar misfortune occur to any of your ships we will be glad to extend the same treatment to your Company." As Captain Johnstone remarked to me, "Harold Brown was long-sighted in his assessment of good relations between the coastal companies," though there were indications the Liverpool owners felt that normal salvage rules should have applied.

In the late fall of 1927, Union's mainliner *Catala*, in command of Captain Alfred Dickson, was southbound from her Stewart terminal when she met with near disaster. At 1 p.m. on Tuesday, November 8, after leaving Port Simpson and heading for Prince Rupert via the southern channel inside Finlayson Island, with Chief Officer Sheppard on duty, she struck fast on a reef opposite the Sparrowhawk buoy. This particular channel had long been recognized as not without risk, the reef in its centre getting its name from a British light cruiser that grounded and was destroyed there in 1874. As a later inquiry found, visibility at the time of the *Catala*'s accident was impaired by glaring light conditions. Had this been anticipated it would have been better for the vessel to have taken the north channel instead of this south one, which was frequently used by those familiar with it to save time in daylight. The vessel hit with a heavy thud, but there was nothing at first to indicate that she had suffered a near-mortal blow. Captain Dickson ordered the boats lowered immediately, and most of the forty-four passengers including A. L. Clements, the assistant manager who, with his wife, was making a round of the route, and the crew, were transferred to a tug which had been summoned. Indian launches also put out from Port Simpson to assist in taking passengers ashore. All were landed safely at the village, forty miles north of Prince Rupert.

It was soon evident that the *Catala* was held "hard and fast," but although she was badly damaged below the waterline, no water had yet entered the hold, owing to the protection of her double bottom. There was, however, a grave risk of the vessel's breaking her back over the reef when the depth of water would fall from 23 feet to only 7 feet at low tide. It turned out that the *Catala* was actually cradled between two pinnacles of the reef; fortunately the ship held fast although listing heavily to starboard. Attempts to pull her off by the tugs *Salvage Princess* and *Cape Scott* failed; photographs show the *Catala* tilted on her starboard side to an angle of 45 degrees with her bow high above water. Within two days after the ship first struck, the powerful *Salvage King* arrived from Vancouver. In the meantime, most of the cargo had been removed by lighters. New efforts to refloat the *Catala* were in vain, and by November 14 the vessel seemed doomed. In fact, she was abandoned to the underwriters; but Harold Brown, who had come north with Mr. McLaren, the builder, had confidence in the strength of the ship, and announced that the Company would accept her back if she could be refloated.

Then followed a fine salvage job carried out by T. W. Allen and W. Jordan of Pacific Salvage Company with Captain Hewison of the *Salvage King*. On the scene in an advisory role was T. C. Warkman, of the London Salvage Association. Working feverishly against time — a sudden storm would have destroyed the ship completely — the salvage crew carefully blasted away the rock pinnacles while patching the hull. On December 5, by incredible good luck and skill, the vessel was successfully refloated and moved to shelter a mile from the reef for temporary repairs before being taken to Prince Rupert. Later she was towed south to Burrard Drydock, to be repaired and partly rebuilt under the supervision of W. D. McLaren at a cost of $175,000. Following a trial run on Howe Sound, when her speed exceeded 14 knots, the *Catala* resumed her weekly sailing on March 30, 1928, under Captain Dickson and Chief Engineer Andrew Beattie.

Reminiscing about the old days aboard our other northern ship, the *Cardena*, Captain Andy Johnstone asked me if I had heard the story about McGregor's "choppers." When I replied in the negative, the mariner's eyes lit up with a playful gleam. "It happened this way," he said.

Most canneries carry an engineer who often stays up-coast all winter and doubles as a watchman. Sometimes, though, he has a special job to do in town, and Mr. McGregor had left North Pacific cannery in the late fall of 1928 — or maybe it was '29 — to get some upper dentures made and fitted in Vancouver. Anyway, he took passage with us and came aboard the *Cardena* the following March, all bright and smiling with his new upper plate. Well, it was blustery weather and a regular gale was blowing when I headed the *Cardena* out into Queen Charlotte Sound the following evening after supper. As cannery officials often did, 'Mac' came up into the pilothouse for a chat and soon departed to go down below rather hurriedly. On the way back to his cabin it appears that 'Mac' was taken violently seasick and headed for the rail between two lifeboats on the top deck. The ship gave a sudden lurch as he bent over the side, and that was the last he saw of his 'choppers.' Now it was always my custom to go down to the dining saloon about ten o'clock for a 'mug up,' and as I walked unsteadily alongside the lifeboats, my foot touched and half trod on something. Before going down to the saloon, I called at my cabin to get a flashlight, as I was curious about what my foot had kicked. To my astonishment it was a set of false teeth, so I went back to the cabin, washed them and wrapping them up in tissue paper, slipped them into my pocket.

When I got below, on account of the weather, scarcely anyone was in the saloon for what we called 'night lunch,' but seated at the officers' table and pouring out his woes to Norman Pattison, the purser, was McGregor. There was 'Pat' and one of our engineers digging into the cold meats, and opposite was 'Mac,' unable to sample anything except hot coffee. Almost weeping, he described vividly to me how he had seen his valuable 'choppers' go overboard — and now all his winter spent in Vancouver was in vain. I held my peace . . . the possibilities of this miracle were too rich to be disposed of lightly. I couldn't imagine what had happened except the gust of wind had somehow blown Mac's 'choppers' back on board, if they really went overside. But when Mr. McGregor and Pat were leaving the table I held the purser back and showed him the little package. 'Bring Mac up to my quarters,' I said to Pat, 'at nine-thirty tomorrow morning, and if you ever tell him I found anything I'll break your bloody neck!'

In the morning I told McGregor that we had a very wonderful medicine chest on board (which was true) and we had everything, even I thought, a couple of sets of 'uppers' . . . that is, if they hadn't been used in the meantime. Very methodically I went through the whole chest in a corner of which I had hidden Mac's teeth, and after much delay pretended to find them. 'Try these, Mac,' I said, 'they may get you by until you can get into Prince Rupert.' Well, McGregor took a couple of trial bites. 'By Jove,' he said, 'these fit a damn sight better than my own!' With this and with many flattering comments on the wonderful medical service of the Union Company, McGregor went happily below. Now, Pattison was a great talker — he'd blab about anything, but I got hold of him again and said: 'It's more than your life's worth to let on about this,' and believe me, he didn't.

It was not until that fall, when he was coming south again, that Andy Johnstone told Mr. McGregor that he was wearing his own teeth. There was always a good deal of fun and banter between the Company's officers and the managers who travelled up and down each season with us. This family atmosphere was a precious one for the Union line.

Little has been written about the small group of dedicated men who ran the office and the operating departments of the Union line during its most productive period between 1905 and 1930. "The Skipper," as Captain Sandy Walker, the marine superintendent, was generally called, and who had been on the scene since 1907, offset a native stubbornness with rare common sense. His great joy was an early Pontiac car. He teamed perfectly with Billy Vaughan, the freight agent who shared part of the same office. Little Billy had a delightful sense of humour, and consistently pulled "The Skipper's" leg without the latter's perceiving it. When I joined the Company, the freight office comprised Walter Keeling from the Boscowitz line, and "Cece" Coville, a well-known city golfer. Alongside, in the wharf ticket office, Douglas Dingwall, back from overseas service, was excitable but well liked in the loggers' agencies; and with him was the capable agent Harvey Anthony. They served the equivalent of the city population many times over.

Generally seen in the wharf shed was the brisk little figure of Teddy Turff, the Cockney head checker who had joined the Company in 1901. This preceded the building of the new freight offices where agents Frank Nealon, Al Newman and Russell Smith in turn operated alongside the marine department.

Superintendent Engineer A. S. de Gruchy, whose office adjoined the machine shop, was succeeded by George H. Foster. The latter died in 1938 and was followed by Robert M. Logan. These three men spanned fifty years in their mechanical supervision of the fleet. Bob Logan, who joined the Union in 1910 from the P & O Line, brought out the *Lady Cynthia* and the *Chilliwack II* from Scotland. The engineering and marine divisions looked after their own certificated personnel.

In the office overlooking the wharf, the treasurer-secretary team of Tom Melton and James Crookall held sway. Jim was knowledgeable in most aspects of the operation, including insurance, and had been bookkeeper since Mr. Legg's days. Jack Larnie, a former Terminal Steam man, assisted Jim and looked after Estates matters. Following Mr. Melton's death, Alan Thomas assumed cashier and paymaster duties for many years, having come to the Company as a young man. He was a quiet, reliable official who found his relaxation on the cricket field. Charles V. Coldwell, "Trix" to his older friends, was port steward and purchasing agent. Charlie Cross, his stores assistant, had served with him on the *Cassiar* in the hectic bar days.

This was the small band that recorded, supplied and kept things moving from behind the scenes. My traffic office was directly linked to "operations," as it issued the Union's schedules to accord with mail contracts, and handled the Company's public information. This office took care of the picnic excursions, and also, for a period, any claims. One old-time custom — a fringe benefit — provided a free staff lunch aboard whichever ship was in port, an arrangement that brought the various departments into closer contact.

The operation was non-stop, like the post office, in its all-round service to 150 calling points. The freight and passenger sections ran smoothly and were affected only by the seasons and by special business. For many employees, statutory holidays meant peak loads rather than a long weekend off. The pursers reported to the accounting department, but were controlled, as were the stewards, through the commissary department. The "upstairs office" and business development came directly under the manager. A daily distribution of mail by Madge Highmoor, "Girl Friday" for several decades, was generally accompanied by pungent comments that stressed priorities. Everyone worked in such intimacy that no doors closed off either the flow of information or the harmless banter.

The Union was recognized as one of the big three in B. C. coastal shipping. The Canadian National steamers which operated on fast direct sailings to four or five main ports were never regarded as directly competitive to the Union schedules. The same feeling did not extend to the Canadian Pacific whose northern steamer schedule largely paralleled our route, and whose officials seemed intent on keeping the Union's freighters strictly to the conference tariff. Rates were regularly discussed at meetings of the Coastwise Operators Association and for the most part, the decisions reached were held to by its members. But some of the smaller companies did not always feel themselves bound on special contracts to the same extent as the main lines, and this often gave them an advantage in a bid for freight service. A more aggressive policy in the Union Company was badly needed at this time to obtain new freight contracts and to negotiate rate flexibility for the cargo steamers. But Harold Brown operated strictly within the existing tariff structure and was often frustrated by loss of business.

In the passenger ship area and in the development of the Union Estates, however, Brown was in his element. Little escaped his notice as he strode round the shore operations. He pounced on untidiness — ropes or gangways cluttering embarkation areas — and for any employee guilty of rudeness or improper conduct, his anger came abruptly. Sometimes the entire office force was affected by his "storms," but dismissals were infrequent, for he was a kindly man. On the few occasions when

The sister ships *Lady Cynthia (above)* and *Lady Cecilia (below)* came from Scotland in 1925 and were soon busy in Howe Sound and on the Gulf Coast. (Union Steamships collection)

The *S. S. Lady Alexandra* carried Woodward's annual staff picnic
of 1,400 to Bowen Island, 1925.
(Author's collection)

Union Steamship directors with ladies at Mt. Strahan Lodge,
Bowen Island in August 1925.
(back, l-r) R. K. Houlgate, Harold Brown (General Manager), Grange V. Holt
(Chairman), R. A. H. Welsford (President) and J. K. Macrae, K.C.
(front, l-r) Mrs. Brown, Mrs. Macrae and Lady Rushton (visiting from Liverpool)
(Author's collection)

The *Chilco* arriving at a float landing, Pender Harbour, July 1925. (Vancouver Maritime Museum)

The *S. S. Catala*, perched perilously on Sparrowhawk Reef, November 1927, was eventually recovered by splendid salvage work.
(Vancouver Maritime Museum)

The *S. S. Cardena* propels the disabled Canadian National *S. S. Prince Rupert* by pulling her off Ripple Rock, Seymour Narrows, where she was impaled, on August 22, 1927 — a magnificent feat by the late Captain Andrew Johnstone.
(Vancouver Maritime Museum)

The *S. S. Chilliwack II*, powerful 1,100-ton British Isles freighter brought from
Glasgow as the *Ardgarvel* in 1927 to replace the earlier vessel.
(Vancouver Maritime Museum)

Three excursion vessels embark more than 3,000 of the Waterfront Workers Assn.
picnickers at Union Pier, 1927 — the Port of Vancouver closes for the day.
(Union Steamships collection)

Harold Brown, appointed General Manager in 1924, became President in 1938.
(Union Steamships collection)

Making a landing at Hardy Bay wharf. Port Hardy was the North Vancouver Island
connecting point for Quatsino Sound, Port Alice and, during the war,
a large air base.
(Vancouver Maritime Museum)

The *Catala* approaches Port Simpson,
an old Hudson's Bay trading centre.
(Author's collection)

Captain John Muir on the *Cardena* bridge in 1931
while traversing a northern fiord.
(Capt. John Muir collection)

"Full speed ahead through gunboat passage."
Captain Andrew Johnstone on bridge of the *Cardena*.
(Photo titled and mailed by an unknown passenger to Captain Johnstone, who sent
it to author two days before the captain's death)

Entire Union fleet tied up at wharf, May 1935, due to Seamen's strike.
(Union Steamships collection)

The *S. S. Catala*, alongside the dock at Anyox, site of the great copper mine and
smelter and a main northern port of call until 1937.
(Vancouver Maritime Museum)

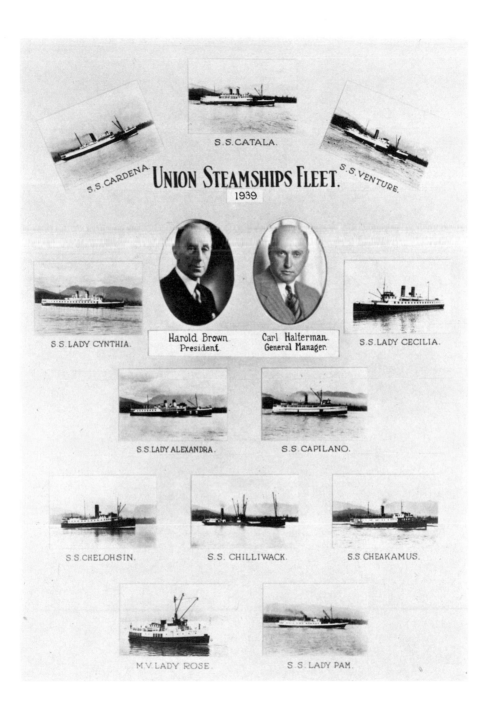

Union Fleet at outbreak of World War II.
(Union Steamships collection)

Waterhouse ships were joined with the Union fleet in 1939.
Pictured are the freighters *Northholm, Eastholm* and *Southholm*.
(Vancouver Maritime Museum)

The *S. S. Gray*, on charter to Waterhouse, was purchased by Union.
(Vancouver Maritime Museum)

Two Canadian National S. S. ships purchased in 1940.
(above) S. S. Prince John, renamed *Cassiar II*.
(below) S. S. Prince Charles, renamed *Camosun II*.
Both vessels were placed on the Queen Charlotte Islands route
throughout the war, the *Cassiar II* being mainly a cargo ship.
(Union Steamships collection)

Awaiting the arrival of the weekend "Daddys' boats."
(above) Halfmoon Bay wharf, the stop for Redroofs.
(below) Float landing at Buccaneer Bay.
(Union Steamships collection)

The *Camosun II* (painted grey) on war service to the Queen Charlotte Islands, 1941. (Mrs. H. S. Putnam collection)

Mr. Brown appeared hazy, it was deliberate. I remember his once calling me into his office and saying: "Sit down and read this letter, Gerald." Sometime before, he had met a delegation of coast loggers, headed by their spokesman Phil Wilson, protesting some freight rates, and this was his reply. Couched in beautiful phraseology, it rehashed the problems in a nebulous way without reaching any particular conclusion.

"It sounds fine, sir," I said, "but I don't quite know what you mean to tell them."

"You don't? That's fine," he said, laughing. "Neither will they!"

For over a quarter-century the Company was fortunate in having the shrewd George McGregor, well-known towboat owner and one of Victoria's most respected citizens, as its Victoria agent. George was a privileged character in the capital city, and in the early motoring days betrayed no concern whatever for traffic regulations, despite his poor eyesight, so that those Company officials who took a ride with him never forgot it. His successor was Walter S. Miles, equally well-known in Victoria.

In the spring of 1928, the president of Canadian National Railways, Sir Henry Thornton, announced that three luxury liners would be built for the British Columbia coastal service. To be laid down in Great Britain were the *Prince Robert*, the *Prince Henry* and the *Prince David*, each of about 5,500 gross tons with a projected speed of over 22 knots. As it was obvious that their size alone would limit their operation to the main ports, the rumour got around that the Union was to be taken over and its way-port routes merged with those of CN Steamships to make way for the new vessels. On April 20, Union Chairman Grange V. Holt denied a story in London's leading shipping journal "Fairplay" about a pending takeover, stating: "It is believed [the] deal would not originate enough freight for that purpose" — to act as feeder for the Railway at Vancouver and Prince Rupert. He pointed out that much of the Union's business "was with pleasure resorts, although it handled freight to and from the canneries and to logging camps along the coast."

But serious negotiations had been underway, unknown at first to the local board. I learned from my father that Richard Welsford was in New York, meeting with Canadian National representatives, including Captain B. L. Johnson, D. S. O., the former Union captain. I heard that the price under discussion was close to three million dollars, but negotiations were suddenly dropped. I always felt that the collapse of the deal was a severe disappointment to Mr. Welsford, as a shipping slump followed closely. Nothing ever appeared in print locally about a possible sale following Holt's statement, but the Union Steamship Company might easily have become a part of the federal government's coastal operation instead of later getting the CPR for its adopted grandparent.

Two blows hit the Company in the midst of a very busy 1929 season. Grange V. Holt was run down by a truck and killed instantly. Manager of the Bank of Commerce and president of the Vancouver Merchants' Exchange, he was highly regarded in the community, and his sage counsel was to be greatly missed by the Union board. He was succeeded by R. Kerr Houlgate, a popular and immaculate figure always distinguished by a flower in his buttonhole. He had been president of the Board of Trade and was a member of the Board's council for many years.

Then, on July 27, 1929, an hour after the departure of the Saturday afternoon steamers, fire destroyed most of the Union wharf shed, the damage being assessed at $120,000. Fortuantely, the main portion of the dock was clear of vessels, and adjacent ships were towed away. As a temporary measure, Pier H. adjoining Union wharf was leased for handling of the northern and logging sailings. Reconstruction of a larger shed began immediately, and the opportunity was taken to improve the loading bays with more modern facilities.

The winter months intensified navigation hazards in the Skeena River slough, and the *Cardena* ran aground at the turn of the tide at 7 a.m. on November 22 on a gravel bar off North Pacific cannery. Captain James Findlay reported that an attempt to refloat the vessel by the *S. S. Salvage Princess*, which arrived at the scene from Prince Rupert within an hour of the accident, had failed. Passengers were kept on board overnight before being disembarked on salvage vessels the following day, when lighterage of the cargo also took place. The vessel was not seriously damaged, apart from crushed plates, and was refloated two days later and returned to drydock, with the *Venture* taking over her route. It was only by utmost care that the Company avoided a major disaster in the Skeena. Apart from early Boscowitz vessels, the Union was the only line to service this key area with passenger ships.

In the off-season particularly, commercial travellers from Vancouver's main wholesale houses formed a regular coterie who booked to and from the coastal points. Frequently, groups of ten or more would travel together on the round voyage, becoming well known to the ships' personnel, and their card games, tall stories and hilarity were a familiar feature of the life on board. Many of them got to know the coast and its characters far better than did the Company officials. At

116

places such as Alert Bay and other fishing and mining centres, they checked with the skipper or watch officer on the length of time the vessel would be discharging, so that they could call on the local managers and merchants. There is no record of a Union ship's ever leaving them behind — the bigger their orders, the bigger the freight next trip! This personal touch in coastal life never really survived World War II, when changing conditions altered many of the Union's familiar wayport itineraries.

CHAPTER 8

1930-1937

Depression is Weathered with Fleet Close-Hauled
Bowen Island and Tourist "Heyday"
Union Ownership Returns to British Columbia

> In season and out we carry on the movement of our
> ships . . . the Union whistle sounds at some port of
> call every twenty minutes day and night. Navigation
> of the coast is an instinct born of accumulated experi-
> ence and constant contact with all kinds of tidal and
> weather conditions.
>
> HAROLD BROWN

With the depression, general business on all Union routes showed a sharp decline, particularly in the mining and fishpacking industries, the latter being dependent on a healthy export market. Harold Brown was faced with curtailing all sections of the Company's dispersed operations.

Valuable links were unfortunately broken with the British interests at this crucial time by the death, on February 5, 1930, of my father, who had been associated with the Welsford company since his youth and had kept in constant touch with Union affairs since Ernest Beazley's days. A man of varied activities, he was a Lord Mayor of Liverpool and took on the strenuous duties of divisional food officer for North Western England during the General Strike of 1926. The loss of my father was followed within two months by that of Major G. B. Haddock, Welsford's chairman, leaving the Vancouver subsidiary with less familiar lines of communication.

For a while, the drop in business was not too noticeable, with the summer excursion fleet continuing to carry record crowds to Bowen Island and to the Sechelt and Selma picnic resorts. A change, though, had come over the logging routes following development of residential facilities by the larger companies, and a fair number of loggers were now staying up-coast for most of the year at places such as Sayward, Englewood and Port McNeill. Still larger centres, such as Powell River and Ocean Falls, had comparatively more clubs and sports amenities than did the big city. On the northern channels, once the season was over, the outlook was grim because of the lack of construction work and bulk cargoes, with the larger companies postponing new projects.

It was ironic that at the height of the Depression, and with the same unfortunate mistiming as at Prince Rupert in 1910, three palatial Canadian National super-liners arrived on the coast. The first of the handsome three-stackers, the *Prince Henry*, 384 feet in length with 57-foot beam, entered service on June 21, 1930, to Prince Rupert and Alaska. These ships, which drew much admiration and created a considerable stir on their arrival (and a heavy backwash when travelling at 23 knots to Victoria), quickly demonstrated that they were too large and unadaptable to the B. C. coastal routes. Thus, at the end of the 1931 summer cruising season, the *Prince David* and the *Prince Henry* were transferred to the east coast, and eventually were engaged in West Indies cruising, for which they were eminently suited. The *Prince Robert* was laid up during the Depression years, and then went into the Alaskan cruise service before assuming her valuable role as an armed cruiser on the Pacific Coast during World War II. It should have been apparent to anyone acquainted with the Union Steamship story that only a special breed of ship could function and earn its keep in year-round operation along the coastal channels.

The Union, along with the business community, was shocked by the untimely death at the age of thirty-five of President Richard Welsford during his visit to the coast on September 5, 1931. It removed the last of the original Welsford board that had fostered the building up of the Company. A reticent man with much personal charm, a former captain of the Rifle Brigade, a keen huntsman, he was well informed on Union affairs, as I found when I accompanied him on steamer trips during the early twenties. He was very interested in technical matters and had much to do with the conversion and construction of our new ships. He inherited the analytical faculty but not the boldness of Welsford's founder, the domineering "J. H."

Over the next few years, under these changed circumstances, the burden of sustaining the Union's fortunes fell heavily on the shoulders of Harold Brown, who became managing director in 1932. The problem was that he was now dealing largely not with shipping men in Liverpool but with trustees representing the Welsford family. Therefore, in assessing for the Vancouver board the immediate needs, including normal ship replacements, he was unfortunately tied to a "no risks" policy. Few people understood this confining situation, and without knowledge of it there was some criticism of the patchwork and reconditioning that followed over the next five or six years to keep the older ships, which were past their economic use, in service. These were not good times for a privately owned Company to "go public," so that needed capital could not be raised. In fact, salaries of office and wharf employees were cut three times in two years. Mr. Brown took pride in the fact that he had never "released" anyone as an economy measure, and this policy helped to keep the Union family together until the worst was over. Gradually, there was a slow recovery. The Union was still held in popular regard by the Vancouver community, and in an encouraging editorial entitled "Piling Up Goodwill," on July 30, 1931, the *Province* said: "The [Union Steamship] Company knows . . . its fortunes are tied up with the fortunes of British Columbia, and that every little thing it can do in these troublous times will be bread cast upon the waters." However the Union dividend, which was a commendable 10 per cent through most of the twenties, was omitted after 1930 and not resumed until after the Company changed ownership.

The year 1929 saw the Union fleet at its zenith, or perhaps one should say, at high water mark, serving over two hundred ports on the coast, even though future amalgamations would provide much greater tonnage. A strategic withdrawal now became essential in several areas to combat the depressed conditions. In addition to the day-steamer *Lady Cecilia*'s being used to serve areas almost a hundred miles beyond Powell River, 1930 was the last year in which the Union maintained three year-round northern routes. In 1931, the *Cardena* called at Bella Coola and Ocean Falls en route to Prince Rupert; and, in the following years, Rivers Inlet was also served on this route during the winter season.

Throughout these difficult days, the Company was fortunate in averting major marine mishaps. There was one narrow escape when, on March 22, 1930, the *S. S. Camosun* in pitch-black darkness, ran ashore on Calvert Island after crossing Queen Charlotte Sound. She refloated herself after being aground for six hours and proceeded to Namu cannery, where the *Cardena* took off most of her passengers. Repairs were carried out at Prince Rupert drydock, much to the satisfaction of that northern community. One side of the business on which these hard times had little effect, probably because the cost was so reasonable, was the northern tourist traffic, and the Union vessels welcomed a stream of cruise visitors from late spring to fall. The masters and chief engineers, particularly Clarence Arthur of the *Cardena* and Andrew Beattie of the *Catala*, played their part well in hosting and entertaining these travellers.

120

There was, of course, always a certain amount of friendly rivalry with the CPR coast ships. Captain Andy Johnstone recalled with some glee when his favourite ship the *Cardena*, in the fall of 1931, was finishing unloading at the Ocean Falls dock, while the CP's *Princess Joan* was simultaneously completing her discharge at the other side of the dock, both ships being northbound to Prince Rupert. His radio operator handed him a Company message stating that it was essential for the *Cardena* to load northbound cases of salmon at Bella Bella, as the cannery had no storage room left. This did not present any problems, but minutes later "Sparks" reported that he had intercepted a similar message from the Canadian Pacific to the master of the *Princess Joan*. Now, this was serious because if the CP vessel reached Bella Bella first, which she could easily do with her faster speed, and occupied the single cannery berth, the *Cardena* would have to wait her turn with a delay of seven hours, and miss the tide in the Skeena River. This was because the *Princess Joan* could load only 500 cases an hour, whereas the *Cardena*, which easily handled 1,500 cases an hour, could be in and out of Bella Bella in little more than two hours. So Andy devised his plan of action. The *Joan* got away first from Ocean Falls, the *Cardena* tagging behind fifteen minutes later. The CP ship was heading for Lama Pass, the normal and rather circuitous route to the Bella Bellas. It was fast getting dark, and before the *Cardena* reached the entrance of Gunboat Passage — a narrow uncharted channel well known to Andy and seldom used by larger vessels — he switched off all lights, even in the main saloon, to disguise his turn-off from the main channel. Then he steamed through Gunboat Passage and had already loaded 1,000 cases of salmon before the *Joan* came in sight. When the *Joan* drew close, Captain Johnstone, who had a foghorn voice, yelled to his opposite number on the bridge: "Don't worry, Cap'n, we'll be out of your way in another hour!"

The *Cardena* was "a happy ship." Tom Lucas, who was a quarter-master aboard before getting his mate's ticket, formed an orchestra from members of the crew. Besides Tom, the band consisted of his brother Ernie, Fred Tite from a Prince Rupert family and Johnnie Walker. It boasted a trumpet, a saxophone, an accordion and drums, and was coached at Vancouver rehearsals by Al Lexington, former member of the Boston Symphony Orchestra. After wearing hours loading salmon in the Skeena, Andy Johnstone would say: "Come on, boys, it's dance time tonight!" The orchestra members would doff their work clothes, changing them for more suitable attire, and play for the passengers all the way to Lowe Inlet, before passing the hat round. The captain made a special effort to beat the *Princess Alice* into Port Hardy by eight o'clock Saturday night. If the tides were right farther south, he'd make a lay-over there while everyone trouped up to the dance hall where the Musical Mariners played for both residents and passengers. After the dance, the loggers would follow the "Pied Pipers" back on board to take the passage south. "On one occasion," Tom recalled, "having promised a dance that night and getting late orders to load salmon at Goose Bay, Andy radioed for extra help from the Chinese cannery workers. The first load came aboard as we touched the cannery wharf, and we got out fifteen hundred cases in thirty-five minutes to keep our date. Andy kept a tight ship, but his crew stayed with the *Cardena* for years."

In the course of their regular northern rounds of the coast, Union vessels and their crews were called upon in many emergencies. One such occasion was when a fire broke out on the Prince Rupert waterfront in 1934 and Captain E. Georgeson, who had succeeded to command of the *Cardena* after Andy Johnstone went to the Pilotage Service, came to the rescue. His prompt action in turning the ship's engines into a fire-fighting unit for pumping sea water, confined the blaze to the cold storage plant. A swarthy, dapper little man, Georgeson joined the Company in 1910 as mate of the *Camosun*, and was a popular figure on the northern routes.

That same year, the *Catala* came upon a sea mystery at Egg Island lighthouse in Queen Charlotte Sound. As the light was not functioning, Captain Dickson stopped his vessel and Second Officer Eric Suffield and two seamen went ashore to investigate. But it was impossible to get the lifeboat close enough to make a landing because of the pounding surf. Without hesitation, Suffield, who was a powerful swimmer, jumped into the icy water and somehow struggled to the rocky ledge of the structure. He discovered both attendants were missing. An overturned boat was later found, but no bodies were recovered. This remains an unsolved tragedy. It is perhaps just a coincidence that some time later at Addenbrooke Light, only sixteen-and-a-half miles north of Egg Island, the lonely keeper was found shot in the back of the head with his own gun.

By 1933, there were definite signs of improvement in trade; consequently, it was very disturbing to me that a decision was taken the following year to sell the fine *Chilkoot* to the Border Line, which company renamed her the *Border Prince*. While it is true that the Union had one of its two splendid freighters tied up and that both had been idle for a period, it was the "conference strait-jacket" on rates — and not the lack of business — that handicapped the Union's representatives in getting more bulk cargoes. When Harold Brown first told me of his intentions, and further indicated that the *Chilliwack* might have to be sold too, I protested more warmly than at any time during my service as his personal assistant. It seemed ridiculous for this exceptionally well-built vessel to be disposed of at a give-away price of under $40,000, and I sensed that pressure must be coming from some quarter to pry this grand cargo ship away from us.

However, the *Chilliwack* was retained (whether due to my remonstrance I do not know) even though many considered her to be the inferior of the two freighters; but the *Chilkoot* should clearly have been released only on charter. This vessel, after being converted to diesel, came back to haunt us like the old *Coquitlam*. Union should have broken up its old ships and, if the need was imperative, sold extra tonnage far away form the North American continent. When World War II broke out six years later, the value of the *Chilkoot* was five times the sum Union received for it.

During the middle thirties, Harold Brown showed his operating officials the blueprints for a new and improved *Cardena* that had been approved by the senior captains. But the cost was around $600,000, and this was considered too high. It was felt that it could be built for less by waiting; as it turned out, the construction of the same vessel five years later would have cost nearly double. This was the price of a cautious policy imposed by absentee owners.

Through these times there was no slackening in expansion of the B. C. coast and in development of excursion business, in which area the Union must have been providing the cheapest transportation on the continent. In 1931, in an endeavour to build up the Sechelt peninsula, Harold Brown moved the motorlaunch *Comox* to Porpoise Bay to run summer sightseeing trips to Clowholm Falls and through the Skookumchuck rapids to Pender Harbour. During the ensuing winter, the direct steamer from Vancouver to West Howe Sound was withdrawn; and, as a measure of economy, the Comox was stationed at Snug Cove on Bowen Island where a transfer was made from the *Lady Cynthia* for west-side points and Gambier Island.

Writing wistfully in later years of the radical change at Bowen Island since the excursion era, Penny Wise of the Vancouver *Sun* called the mid-thirties "Bowen Island's heyday — It was the Union Steamship Company at the peak of its passenger service, providing transportation and family fun for one and all." In this "gigantic romp," as she called it, Union ships from 1921 onward carried nearly two million passengers to the "island playground." An island visitor also observed: "Bowen Island, developed as a family and vacation resort, still preserves its pristine beauty . . . it is the artist's delight and the camper's paradise; special attention has been given to the amusement and safety of children and all the amenities of resort life are to be found. Care has been taken to protect the natural charm of the island."

By 1935 it was the best known "tripper resort" on Canada's west coast, and always linked with the *Lady Alexandra*. As this popular vessel steamed into Snug Cove, a gay throng in every conceivable attire gathered to greet new arrivals. Within fifteen minutes of landing, most of the visitors would be swallowed up in the Union Estates' woodland areas, which spread back from the close-in picnic fields and beaches for a thousand acres.

When they first arrived from Montrose, both the *Lady Alexandra* and the *Catala* had their holds filled with ballast of several hundred tons of golden sand from Scotland's east coast. This was discharged by barges in Deep Bay, Bowen Island, greatly improving the resort's main bathing beach. It was a misfortune that Harold Brown's project for a holiday pier there, complete with a marine pavilion, did not materialize. Suffice to recall a few features in which Bowen Park was generally considered beyond compare. On summer days its inshore boating, which included canoeing and remarkably good fishing, was notably safe. There were few large vessels around to disturb water-skiers or anything to upset the peace of holiday-makers in this delightful setting just an hour from the city. Around the hotel, the lawn bowling green was first-class, and the six hard tennis courts were good enough for the staging of Pacific Northwest Championships. On Labor Day weekends, these were star attractions, the only hazard being the weather. This long preceded the granting of the resort's club licence. A little back from the lodge lay the Estates' farm and stables, and the island trails were perfect for horseback riding. The special-events calendar included campers' sports, a swim gala, frequent band concerts, the United Scottish Societies' picnic, and highland dancing organized by George Gibson, a long-time Union constable. Speedboat trials were a spectator attraction, and Frank Scott's vaudeville troupe gave weekly shows at the shell on number one picnic ground. There was also a small chapel for interdenominational services.

From the early twenties to late forties Bowen Island was promoted by the Union Company for mass transportation at lowest cost. Until after the war, a dollar covered the return fare, and an extra 50 cents bought the hotel luncheon. A weekend at the hotel, inclusive of meals and boat fare, was offered for $5; a "midweek" from Tuesday to Friday for $10.50, and an all-inclusive week for $25. It was not surprising that particularly on weekends the resort fairly hummed with life. For the younger crowd, Saturday night activities centred on the Pavilion dance, to which the *Lady Alexandra* brought five or six hundred "moonlight" excursionists, and perhaps half that number on Wednesday evenings, who got both the trip and dance for what Mr. Brown called "the nimble dollar." Barney Potts, Percy Lee, Dal Richards and other popular Vancouver bandleaders played aboard the "Alex" and at the pavilion. Until the late thirties these popular moonlight cruises were run seasonally in fair tranquility, though couples sometimes missed the return steamer whistle.

It was much later before a serious liquor problem was encountered with wartime rowdies, when extra precautions had to be taken on Saturday night sailings. The "booze cruise" label, indiscriminately pinned on these sailings afterwards, was grossly unfair, for the cruises had been noted for fun and romance since 1924 and not for drinking. The atmosphere was rather the air of romance which Penny Wise recaptured: "Soon from the dance pavilion came the music . . . How Deep is the Ocean . . . We Just Couldn't Say Goodbye . . . or maybe Frank Bolney's Aloha from Captain Yates's bridge of the *Lady Alexandra*, as the vessel backed serenely into the night."

Long-service managers of Bowen Park prior to 1940 were H. J. Haslett, and Mrs. Latham at the hotel; and the friendly Vospers, with William Semple and Stuart W. Jenkins in turn running the Estates' office. Agar Vosper, a soft-spoken Plymouth man, controlled a smooth operation during the peak period of Bowen's popularity before leaving in 1939 to reside on Lasqueti Island. He was replaced as superintendent by "Stu" Jenkins, president of the local branch of the Canadian Legion. Three years later, Jenkins joined the Union staff in Vancouver. Pat Wylie transferred from the catering and purser's end to take over at Bowen Park until 1945. In July and August, "Estates men" were kept on the go tending the wants of streams of picnickers especially on rainy days when the large pavilion was opened for shelter and indoor amusement. On bumper weekends, the larger organized parties taxed the capacity of ships and the Union's traffic staff alike. Over a few short weeks, while the considerable local revenues were being harvested, Bowen and other resorts necessarily took a bit of the spotlight away from the general steamer routes.

Each summer, the Union Company developed additional excursion traffic from the "out-ports" of New Westminster and White Rock. A number of special chartered trips were run from New Westminster dock direct to Bowen Island, with the *Lady Alexandra* proceeding up the Fraser River overnight or in the early morning to pick up the excursionists. Another popular run was the round trip to New Westminster, with the "Alex" taking sightseers up the Fraser, to be later returned in chartered buses to Vancouver. One well-received daylight excursion was the *Lady Alexandra*'s occasional trip between White Rock and Victoria – a four-and-a-half hour sail. On August 20, 1931, an excursion sponsored by the local Surrey Legion was run from White Rock, leaving at 8 a.m. with 900 passengers for Victoria. George Thrift, an oldtime White Rock realtor, was our local representative, and Tom Reid, MP, led the picnic parade on board, playing his bagpipes. The outing was so successful that the ship made two trips each season, the second one sponsored by Langley municipality, drawing passengers from all parts of the Fraser Valley.

I always enjoyed promoting the White Rock excursions with the help of the late Fred Tonge, one of Vancouver's creative advertising postermen and publicists, who had a dry flow of Lancashire humour. Weeks before an excursion, Freddie and I would spend a day in the Surrey and White Rock area, postering the district. Then, very often, we would drive down together early in the morning of an excursion day and sail with the Legion to Victoria. On occasion, I would travel to White Rock overnight on board the "Alex" with the whistle sounding every fifteen minutes from 7 a.m. to wake up the neighbourhood. The trips were always fully booked, and the only misgiving the Company had was whether the long, narrow White Rock pier would stand up, as a hard landing could have put it out of commission. With this hazard in mind, Captain Boden or Captain Yates always approached the end of the pier with utmost caution, and the embarkation and unloading were most carefully supervised. There were no mishaps to mar these outings to Vancouver Island.

Another featured day-cruise threaded Jervis Inlet, once called "the wonder fjord of the world." The *Lady Cecilia* steamed beyond Pender Harbour as far as Prince of Wales Reach and into Vancouver Bay, where Captain George Vancouver dropped anchor on June 17, 1792.

The outstanding excursion introduced in the lean thirties in 1933, and which met with instant success, was the day-long return trip to Powell River and Savary Island. This one happened to be my particular "baby." I had received a bid from an organized group for a charter trip to Nanaimo, which was within the unofficial CPR sphere of interest;

126

and on Mr. Brown's suggestion, I talked it over with Henry Schofield, their local passenger agent. As anticipated, he did not welcome this intrusion at all, saying: "Why don't you take a look at Powell River? Your *Cecilia* or *Cynthia* full-out could easily make a day run of it." Harold Brown was as taken with the possibilities as I was, and stemming from this casual remark was born the famous Powell River-Savary Island excursion.

Lovely Savary was included for its beauty and publicity value, and to offer Union excursionists greater variety. Harold Brown was enthusiastic in describing Savary as "the South Sea Island of the North Pacific," and set an unprecedented fare of $2 for the round trip of 160 miles. The opportunity to stop off for several hours at Powell River, or to spend an hour on Savary with its magnificent sand beach, caught the imagination of Vancouverites and visitors alike. Later the round trip fare rose to $3.50, but it was always the best one-day bargain in local waters.

It was well known that the local residents used it for regular travel, but their goodwill was needed and the trip was a great stimulus to the Union's business generally. Old William Gardiner and Harry Audley, the chief stewards, had bumper days handling three and four sittings in the dining saloon. For more than seven years, these runs averaged over 400 passengers a trip. More than 75,000 passengers were carried on 172 Savary excursions, which ran twice and sometimes three times weekly. To my knowledge, there was nothing on the North American continent to equal such a tourist delight for the price.

Meanwhile, both the day-steamer traffic and the Pacific Great Eastern Railway passenger business on Howe Sound continued to increase. For five years, starting in 1934, the Union Company provided a direct steamer, either the *Lady Evelyn* or the *Capilano*, leaving three times weekly at 7 p.m. and later at 12 noon for Squamish. Then, during the war years, the traffic reverted to carriage on the regular Howe Sound steamer. In retrospect, it would have been sounder for a special steamer to have been built conjointly or chartered for the PGE railway connections, as there was a conflict of interest with the Company's local traffic from Britannia and Bowen Island. At no time did the Union Steamship Company receive any financial guarantee from the railroad beyond payment of the ordinary passenger and express rates. Nothing came of several discussions with the PGE management about a rail steamer, and another twenty years was to elapse before the rails finally came through to Horseshoe Bay and North Vancouver from Squamish. The prominent role played by the Union Steamship Company in providing the vital southern link of the Railway without mishap through the intervening years is part of the development story of British Columbia.

One of the most sought-after Union trips was the six-day cruise of the *Camosun* and later of the *Catala*, to Rivers Inlet, Ocean Falls, and via the beautiful Dean Channel and North Bentinck Arm to Bella Coola (Pleasant Valley). This was the prosperous site of ancient Indian and early Scandinavian settlements, and later the thriving centre for loggers, ranchers, and big-game sportsmen. It was the arm of the sea reached by Alexander Mackenzie in 1793. On a prominent rock in Cascade Inlet, just off the main steamer channel, he inscribed "Alex Mackenzie, from Canada by land, 22D July, 1793." On these cruises, visitors always had time to visit the progressive Bella Coola townsite. This was the region where T. A. (Tommy) Walker, one of the province's best known guides, made his headquarters, later developing a fine hunting and fishing lodge at Stuie, thirty miles from Bella Coola. Tommy, who used to dispatch pack-trains trading up to Anahim Lake, also maintained fine saddle horses for hunting parties seeking moose, bear and a variety of small game in the magnificent wild country of the area. Later on he arranged for the booking of trail-ride groups of about a dozen visitors weekly, chiefly Californians, with our vessel bringing up a new party and exchanging the previous group each trip. This expedition by sea and horseback cost only $150. I can testify to the rugged trail beyond Hagensburg, which resembled a track through forested undergrowth rather than a road. After the visit in 1937 of Governor General Lord Tweedsmuir, who travelled north from Bella Coola in the *Cardena*, Stuie became Tweedsmuir Lodge and the surrounding area was named Tweedsmuir Park.

The splendid old *Camosun*, which ran steadily for twenty years on the main northern route, and after 1925 to Bella Coola, was sold for scrapping in 1935. Oldtimers will still recall her chief steward for many years, Dave Singleton; also purser Russell Smith and the fine crew who sailed under Captains Dickson, Findlay, Boden and Sheppard. The *Lady Evelyn* was also withdrawn and scrapped the following year, but there was no replacement in sight for either vessel. Although the need was urgent, the only relief obtained was the old *Chilco*, now the *Lady Pam*, which had been temporarily withdrawn in 1936 to have her accommodation completely remodelled. Although her licence was now reduced to 150-passenger capacity, she performed useful service on West Howe Sound and other local routes for another ten years.

Captain Harry Roach's association with this particular vessel is quite remarkable. A native of Cardiff, his first job on the coast was deckhand on the *Santa Maria*, as this vessel was named when she ran for the All Red Line. Later, he was first mate in her as the *Chilco*, under Captain W. (Billy) Mounce, and still later he became her master when she was renamed the *Lady Pam*. Succeeding skippers of this vessel included Captains Bob Naughty, Lorne Godfrey and A. C. McLennan.

About this time, in the month of October, I took a busman's holiday with my wife aboard the *Venture*, which was operating in winter relief of the *Cardena*, and got a personal glimpse of Captain John Boden in faster action than I had anticipated. He entered the tidal Skeena, and skillfully piloted the ship into several cannery wharves to load salmon; finally, at Haysport cannery, he barely had time to get out on the tide, with 3,000 cases to load in two hours. Noticing him anxiously checking his watch, I joined several passengers in handling a salmon truck. All went smoothly until my last load, when the truck stuck on an uneven plank and, as I held on grimly to 150 pounds of salmon, my ankle snapped. Of course I should have let go and risked smashing a few cases. Within minutes John Boden had the gangway up and was "full speed" for Prince Rupert, where he slung me overside on a pilot-board to a waiting ambulance. When asked some time later for my suggestions on how to avoid similar longshore mishaps, I wrote simply "More experience" (in obvious reference to my own lack).

The mates, responsible for handling the Union cargoes as well as taking regular watches with the master or the pilot, were perhaps the hardest workers in the fleet. Seven well-known officers, who were mates in practically all the vessels for a decade from 1928 were: J. Halcrow, L. C. King, J. Hackett, J. J. Hunter, J. McLeod, V. Hayman and J. E. Summerfield.

Lawyer J. K. Macrae, K. C., whose service as a director embraced the whole expansion period from 1924, succeeded to the chairmanship of the Company upon the death of R. Kerr Houlgate in 1936.

The only new ship to be laid down at this period was the small motor vessel *Lady Rose*, whose prime purpose was to take over the winter service to West Howe Sound, which was being maintained by Captain Yates with the 53-foot *Comox*, operating via Bowen Island. Since the *Comox* ferry was obviously too small, the new vessel was ordered in Scotland at a cost of $100,000. Although well designed, she had insufficient capacity by at least a third to fit into the Union's operating requirements. She was launched as the *Lady Sylvia* at the A. & J. Inglis Pointhouse Shipyard in Glasgow on March 17, 1937, and christened by Mrs. J. F. Jupp, a daughter of the late J. H. Welsford. It transpired that there was a registry duplication, and the small motor vessel was renamed *Lady Rose* after her arrival in Vancouver. Of 199 gross tons, she was 105 feet in length, breadth of 21 feet, and had one 220 BHP six-cylinder diesel propelling unit to provide a speed of 11½ knots. This engine, on the vessel's first arrival, was controlled directly from the bridge, but this system was quickly changed for safety and maintenance reasons soon after she entered service. She was an economical little craft, with an enclosed cabin aft containing a lounge and a small coffee bar. An open upper-deck with seating space qualified the *Lady Rose* for a summer licence to carry 130 passengers, but her winter ticket for only 70 passengers was disappointing and restrictive. She could handle about 20 tons of general freight forward on the main deck.

She had an adventurous crossing to the Pacific, after leaving Glasgow on May 7, 1937 under Captain W. E. Smailes, who had a crew of only nine. She ran into foul weather going south to Las Palmas and again off the coast of South America; and, even after traversing the Panama Canal, Captain Smailes had to fight seven days of storms and mountainous seas before rounding Cape Flattery on July 10 and entering Vancouver harbour the next day. She was quickly put into summer service but, while very manoeuvreable, her limitations as a utility vessel were obvious, and her size precluded her employment in relief.

Two weeks after the *Lady Rose* arrived, an announcement was released on August 1, 1937, that the majority Welsford interest in the Union Steamship Company had been bought by a group of prominent Vancouver business men. The controlling shares were purchased in England with M. J. K. Allen and F. F. Buckerfield representing the Vancouver group, and Welsford's Industry Steamship Company acting for the Welsford family. The figure I heard quoted, close to $1 million, was a third of the amount discussed secretly with Canadian National Steamships in the halcyon days of 1928. It was certainly a bottom price for the historic Company, but the equipment was old, necessitating frequent repairs, and there was much to be done to bring the fleet up to date.

In December 1937, when the Christmas trek of southbound passengers was starting, the *Catala* had an amazing escape from disaster. After embarking hospital personnel from an extra call at Ocean Falls, she was south of Kennedy Island heading for Prince Rupert when a light was mistaken for the blinker on Herbert Reef. The ship grounded heavily about 10 p.m., losing the fuel oil in the main tanks when her double bottom was ripped open. Third Officer Angus McNeill said: "She was held fast on the reef for three hours but freed herself at high tide and reached Prince Rupert harbour, with lifeboats swung out, on the fuel in her settling tank." All cargo for more northerly points, as well as for Prince Rupert, was discharged immediately. Upon inspection, Lloyds' agent found that the engine room and everywhere below deck was dry, protected by the torn double bottom, and issued a permit to complete the voyage back to Vancouver.

"When Captain Sheppard entered the dining saloon, where the chief engineer was sitting, with word that the *Catala* had a clearance to return south," Angus recalled, "Andy Beattie in his excitement promptly fell off his chair, exclaiming 'We haven't even got enough fuel to carry us back.' " So the crew was set to work shoring up the bulkheads and lower deck with lumber intended for Kincolith "until it seemed like a forest down below," and the vessel rode safely home on her tank tops. Andy got his oil by high suction from over the water in the wing tanks, with only a small reserve in hand. "We got precious little sleep," he recalled, "and it was an anxious time for Captain Ernest Sheppard as well as for Chief Officer Harry McLean, making all stops with so many passengers aboard."

The Company despatched a vessel to Sayward for escort over the last lap, and it was a very relieved superintendent who hurried on board at Union pier. When drydocked the staunch ship was found to be "completely tight," although someone exclaimed: "You could drive a loading truck through her double bottom!" Like her predecessor, the *Camosun*, the *Catala* was a miracle of strength for the Union's needs. Together with the *Cardena* and the *Venture*, the four passenger vessels which were specifically built for the northern trade, operated for a total of 136 years and logged an aggregate of six million miles without losing a passenger.

Harold Brown remained as president of the Company under the new ownership and the chief operating officials were retained. The only important change was the appointment of Carl Halterman as assistant general manager in 1938. He joined the Company from the Anglo-Canadian Shipping Company, and had also been prominent in local chartering and in the grain trade. The new Board of Directors comprised Harold Brown (president); M. J. K. Allen (vice-president); J. K. Macrae K. C. (chairman); and E. E. Buckerfield; Gordon Farrell; F. H. Clendenning; W. B. Farris K. C.; J. S. Eckman; J. R. Murray and G. M. Warren. The floating equipment comprised twelve ships, operating on seven main routes. With the return of the Company to British Columbia ownership, after a quarter century under Liverpool control, there was keen expectation of an expanding future for the busy red-funnelled ships.

The outbreak of war within two years and changing economic conditions in the coast industries had a considerable bearing on the extent to which these high hopes were borne out. One thing never changed: the torch of Union traditions handed on to Harold Brown from Gordon Legg, Henry Darling, John Barnsley and Ernest Beazley was still alight, even if it flickered a bit during the Hungry Thirties.

CHAPTER 9

1938-1945

Waterhouse Ships Join the Union Fleet
Coast Industries in the "Black-Out Years"
Loss of the Northholm

The City of Vancouver is bound up in the general development of the coast. In the future of Vancouver the Company has the greatest faith and in that development they are endeavouring to play their part without regard to any purely commercial consideration.

HAROLD BROWN

Following return of the Union Steamship Company to local control, and the considerable attendant publicity, general up-coast and excursion business showed some improvement. During 1937, 171,000 passengers were carried on day-vessels, including Bowen Island trips. It was fully expected that a building program would be undertaken to provide at least one new vessel for the northern trade. However, the matter was again shelved when it was decided not to proceed with any fleet additions owing to prohibitive construction costs. Harold Brown and the local directors had been "holding the line" and making the best of things with the old ships for the last seven years of Welsford control, and this further postponement by the new owners put a heavy strain on these vessels when new tonnage became unobtainable through the war years.

Instead, some improvements were carried out on existing vessels at a cost exceeding $100,000. After twenty-six years' service, the *Chelohsin* was withdrawn for a complete reconditioning, her hull being replated extensively and the passenger accommodation being attractively remodelled. And with the idea of using the *Cheakamus* on more routes, her accommodation was also modernized.

The *Catala* entered the news on Sunday, January 30, 1938 when she answered an SOS at 8 a.m. from a U. S. Navy plane, one of six en route to Sitka, which had been forced down by engine trouble off

133

Goose Island near Bella Bella. Captain Findlay turned his ship, getting a further message that the five airmen were abandoning the plane for a rubber dinghy, and at 11 a.m. he reached the area in a blinding snowstorm. Off the Broken Rocks he came on a small fishing boat which had just picked up the airmen. They were promptly taken aboard the *Catala*, suffering from exposure despite their protective clothing, and farther up the coast transferred to the *U. S. S. Teal*, which had been alerted by the squadron commander. Assistant Purser Harold Crompton, later a senior Company official, had his photos of the rescue published in the *New York Times*.

The Company lost two of its senior and best-known officials in 1938. George H. Foster, the superintendent engineer, who had been with the Union since 1900, died in January. Since 1923, he had devoted himself to the fleet's upkeep with quiet proficiency, and no one was better liked than this modest professional who found time for anyone with a problem. Robert M. Logan, who succeeded him, enjoyed an excellent reputation as "Chief" in several of the northern ships. Captain Alexander (Sandy) Walker, who seemed an inseparable part of life on the wharf, where he presided as "terminal boss" for thirty-one years, retired in June 1938 and died in December 1939. He was succeeded by Captain John Muir, who had been appointed Travelling Supervisor of marine services earlier in the year. Arriving on the coast in 1912 aboard the *S. S. Orontes*, his first job was as quartermaster in the *Cassiar*. Jock Muir served as master in no fewer than twelve Union vessels and was well equipped to take over the marine services' helm. He made news on March 20, 1929, while in charge of the *Chilliwack*, when he rescued five passengers from an American seaplane that had been forced down and was drifting close to the precipitous shoreline of Grenville Channel.

After the opening of Vancouver's Lions Gate Bridge in 1939, the Union Company acquired for its Estates division 150 acres at Whytecliff in West Vancouver. Its purpose was to provide a ferry terminal to develop additional traffic now moving to Bowen Island via the North Shore and Horseshoe Bay. The scenic residential area overlooking Howe Sound was disposed of by lots, but Cliff House was retained as a tearoom and supper-dance resort. Those were the days when the Cliff House menu listed a fish dinner for 75 cents, steak for $1 and chicken for $1.25, with cocktail, soup and dessert included. The ferry service, for which a new landing was built, opened with the inaugural trip of the *M. V. Comox* under Captain J. R. Browne on May 19, 1939. The venture was well supported with 10,000 passengers transported between

Whytecliff and Bowen in 1939 and 15,163 during the following summer. On May 24, 1940 the *Comox* rescued five persons from a capsized yacht in Howe Sound. They had been in the water for an hour before Captain Browne spotted them. For the summer of 1941, the *M. V. Bowen* was acquired to give a more frequent schedule alongside the *Comox*, and altogether 22,542 passengers were moved in this ferry crossing.

On February 1, 1939, Carl Halterman was named general manager to succeed Harold Brown as the operating head, as the Union prepared to celebrate its Golden Jubilee. This coincided with the Royal visit to Vancouver, and commencing on May 25 the Union day-boats operated a series of special southbound sailings to bring nearly 4,000 settlers and school children from Howe Sound and mainland points to join in the city's welcome to King George VI and Queen Elizabeth. The *Lady Alexandra*, the *Lady Cynthia* and the *Lady Cecilia* were assigned good harbour locations when Their Majesties sailed from the CPR pier aboard the *Princess Marguerite* in the late afternoon of May 29. As many as six Union ships left the Union pier at 4 p.m. with 2,500 passengers, to follow the Royal ship and destroyer escort as far as Point Atkinson.

The outbreak of World War II was fewer than five months away when Bowen Island "Playground" prepared for another bumper season. Band leader Harry Pryce and his Merry Mariners were engaged for the pavilion, which had been fitted up with a new spring floor. Spencer's Remnants — which had been organized by veterans of World War I — left aboard two steamers for their annual carnival and dance at Bowen Island, and another season was in full swing. Bowen Inn was modernized with enlargement of the dining room overlooking Howe Sound.

Unsettled conditions in the Orient had already upset local trade as rumbles from the explosive situation in China reverberated across the Pacific. Then, in September 1939, hostilities broke out in Europe, and Canada's entry brought blackness and silence to the British Columbia coast. All vessels operated under difficult conditions, using navigation lights only and with silenced radios; and all ports were blacked out. Later there would be degaussing cables and paravanes for anti-mine protection, pilothouses reinforced with cement blocks, and stern guns manned by naval ratings. Information on departure and arrival times was soon omitted from the schedule for vessels operating in outside waters, intending passengers having to apply in person for sailing information, especially at this time when Japanese submarines were reported to be operating off Vancouver Island.

It was an eerie experience to take passage on the *Catala* or the

Cardena on the northerly routes, with passengers consisting mainly of servicemen travelling to Air Force and military bases along the coast. Each vessel carried two and sometimes three engineer trainees for the Canadian Navy and Chief Engineer John Hogan in particular earned much credit for his fine training program. Many Union men left for active service among whom were Captains W. McCombe Sr. and Eric Suffield. The younger officers included B. G. Owen-Jones; Jack McLeod; W. McCombe Jr.; M. A. Benson from the pursers' department; and Douglas Halliday, my traffic assistant, who was a lieutenant in the B. C. Hussars and died from an illness contracted in the line of duty. Miles Robinson, one of the fleet's chief officers, was in charge of the submarine gates at the entrance of Prince Rupert harbour. Jack Gledhill, Harold Brown's secretary, joined the RCAF and became a squadron leader.

At this time, the Union Company purchased the vessels and freighting interests of Frank Waterhouse Company of Canada, in the cannery trade for many years, and our competitors for bulk cargoes. The Waterhouse manager and part owner was the ebullient R. L. (Rap) Solloway, who had joined the Company in 1915 before serving overseas. Those close to the scene felt that this takeover was aimed as much at getting their freight contracts and tramping "know-how" as in obtaining their vessels, which had an average age of twenty-five years. However that may be, tonnage of any kind was at a premium, and in the atmosphere of the first months of war there was much to be gained by deploying the combined fleets to best advantage on the coastal routes.

Waterhouse vessels taken over were the *Northholm*, built by J. Towers Co. of Bristol in 1924, 150 feet in length, 25 feet in breadth, with cargo capacity of 550 tons; the *Southholm*, built in 1919 by Canadian Car & Foundry, Fort William, 200 feet with 32-foot breadth, capacity 1,100 tons; and the *Eastholm*, a small wood freighter constructed in 1913 by A. Moscrop, Vancouver, 93 feet with 24-foot breadth, and 250-ton capacity. In addition, three chartered vessels came with the deal: the *Gray*, built in 1909 at Workington, 182 feet, 28-foot breadth and 650-ton capacity, which was later purchased and reconditioned by the Union Company; and the *Salvor* and the *Bervin*, the latter being the original *Coquitlam* which had been put together by Henry Darling in 1891 and now came back to the Union like a homing pigeon.

The Waterhouse company, with its headquarters now moved to a section of the Union general office, was kept under the continuing management of R. L. Solloway and his traffic and marine assistants, Sterling H. Beek and Captain Fred Talbot. The Waterhouse division took over the heavy freight and tramping end of the business, though in retrospect some thought might have been given to retaining this cargo group as a fully independent operation. For a long time, the Waterhouse ships had provided keen competition for the Union, and keeping them in a separate company and utilizing their tramping experience might have been a means of counteracting the activity of other "independents." It might also have avoided too great an overhead expansion of the Union line at this time, and kept the parent company from losing sight of its basic coastal objectives that had paid off so handsomely in the past.

In spite of restricted private and commercial travel, and suspension of all tourist travel in 1940 on overnight sailings, the northern ships were kept filled to capacity, taking naval personnel and military contingents to defence points, as well as moving RCAF groups to Port Hardy, Bella Bella and Prince Rupert.

On June 8, 1940, it was announced that the Union Company had bought the two smaller Canadian National steamers, *Prince Charles* and *Prince John*, and with them assumed responsibility for the Queen Charlotte Islands' subsidized service. Action in this direction was no surprise since it was common knowledge that talks had been held with senior Canadian National officials. Only the outcome was surprising. Shortly before, Mr. Halterman called for my report on how the Union and CN services could best be joined with operational improvement. I advised that no important economy was possible with acquisition of the Canadian National vessels alone, since their larger ships, wholly engaged on direct services to three or four main ports, could not be satisfactorily alternated with the smaller Union way-port vessels; also, that the Queen Charlottes were best served by a separate or connecting steamer. I pointed out that in a joint wartime operation which would include the Canadian Pacific, there could be a substantial saving with the CP's *Princess Adelaide* alternating with the fast CN ships and leaving the intermediate areas of Bella Coola, Skeena River and Nass River to the Union ships. Only part of my advice was followed when the Queen Charlottes route was taken over with the two old CN vessels being engaged on it. If the government intended that the Union Company look after this area for the war period, it ought to have been on a working agreement only, I felt. The truth came out in a CN release from Montreal, and published that month in *Harbour & Shipping*: "The Queen Charlotte run is being dropped because it has always entailed a loss to the CNR, even with the payment of a subsidy." Subsequent events bore out this statement, even though the RCAF movements and government timber contracts in the Queen Charlottes produced very substantial revenues for the Union during the war years.

One of the vessels taken over, the *Prince Charles* of 1,344 gross tons, was launched in 1907 as the *St. Margaret* by Ailsa Shipbuilding Company for the North of Scotland & Orkney & Shetland Steam Navigation Company. She was 242 feet in length, 33-foot breadth, with a coast licence for 178 passengers and up to 150 tons general cargo capacity. Although her accommodation was grossly outdated, the vessel was adequate at this stage to maintain the Queen Charlottes service, in which she was continued after being renamed *Camosun II*. Canadian National had been running her on a fortnightly schedule from Vancouver via the Islands to Prince Rupert and return. With the heavy demands of wartime traffic, we used her 13-knot speed to institute a new ten-day schedule to the Queen Charlottes.

The other CN vessel, the *Prince John*, built by Scott & Sons, Bowling, Scotland, was launched in 1910 as the *Amethyst*, 185 feet with 28-foot beam and cargo capacity of 400 tons. She was fitted with 40 tons of "reefer" space for frozen fish, before being put into service under the historic name of *Cassiar II*. She was maintained on her Queen Charlotte Islands route via Prince Rupert, and alternated with the *Camosun* on direct islands sailings from Vancouver. Her licence, with her deck bunks, was for 85 passengers, but the cabin space for only 38 berths was cramped and uncomfortable. From the outset, it was a question of keeping the vessel going to meet the transportation emergency. *Cassiar II* was always a good sea-boat and, when required, made the direct run from Vancouver to the South Islands in about forty-eight hours.

At this time, the timber produced in the Queen Charlotte Islands — chiefly in Cumshewa and Skidegate Inlets and Masset Inlet — was hemlock, spruce and cedar in that order of production. It was the best timber in the province and could not be readily obtained on the mainland. The Islands spruce fir was vital in airplane construction, as well as in the manufacture of newsprint at the Powell River mill, and Harry McQuillan of Aero Timber Company said that the area could supply over a hundred million board feet yearly in perpetuity. Over a thousand men were employed in logging and auxiliary industries there during the peak of the wartime demand. The Canadian Government took over Allison's Camp in Cumshewa Inlet to establish Aero Timber Company which operated five locomotives on a logging railway that bridged a lake four miles inland and extended with branch lines for eighteen miles to various logging areas. Another huge operation at this time was the RCAF base at Alliford Bay, with large hangars and supplies to maintain this western defence station; and there was the airstrip at Sandspit for land planes, one mile from the Pacific Mills camp and thirteen miles by road to Alliford Bay.

These mammoth projects were supplemented by the important fish-liver oil industry at Pacofi to the south, by fishing off Skidegate Inlet, and by the logging and cannery plants in Masset Inlet, which drew workers largely from the resident Indian community. The Masset Co-operative Association cannery at Naden Harbour put up 20,000 cases in 1943.

Milder weather in the Queen Charlottes permitted almost continuous year-round logging and the areas were kept busy timber cutting to accommodate summer booming, since towing weather from the Islands was good for only two or three summer months. With the loggers staying on through the winter, camp closures were limited to a few weeks at Christmas, which meant an anxious time getting the loggers home and back on a special Union shuttle service, with capacity loads being carried in the worst weather. Navigation, too, was difficult in the Islands area; there was a reef off Cumshewa Inlet which had to be circled in approaching the small camp landings.

With the larger number of sailings to provide for, more Vancouver docking and loading space for the northern ships was obtained by leasing a portion of Pier H. Under the pressure for more logs, some closer-in logging camps moved their landing floats constantly, occasionally into positions that required utmost care by an approaching steamer. Boardman's camp was always shifting to another bay. Once, after Captain Harry Roach's vessel was safely tied up, Mr. Boardman called to the bridge: "You've done just fine, Captain! We'll be here quite a while." "How long will that be, Mr. Boardman?" asked Harry. "It'll be two weeks anyway!" came the unruffled reply.

To assist the war effort, the Company sponsored some local "win-the-war" cruises, with free tickets to purchasers of War Savings Stamps, the officers and crews donating their time. On the evening of July 29, 1940, six ships took out over three thousand passengers. Captain John Muir led the marine parade with Captain H. E. Lawrey in the *Lady Cynthia*, followed by the *Lady Cecilia* (Captain Lorne Godfrey), the *Lady Alexandra* (Captain E. Suffield), the *Lady Pam* (Captain Harry McLean), the *Capilano* (Captain W. L. Yates), and the *Cardena* (Captain John Boden). Off Howe Sound the southbound *Venture* joined the parade and nipped into the lead place, while the *Lady Rose* tooted her whistle and tagged behind, completing a cruising fleet of eight Union vessels. A week later on August 10, the *Lady Alexandra* was host to the entire 2nd Battalion Irish Fusiliers, who marched down the pier led by Lt. Colonel K. A. McLennan, for an evening sail on Howe Sound.

Gasoline restrictions now forced thousands more to seek relaxation by taking short boat trips to Bowen Island and Howe Sound. The *Lady Cynthia* emerged from an extensive refit with a new appearance, her dummy aft stack removed and the observation cabin extended to full width. The Union fleet, including the Waterhouse ships and the Canadian National additions, now comprised seventeen vessels with a total of 14,824 gross tons, excluding the small ferries *Comox* and *Bowen* engaged in Howe Sound. During 1940, 210,651 passengers embarked at the Union pier, and the total carried north and south between all ports reached 424,000. Travel conditions were of course abnormal with the constant movement of service personnel and the greatly increased logging boom, but the figures indicated a growth of over 50 per cent in five years. It has to be remembered that with this expansion the Company was faced with heavy increases in the cost of fuel oil, insurance, and longshore wages, while the general overhead expense also continued to mount.

On the main passenger routes, the *Catala* and the *Cardena* were fully extended in serving the RCAF Station at Bella Bella, and points to Prince Rupert and Stewart, the last port being exclusively looked after by Union ships from 1940. To ease the pressure on the northern ships, in 1942 the *Chelohsin* was assigned to an intermediate service, sailing bi-weekly as far as Port Hardy, the main port not only for Quatsino Sound and transfer to Port Alice but also for the RCAF base. Special arrangements also had to be made to supply and relieve the defence base on Yorke Island at the head of Johnstone Strait.

Locally, the Bowen Island resort offered one of the few convenient holiday spots, especially at weekends, open to a city population swollen by shipbuilding and other defence industries. Close to a hundred thousand persons visited Bowen Park by direct steamer and the ferries during the uneasy summer of 1941. Brief vacations were the order of the day, and it was easy for shift workers and off-duty servicemen and their families to hop aboard a short trip steamer at the Union dock. At this time, the setup of the Union Estates division of the Company, which had controlled the properties at Bowen, Sechelt and Selma since 1926, was altered to become a special department of Union Steamships Limited.

Gerald McBean joined the Union in 1941 as assistant manager, coming from the Canadian Transport Company, a subsidiary of the H. R. MacMillan group. He brought to the Company twenty years' shipping experience, having been associated with the Canadian government merchant marine for five years and with the Canadian Robert Dollar Company.

An event of considerable significance occurred during the year, that affected the whole future of the Union Steamship Company, although it was first known to a comparative few. As Harold Brown succinctly related it to me: "A CPR vice-president sat down and put his hat on my desk this morning, telling me in few words we were now working for them!" This was his first intimation that the controlling shares had been bought privately from one or more of the British Columbia owners, who had purchased the Welsford interest in 1937. From his language, I gathered that the "Chief" was by no means enamoured of the manner in which control was obtained through one of the CP subsidiaries, the Consolidated Mining & Smelting Company. Mr. Brown felt that "they might have knocked at the front door." However the transfer of control passed off with friendliness and courtesy. The CM&S general manager, T. W. Bingay, joined the Union board, and at no time was there any interference with the day-to-day operations. Personal relations with our Canadian Pacific opposite numbers were always congenial. The fact remains, however, that, lacking the same individual freedom of action, from 1941 onward the prospect of continuing development hand-in-hand with the coast communities that had been the Company's goal for so long now seemed rather visionary. But the oldtimers of the Company accepted the difficulties and carried on the Union traditions that were instinctive.

With the entry of the United States into the war in December 1941, the Waterhouse ships participated in increasingly heavy cargo moves to the north, and gave service to the United States Transport. The *Cheakamus* was converted into a towboat, and a hull was purchased for use as the barge *Commando* to handle the emergency freight which was offering. She was sold for $75,000 to the United States government as a salvage tug in 1941 by which time the *Cassiar II* was providing considerable relief to the northern steamers.

The *Lady Rose*, which had been used on several daylight runs to move military personnel to the fort on Yorke Island, now was requisitioned by the Canadian government for naval and air force transport on the west coast of Vancouver Island. The difficulty experienced by both Captain John Muir and Superintendent Engineer Logan in getting qualified men for the ships and shore staff was keenly felt.

At the close of 1942, Harold Brown retired as president but continued as chairman of the board after going to reside in Victoria. He was succeeded by Gordon Farrell, with F. H. Clendenning and J. S. Eckman as vice-presidents, and Carl Halterman as managing director. With the situation becoming more and more threatening, particularly in the Pacific area, operations in outside waters and all ship movements and long-distance marine calls were rigidly controlled. Vessels were sometimes called on at short notice for special defence service, as when the *Cardena* crossed the gulf to Sidney, to pick up a complete RCAF squadron for duty at Annette Island in Alaskan waters.

A tragedy occurred on January 16, 1943, when the Union-Waterhouse freighter *Northholm*, under Captain Frank (Paddy) McMahon, foundered in a howling gale off Cape Scott at the northern tip of Vancouver Island, with the loss of fifteen out of the seventeen-man crew. Harrowing details of the disaster were related to me by one of the two survivors, Chief Officer (later Captain) Ray W. Perry, a hardy Newfoundlander who had worked aboard fishing boats off the Labrador coast from the age of nine.

> We left Port Alice early Saturday morning the sixteenth of January with a full load of pulp for Vancouver. Soon after twelve noon under Cape Scott, some eight hours from Port Alice, I was in charge on the bridge when the *Northholm* met up with a nor-westerly raging up to fifty miles an hour. The vessel took a heavy pounding and began to take water into the engine-room. The hatch covers were on but the *Northholm* with only a single bottom must have got several plates opened up, as the ship gradually took on a serious list. At first there was no indication the vessel was in danger of foundering, but with the engines now stopped the order was given about one o'clock to abandon ship. I had charge of one of the life-boats which we got launched under appalling conditions with eight of us altogether including Second Mate David King. By this time the second boat could not be swung out on account of the list and then suddenly before 1:30 p.m. the vessel heeled and went down by the stern, with no possibility of anyone surviving in the icy waters. In the freezing weather and high seas it was difficult to do more than keep afloat in the area between about eight and ten miles from shore, but finally at sundown I managed to get a small sail hoisted and headed for land.

There were no lights on either ship or shore during the war. It was his Newfoundland experience in small boats, he said, which saved his life, but five of those in the chief officer's boat perished from exposure.

142

Finally, nearly twelve hours after the sinking, Ray Perry and seaman A. H. Gerbrandt managed to struggle ashore after a sixth crew member died in the lifeboat before they could beach it. The two half-frozen and exhausted men succeeded in finding shelter under a tree and starting a fire. Ten hours later, at noon the next day, they were spotted by a trapper, Burnt Ronning, who assisted the men to his cabin two miles away, where they were gradually revived. Throughout Monday they remained penned in the cabin by a snowstorm, but on Tuesday, seventy-two hours after the vessel had gone down, Ronning reached a telephone near Shushartie Bay and gave news of the tragedy. The Union office in Vancouver was already aware that a disaster must have befallen the *Northholm*, and the Canadian Navy went quickly into action and picked up Perry and Gerbrandt by a patrol craft.

Neither of them suffered the loss of any limbs from frostbite. A subsequent wartime inquiry did not find a conclusive explanation for the sinking, which appeared to have been the result of a powerful sea literally opening up an old freighter at the seams. In addition to Captain McMahon, who had joined the Waterhouse Company as a deckhand, Chief Engineer Alexander Findlay, Second Engineer McLennan who was also a Newfoundlander, Second Mate David King, the Third Engineer Nelson Macarle and a total of ten seamen and engineer artificers lost their lives. These were hazardous days for the coastal vessels and crews engaged in keeping open vital communications.

For a short period in 1943 the Company took over management of the two 4,700-ton vessels *Kennington Park* and *Manitou Park* from the Park Steamship Company, until they were requisitioned by the Shipping Board for service elsewhere. This was the third period in its chequered history that the Union had deep-sea vessels under its control, and all were short lived.

While gross revenue was at an all-time high for the Company at this time, the increase was principally due to the war movements and was unrelated to normal coast developments. War profits taxes took all but a small margin of the extra earnings, and the long term outlook was by no means overly optimistic despite another record total of 472,000 passengers transported over twelve months.

The continuing safety of the passenger ships was amazing throughout these "black-out years" and must be attributed to the care exercised by Captain John Muir's marine department. In the winter months it was a heavy responsibility dispatching the northern ships, especially the capacity-filled Queen Charlotte Island vessels, and often entailed a lonely vigil checking their safe movements and arrivals at all hours. New masters — the former pilots of the early thirties — including Captains McLennan, Roach, Malcolmson, McLean and McNeill, were navigating the channels with unerring skill. Captains A. E. (Wally) Walsh and Harry Biles were rotating as shore mates, ensuring the fast turn-rounds demanded by wartime schedules.

There were always lighter moments, and a good deal of friendly banter went on between traffic and marine staff, but an excellent understanding existed. One incident concerning local traffic comes to mind. Orders were most stringent about keeping passenger loadings within legal limits both at Union Pier and up-coast, but it was not an easy matter to control the peak loads that sometimes boarded a vessel southbound along the Gulf coast or at Bowen Island dock. One Sunday night Captain Wally Walsh was on duty at Union dock and could tell by the appearance of the incoming *Lady Alexandra* that she was probably overloaded; he also saw two Customs officers waiting in the wings. As Wally related afterwards, "It was obvious that the large crowd required special service, and we needed to turn the 'Alex' around fast, so I ran out four gangways — extras to both the main and forward decks. The inspectors gave it up in disgust — they couldn't check two-a-piece, could they?"

In the business office, Jim Crookall, accountant and secretary, was joined at the end of the war by George B. Rea, C. A. from Glasgow. The administration of the combined Union-Waterhouse fleet had to deal with a much-expanded operation; the number of employees afloat and ashore now totalled over seven hundred.

To meet the ever-increasing cargo demands in 1944, the 165-foot motor-vessel *Island King* was purchased for Waterhouse operation. Of 591 gross tonnage, 165 feet in length with 28-foot breadth, she was built in 1920 at Brevik, Norway as the *Granit*. This handy vessel, later renamed *Chilliwack III*, had capacity of 800 tons and was invaluable on the Port Alice weekly pulp run. To get the best out of available tonnage for passenger service, the wooden *Capilano* was reconditioned and a buffet saloon added.

This was the year that the Selma property was sold to private interests. It had served its purpose well in encouraging steamer traffic, but now large excursions were reduced because of the war and the Sechelt resort was more accessible.

Harold Brown died in Victoria in 1945, following partial retirement two years earlier. He had presided over the Company's greatest passenger expansion between 1924 and 1939. President of the Board of Trade, a brilliant and sought-after speaker, he was a pastmaster of coastal goodwill. "People are apt to be a little difficult to handle," he once wrote in a rare understatement; "exceptional tact is necessary in keeping friendly and neighbourly relations. The call of the Union Steamship boats should be a welcome incident . . . this forms the best security for preservation of our coast business."

Harold Brown had a ready wit, was a born story-teller and was very fond of music. Early one morning Mr. Welsford, who had been spending the weekend at Bowen Island, entered Mr. Brown's office in cantankerous mood with a mile-long list of complaints. Before the president could get fairly started "H. B." told him: "There's something I have to do right away." "What's that?" "Fire the chef at Bowen Inn; It's evident he cooked you a very poor breakfast!"

I always enjoyed one of his Italian war stories (and incidentally, he suffered from recurrent malaria as a result of his Mediterranean service). It concerned General Sheridan who had telephoned at the end of a hard day in 1917 and ordered Major Brown, who ran the Italian troop trains, to switch a vital supply train en route to the front from the fast coast route to a more circuitous mountain line to avoid air attack. Part way through his soup that night, "H. B." nearly choked when he realised that he had forgotten to telegraph the route change. He decided to ride it out. Half an hour later, the general was summoned to the telephone and Major Brown figured that his goose was cooked. Finally General Sheridan called out: "Brownie, the front line can't wait for those supplies. If you ever did anything for me, get that train back on the coast route!" In a daze "H. B." went to his office, waited for a reasonable time, and re-entered with the good news that the train was back on coast route orders. "I always said you were a bloody marvel," said the General.

Many years after her husband's death, Mrs. Brown, who at the time of writing is still living in Victoria, gave me his well-marked copy of Shakespeare, saying, "I think Harold would have liked you to have this, Gerald." Underscored in the *Merchant of Venice* was the famous passage beginning: "The man that hath no music in himself, / Nor is not mov'd with concord of sweet sounds, . . ." and ending "Let no such man be trusted — Mark the music."

CHAPTER 10

1946-1950

War's Aftermath on the Coast
The Coming of the Corvettes
A Diamond Jubilee is Celebrated
Farewell Chelohsin

We will take the age-old liberty of indulging in a
birthday wish . . . that the links with the coast, which
were fashioned long ago, will be strengthened and not
broken.
                    GERALD MCBEAN (Golden Jubilee - 1949)

In 1945, Gerald McBean took over active management from Carl
Halterman, who became vice-president in charge of operations. With
the end of the war, several moves were made to secure replacement
tonnage. First, a China coaster type, under construction at Victoria
Machinery Depot, was taken over for completion to the Company's
specifications. This staunch freighter of 1,336 gross tons, named the
Chilkoot II, was 214 feet in length with 29½-foot beam, a carrying
capacity of 1,500 tons and refrigerated space for 30 tons. Captain Fred
Talbot, the Waterhouse marine superintendent, designed the changes in
her deck and cargo gear. She was handed over to Union Steamships for
commissioning on June 26, 1946, and was put in command of Captain
D. A. Connell on a weekly run to the Port Alice pulp plant around the
northern end of Vancouver Island.

When the cessation of hostilities permitted the removal of gun
mountings and protective armour from wheel housings, the fleet gradually assumed a more normal appearance. Caution was still needed in.
outside waters off Vancouver Island, where more than a hundred
floating mines — whether Japanese or Russian was never clearly established — were located over the next two or three years and disposed of
by the navy. The *Lady Rose* was returned from naval transport service
and, after re-conditioning, resumed West Howe Sound service. Two old
units, the *Lady Pam* and the *Gray*, were sold — the former for use as a

breakwater after being hulked in Oyster Bay, while the barge *Commando* was broken up.

By late 1945, the Cumshewa Inlet logging camps in the Queen Charlottes had reduced their crews to barely a hundred men at the Morgan's and Kelly camps, and the Aero Timber operation was practically shut down. The large Alliford Bay station of the RCAF was closed on September 15, Under these circumstances, the *Camosun II* was quickly sold to Greek owners and left Vancouver on September 6 under the name *Cairo*.

The provision of new passenger tonnage posed more problems than did the replacement of cargo vessels. Serious deterioration since 1939 was now evident in the condition of the passenger vessels, and only the old *Cassiar II* was left to maintain connections with the Queen Charlotte Islands. The *Venture* was overdue for retirement, and was sold in September 1946 to Chinese interests. It is sad to note in passing that this splendid and carefully husbanded sea-boat, now named *Hsin Kong So*, was damaged by fire in Honolulu harbour on November 12, 1946, then destroyed by another fire at Hong Kong on February 2, 1947. By the end of 1945, besides the *Cassiar II*, the only Union passenger vessels available to continue on the northern routes, as well as to service the logging areas, were the *Catala*, the *Cardena* and the *Chelohsin*.

Late in 1945 the Union purchased three Castle Class corvettes, which had been engaged in the North Atlantic convoys, from the War Assets Corporation at a cost of $75,000 each, for conversion into passenger-freight vessels. This eventful step was taken to get badly needed replacements speedily and to introduce a higher standard of accommodation on the passenger routes to cope with postwar demands. Despite rising costs, an earned surplus of $461,000 at the end of 1945, after a dividend of 30 cents a share, made the time seem ripe for expansion, and it was expected that at least one converted vessel would be in service by the following midsummer.

The haste, however, with which this decision was made stands out in sharp contrast to the hesitation in laying down any passenger ship replacements for the northern services since the *Catala* was built in 1925. The operating officials received only the sketchiest outline of the corvette plan upon which to project any meaningful forecast of trading results. To my knowledge, no conversion plan in detail was examined by either the marine or engineering staffs in advance of the purchase. Whereas in the takeover of a wartime freighter its cargo capabilities were at least approximately known, this was by no means the case with the corvettes, which were built as expendable gun platforms with engines designed for naval rather than economical commercial use. The requirements of the Company were clearly those for a northern vessel, of which detailed plans were drawn before the war, to accommodate up to 150 first-class passengers, including a third premium space for the tourist season, and capacity to handle 300 to 400 tons of general cargo, with a service speed of 16 knots. Only a diesel-engined ship could provide these requirements within the limits of a handy coaster in the 250-foot range that the Union way-port calls made essential. One such vessel laid down at this time, and a second ship of a smaller type to replace the *Chelohsin*, could have "held the fort" for the Union over many years.

Instead, with the corvette plan it was estimated that these naval vessels, which cost the Navy $900,000 each, could be converted into commercial use for an expenditure of under half a million on each vessel. This projection seems to have entirely overlooked the suitability and economy of the ships on the coastal routes when converted. However, a press release from the vice-president on November 13, 1946, read in part: "The Company felt that [it] . . . could not carry on efficiently without the programme of renewals and expansion and when these Navy surplus ships could be made to fit into our operation it was the opportune time to make use of them, although the revenue from the present tariffs . . . does not justify the capital expenditure." This was an admission of trying to make Union's trade fit the ships instead of vice versa. An earlier Company statement in September 1946, quoted by *Harbour & Shipping* said: "The ships are expected to adequately care for the Northern and Queen Charlotte service for some years."

Neither the conversion troubles initially experienced with the steam plant of the corvettes, nor the fact that their cargo capacity in actual service might be reduced to barely two-thirds of expectations, was anticipated. Nor was their operating cost, which was nearly half as much again as the *Cardena*, fully appreciated. Then again, their new luxury-type accommodation was designed with an eye to the seasonal tourist trade rather than to meet the year-round needs of the B. C. coast. The *Financial Post* (December 14, 1946) said the corvettes were "equipped as miniature luxury liners and refitted as passenger carriers, and it would cost, in addition to the $1,500,000 spent on these vessels, an additional $600,000 to bring the fleet up to scratch."

Having got what Carl Halterman believed to be an attractive deal, the approved conversion plans were carried through efficiently in local shipyards, and the interior accommodations were greatly admired. Private debentures to cover the conversion work were issued for a total of $1,750,000, half a million more than the original estimate.

The first of the new vessels was converted by West Coast Shipbuilders under the supervision of its general manager and founder, W. D. McLaren, and was named *Coquitlam II*. One of the happy Union customs was the retention of its historical names, this one coming from a tribe of Salish Indians in the Fraser Valley. The word means "a small red salmon," which once teemed in the Coquitlam river. This vessel was the former *HMCS Leaside*, originally built by Smith's Dockyard Company, Middlesborough, in 1944. With length of 236 feet, 36½-foot breadth, and 1,845 gross tonnage, her conversion provided a fine enclosed saloon deck with berth accommodation for 114 first-class passengers, nearly all in outside two-berth cabins. The twenty-five upper-deck rooms were equipped with shower or tub-bath and a toilet and included two deluxe suites with twin beds. The vessel, with a licence for 200 persons, had most attractive public rooms with a tastefully furnished lounge. Forward on the promenade deck was an oak-panelled observation room with low glassed windows, the walls being decorated with murals depicting Indian scenes. A club-style dining room seated sixty. Her engines of 2,750 h.p. gave an operational speed of 14 knots, with a maximum of 15. Her cargo capacity was about 250 tons, including a 25-ton refrigeration chamber.

The sister ship to the *Coquitlam* was the *Camosun III*, the former *HMCS St. Thomas*, built by the same firm at Middlesborough in 1943. Camosun (or Camosack), meaning a "deep narrow gorge" or "swift running water," was the Indian name for the native settlement where Victoria now stands. The vessel's conversion work was awarded to Vancouver's Burrard Dry Dock Company in 1946, and, apart from the darker panelling (mostly in mahogany and walnut through the public lounges), the general accommodation followed the same pattern as the *Coquitlam*'s. Both vessels had been counted on to handle August and September bookings, but their completion was delayed three months.

Late in the fall, on Friday, November 8, 1946, the *Coquitlam* sailed on her maiden voyage to Prince Rupert and Stewart under Captain John Boden. Her chief engineer, Fred E. Smith, had worked for years as second engineer of the first small *Coquitlam*. Describing the new coast luxury ship, reporter Bill Fletcher of the Vancouver *Sun* wrote: "Bright and jaunty in her shiny white coat, she is the toast of the North!"

The converted ships had a bow rudder installed. Their equipment, including radar, depth sounder and direct-transmission steering gear, was designed to ensure maximum safety.

The *Camosun* left Vancouver on Wednesday, December 11, under Captain E. Sheppard, on a new postwar run to Ocean Falls, Prince Rupert and Ketchikan, Alaska. The chief engineer on this maiden trip was Fred Matheson, and the chief officer, J. E. Summerfield. I was Company host and welcomed aboard representatives from the various communities en voyage. We met with a cordial reception from Pacific Mills officials and local merchants at Ocean Falls, where there was a new suburban housing project.

I also recall vividly the striking population growth at Prince Rupert to nearly 12,000, and the huge assembly area at Port Edward, now almost deserted, which had been used by American forces in transit to Alaska and the North Pacific. Two other Union vessels, the *Catala* and the *Cassiar*, greeted our arrival at Prince Rupert, together with local dignitaries and Frank J. Skinner, our enthusiastic northern agent. Our arrival at Ketchikan marked the re-entry of the Union into southeast Alaska after nearly forty years. Because of the Jones Act, a regulation restricting the carriage of cargo between U. S. ports to American vessels, Ketchikan was only a passenger port for us. There was still considerable U. S. service movement through Ketchikan, and the call was worthwhile for a time as a seasonal tourist attraction.

Last of the trio to enter service was the newly christened *Chilcotin*, the former *HMCS Hespeler*, which assisted in destroying a German submarine in the Atlantic. Her Indian name means "the men of Chilco or warm water." She was built by Henry Robb Limited of Leith in 1944, and was the second corvette to undergo reconstruction at West Coast Shipyards. Similar to the other vessels, the *Chilcotin*, with accommodation for 106 passengers, was specifically designed for operations in the Alaska cruise service, with relief only when required in the off-season on the northern route. She was ready for service by May 1947, and sailed May 21 in command of Captain A. C. McLennan and in company with the *Princess Norah* of the Canadian Pacific. The two vessels had been engaged to take a convention of Shriners to Prince Rupert, where our new ship got a rousing welcome. Other officers of the *Chilcotin* on her maiden voyage were Chief Engineer G. Craigen, Chief Officer A. E. Walsh, Second Officer Robert Ashmore and Third Officer Geoffrey Hoskins.

On June 7, the *Chilcotin* inaugurated a series of outstanding ten-day cruises to Skagway. Her itinerary included a daylight sail through the majestic Gardner Canal, with sightseeing visits ashore at Prince

Rupert, Ketchikan and Juneau. Her cruise schedule offered passengers a memorable side trip to Carcross, following the trail of '98 on the historic White Pass and Yukon Railway, while the vessel was docked for fourteen hours at Skagway.

This was the most successful cruise venture ever developed by the Union and the name *Chilcotin* became almost synonymous with Alaskan cruising. Its success was repeated for many years under the direction of Harold Crompton, some eleven or twelve seasonal trips being booked to capacity, mostly from California at a cost ranging from about $250 to $375. Later, following the current trend, the *Chilcotin*'s facilities included nightly motion pictures, a refreshment bar in Alaskan waters and a cruise director and hostess for the recreational program.

These trips had their lighter moments and occasional romances. There was a preponderance of female passengers, who frequently out-numbered the males by as much as three to one, and this, coupled with the fact that the Union had many good-looking officers who did their best to mix congenially with the tourists, created obvious problems. One lady traveller, a skilful artist, left the painting of a nude siren affixed to the ceiling of a certain officer's cabin. His wife, who discovered it when she went on board several trips later, was furious and insisted that the masterpiece be removed forthwith. One of the Company's most popular skippers, the late Captain Harry McLean, met his future wife aboard a *Chilcotin* cruise, and I well recall watching the vessel as it pulled away from Union pier following their wedding ceremony with Mrs. McLean in her bridal dress on the bridge of the ship.

On the local scene an Estates change occurred when Edwin G. Enwright, one of the Union's younger men, who had been a purser, was sent to Bowen Park. The following year he was appointed superintendent in Vancouver of the Bowen and Sechelt properties. F. A. Billington was named local Estate agent at Bowen Island. Described by Enwright as an "outdoor practical man of sterling worth," Fred grew up on the island and spent over twenty years in the Estate employ. Mr. and Mrs. W. C. Deadman took over the seasonal management of Bowen Inn until 1952; and at Sechelt, which was no longer being used as a picnic venue, Ernest W. Parr Pearson took over in 1948 as resident agent from Bert Hackett, who had been a central figure in the community since 1928.

In August 1946, the Union Company announced a further purchase of four Bangor minesweepers, much smaller than the corvettes. The vessels were the former *HMCS Bellechasse, Miramichi, Courtenay* and *Chignecto*, each of 614 gross tons, 180 feet in length, with a maximum speed of 17 knots. It was expected that they could be converted for carriage of 500 day-passengers and perhaps 50 to 75 tons of general cargo at a figure generally believed to be about $800,000 for the four-ship conversion. The purpose was to offer more of a "passenger express" on local service — an improved version of the new Gulf Lines' service along the Sechelt peninsula, to which further reference will be made. Plans were drawn up to power the new Bangors with diesel engines for a speed of 14 to 15 knots, one as a night ship with cabin accommodation, and the other three for day travel on local runs.

However, shipyard costs remained high and with operating expenses, especially for wages and fuel oil, skyrocketing to 134 per cent over 1939, the Bangors conversion plan was deferred and then scrapped, the four vessels eventually being resold. It turned out to be a wise decision with difficulties already arising from the corvette conversions and considering the gloomy outlook that developed for day steamers on the coast. There was more to be said for converting one of them to a small overnight cabin ship to fill the gap on the nearby routes.

In May 1946, Gulf Lines Ltd., a local company organized by Commander Ted LePage and several naval veterans, started a fast passenger and express service with the *Gulf Wing*, a redesigned Fairmile corvette. He had been to see me earlier on "a fishing expedition," to find a spot for the Fairmile, at which time I suggested a feeder service and charters in the Pender Harbour-Jervis Inlet area. However, the company was looking for bigger game and started a competitive run to Powell River, calling at main stops such as Sechelt and Pender Harbour. This small competitor had an effect much greater than in normal times on a public tired of delays and wartime restrictions. It picked up a fair slice of business on the route of our *Lady Cecilia*, which badly needed streamlining. A second vessel, the *Gulf Stream* (the former navy patrol ship *Wolf*), was fitted up for the carriage of 225 passengers. This vessel was wrecked in October 1947 on Dinner Rock, near Savary Island, and sank with the loss of five lives. A third ship, the former Bangor *Truro*, renamed *Gulf Mariner*, was brought from the east coast in December 1946.

This competition spurred us into speeding up our south coast passenger schedules, and we had four direct Powell River sailings by the end of 1947. The result, however, was the opposite of what might have been expected, and I believe the ease with which our older and costlier ships like the *Lady Cecilia* were discomfited by these small, handy craft was a key factor in deterring the Union board from making any day-steamer replacement. The enterprising young Gulf Lines company survived the Union's later withdrawal on this route by only one year; they too were compelled by the impact of the new coastal ferry-road transport system to quit the service from Pender Harbour and Sechelt in April 1951.

All coastal passenger and freight rates had been pegged during the war, despite the disparity with increased costs. It was not until 1946 that Gerald McBean secured a moderate revision in the government subsidy contract, when the coastal companies were at last permitted under supervision of the Maritime Commission to raise their fares and freight charges.

Radar installations were completed on all the Union ships by Captain Eric W. Suffield, who returned from war service and was appointed acting superintendent in October 1946. A gallant officer, if something of a martinet, veteran of both wars who was cited twice for rescue at sea, Eric Suffield played an important role in the Union's affairs over the next decade. He replaced Captain John Muir, who had to withdraw temporarily because of ill-health after the strenuous war years. Captain Muir was appointed general superintendent in April 1947 and retired the following year. John Henry Gilligan had been made assistant superintendent engineer to Mr. Logan in 1940, and worked alongside him in the war years. Gilligan had been with the Union since 1916 except for a spell with the Royal Canadian Engineers in World War I, and was always a busy figure in the fleet maintenance department until his retirement and death in 1950. "Chief" Duncan McGregor, who had come ashore in 1946 to the engineering staff, succeeded Johnny Gilligan as assistant in 1949.

In the immediate postwar period, the staff atmosphere was particularly friendly and helped by Captain (later Brigadier) E. G. Eakins M.C., who was personnel director for several years after returning from overseas. C. W. (Chuck) McLean, who had succeeded Charlie Coldwell as purchasing agent, was made assistant general manager in September 1947. About the same time, E. D. Cottrell, former vice president of the Canadian Pacific Railway, and Gerald McBean joined the board of directors. At this time there were some sad losses among the mariners. No fewer than three senior masters and one chief engineer, Andrew Beattie, died at their posts — worn out, it was generally felt, by their heavy wartime responsibilities. Captain John L. Malcolmson, born at Lerwick in the Shetland Islands and a great favourite with the settlers and campers on West Howe Sound, died aboard the *Capilano* in the excitement following jamming of the rudder and the disabling of the vessel as it backed out of New Brighton on February 5, 1947. On September 23 of the same year, Captain Lorne Godfrey died aboard the *Cassiar*, which he had commanded for four years. A brother of Air Vice-Marshal Earl Godfrey, Lorne was one of the Union's most versatile freighter captains.

Then, on December 21, our best-known logging captain, Robert Wilson — "Cap'n Bob" as he was called up-coast — collapsed on the bridge of the *Cardena* en route to bring a load of loggers home for Christmas. He refused to have the vessel turn back, and Chief Officer Jack Summerfield went full speed for Campbell River where the popular skipper succumbed on reaching hospital. Perhaps his epitaph lies in this story told by a shipmate. An American visitor and boat-owner, reluctant to risk his small craft in the passage through narrow Chatham Channel, rode on the bridge of the *Cowichan* with Captain Wilson to get first-hand knowledge. "Say, Cap'n," he asked Bob, "How much tide d'you need to get through these narrows with your ship?" Came that broadening smile, with head thrown back, as Bob Wilson replied: "Good gracious, man, we often come through here on the heavy dew!" Such a man helped create the Union legend.

Maybe the law of averages also caught up with the Union ships after their fine wartime record, as there were several mishaps, all fortunately without loss of life or injury to passengers. On the night of June 15, 1947, the *Lady Alexandra* was returning from a special trip to Britannia and Squamish with Chief Officer B. G. Owen-Jones on the bridge. In a blinding rainstorm, she struck a rock a mile south of Brunswick Point on the east shore of Howe Sound at 11:12 p.m. and was badly holed. Captain Billy Yates took charge, putting the pumps to work and floating her off the reef two hours later with the rising tide. Despite the inrush of water in the hold, which exceeded her pumping capacity, Captain Yates safely made the seven miles across the sound to Bowen Island wharf under the ship's own steam. After the eight southbound passengers were returned to town via Horseshoe Bay, the *Lady Alexandra* was temporarily repaired and towed back to Vancouver.

The most serious mishap in 1947 occurred when the *Lady Cecilia*, with the chief officer, James Galbraith, in charge, went hard aground on Tattenham Ledge, Buccaneer Bay, forty-two miles north west of Vancouver shortly before 4 p.m. on Tuesday, December 23. She was bound for Powell River under Captain Walsh to bring south a Christmas load of mill workers. (It was a similar "special" that had cost the Company the *Cowichan* twenty years earlier, and I sometimes felt these runs were not worth the extra steaming or risk involved in the

154

wintry season. As with planes, it seemed to be the charters and not the regular "milk runs" that got into the most trouble.) Twelve of the thirty-eight passengers disembarked and were taken over to Secret Cove to make connections, while the *Catala* left the Vancouver "bull pen" in relief as usual to complete the trip. The *Lady Cecilia* resisted the efforts of three Straits Towing tugs to pull her free during the next two days, and remained stranded throughout Christmas with 75 feet of her bow plates torn. Finally on December 26, as reported by the Vancouver *News Herald*, "Four tugs grappled with the craft — the *Commodore*, *Belle*, *Union Jack* and *Mary Mackin* — for three quarters of an hour before beaching the vessel in the sandy bay, otherwise [the vessel] might have been abandoned." It was a fine piece of salvage work. The holes were patched while powerful pumps of the *Salvor* were worked to keep her dry, the whole operation being supervised by Mr. Warkman of London Salvage with expert crews from Straits Towing & Salvage Co. Ltd. She was returned to Vancouver harbour at 10 p.m. on December 27.

Through the summer of 1947, the *Camosun* took a capacity load of tourists on the round trip to Ketchikan. By October, however, Mr. McBean had become concerned about the future, with Prince Rupert's population declining again to under ten thousand and much of the wartime housing being abandoned. It became a question of either withdrawing the *Camosun* or extending the route farther north for additional business to the Alaskan ports of Petersburg and Wrangell. The latter choice was made. The vessel had the necessary time on her weekly schedule, but it involved a round trip of 1,800 miles, passing through Wrangell Narrows in daylight. On October 22, the *Camosun* sailed on her new route under Captain Harry McLean, accompanied by Captain Suffield, Captain Alex McLennan and Harold Crompton. Fred Matheson was chief engineer, with senior purser A. W. Robinson and chief steward Harry Keen. The route extension was, however, a disappointment, as it came too late in the season, and the vessel was soon withdrawn and laid up.

Within thirteen months from the sailing of the first corvette, the climate of opinion at Union headquarters changed to one of near pessimism. Only the *Chilcotin*, converted specifically to a cruise ship, had successfully filled her purpose; in fact, she exceeded the revenue estimates. It had become clear that the new vessels were expensive luxuries in the off-season on Union's northern routes, and in the haste for cheap replacements after the war, it was feared that the Company, like the Canadian National in 1930, might have acquired a couple of "white elephants." In the words of a *Coquitlam* captain: ". . . the converted ships proved very comfortable sea boats and most popular with the travelling public, but were poor freight carriers for their size, very slow in loading and discharging. They were lacking in 'tween deck space and the handy and economical facilities of vessels designed and built for our special type of trade."

In December 1947, Mr. McBean notified the main coast centres and the press that the Company would be laying up all three corvettes in January, and that the entire northern services for the rest of the winter would be maintained by the old favourites, *Catala* and *Cardena*. It was planned to run the *Catala* on the main line to Stewart, and cross the *Cardena* via Bella Coola and Prince Rupert to the Queen Charlotte Islands. Protests from all coastal areas were, however, so heavy that it was decided that this move was too drastic; as a compromise, the *Coquitlam* was placed on a ten-day schedule to the Queen Charlottes and Prince Rupert, with the older ships maintaining the inside-passage routes.

The new master of the *Coquitlam* on her Islands run was Captain Alexander Campbell McLennan, a quiet and resourceful mariner with an enviable safety record. Paul St. Pierre once wrote about him in the Vancouver *Sun*: ". . . he started sailing in the days of wooden ships and iron men," describing him as "a short, jolly man who'd look well in a Santa Claus suit." Born at Kyle, Scotland, he shipped as a youth aboard a Hebrides trawler to drag for cod off Greenland, and got his ticket in the Scottish coastal trade. Before joining the Union in 1921, he served in minesweepers during the war. Angus McNeill, Captain McLennan's second officer on the old *Camosun II*, tells of this amusing experience with "Big Mac" in 1943 while running to the Queen Charlottes.

"It was terrible weather, in fact a gale was blowing across Hecate Strait, and Captain McLennan twice turned the ship back into Prince Rupert harbour. He set out once more and, greatly to my surprise, as I felt for once the "Old Man" might be losing his nerve, he came back a third time."

After the storm, when he next went up to the bridge on watch neither of them spoke for a while, and then suddenly the captain turned on Angus: "Don't look at me like that," he barked. "If you think I'm going to drown myself, you're crazy!" Nothing more was said, but the explanation of the skipper's antipathy to the *Camosun II* was revealed two years later when the vessel was sold to the Greeks. "Well, I'm very happy to see the last of her," he told Angus. "Twenty-five years ago I was second officer on that ship when she sailed the Scottish lochs

156

under the name *Chieftain*. My captain caught me out making love to a highland lassie one day in the steerage, and that was my finish. I had the strange feeling the ship had followed me out here to get me." So the sailor's spell was broken. This consummate mariner died on the job in April 1950, only two weeks after he had given up his command of the *Cardena*.

By 1949, the Company had borne the brunt of its disappointment over the new ships. It had found out exactly what the new ships could do, which was neither as good or as bad as expected; and from this time onward, except for the *Chilcotin*, they were deployed on the subsidy routes on schedules that cut the winter loss to a minimum, while taking advantage of the summer tourist trade. For two summers, the *Chilcotin* was fully booked on weekly tourist trips as far as Ketchikan only, before resuming her popular nine-day cruise to Skagway.

In 1949, the Company achieved better results by changing the *Coquitlam* to a regular weekly route to the Queen Charlotte Islands via Prince Rupert and the chief mainland ports, crossing to Masset Inlet or the South Queen Charlottes on alternate weeks. On this schedule, the subsidy route was maintained relatively unchanged through the postwar years. It had the blessing of the Canadian Maritime Commission, and I pleaded with the settlers, if they ever knew a good thing, to lend their support to this invaluable steamer link. It took care in landing, and some luck, for a Union ship to avoid being tagged for a wharf damage claim. The old Allison wharf in Cumshewa Inlet, for example, was in a parlous state after the war. "Why don't you get your wharf fixed?" Angus McNeill called out from the bridge to the manager, who was nicknamed "Panicky Bill." "I'm waiting for you to knock it down!" came the quick response.

Throughout the summer, the *Coquitlam* was crowded with tourists. Marion Angus, writing in *Seaports and Airports* about the romances of this trip which she took via the Inside Passage and across to "Canada's Westerly Isles," said:

> . . . it was full of mystery, enchantment, history and legend. From these Islands the fierce Haidas used to make war-like raids on southern British Columbia and brought terror and destruction to the milder tribes . . . Here are the remains of old totem poles, community houses and burial boxes of the Haidas whose totemology epitomized the best of B. C. art and culture . . . Here too linger the ghosts of early Spanish adventurers."

As a tourist vessel, the *Coquitlam* was indeed in her element, but the season was all to short — only five months.

157

The Union received another jolt in mid-summer 1948 when the *Cardena*, bound for Rivers Inlet, grounded on a reef near the entrance of False Bay, fifty-five miles northwest of Vancouver. It was foggy in the early morning of July 16, with Chief Officer Angus McNeill on watch, when the vessel, carrying 180 passengers and crew, struck heavily off the dangerous Lasqueti Island coast. Passengers were in bed when the crash occurred, and many were thrown from their bunks. Captain William McCombe immediately ordered the boats lowered, and lifeboat stations were quickly manned. The nearby lights of False Bay wharf were reassuring to the passengers who realized that they were close to the shore. Reported the Vancouver *Sun* on June 17: "Women and children went first in an orderly procession. Two power boats set off from False Bay to tow the last of the lifeboats ashore and bring in the mail."

One of the *Cardena*'s oil bunkers had been badly holed, pouring a thick coating of oil over the water which made it hard to make headway with the oars. At False Bay, the settlers had been waiting for the usual radio call about 11:30 p.m. when word came that there was a big boat on the rocks in the channel. They did not know then that it was the *Cardena*.

Mrs. Charles Williams, who ran the False Bay general store, took care of more than a hundred people overnight, packing them in every corner of her house and store. Captain McCombe and his officers stayed on board the stranded vessel, which at daylight and low tide was seen perched for two-thirds of her length on a rocky ledge but with her bow free. First efforts of the Straits' tug *Salvor*, which was summoned by telephone, after careful examination of the hull, failed to loosen the ship, but later she was pulled free into deep water. Her double bottom had saved her from flooding although two holds had been punctured. She made it back to Vancouver for drydock under her own steam, escorted by the *Salvor*. A number of plates had to be replaced but the damage was less than expected – a tribute to the well-built *Cardena*.

The serious mishaps were as costly to the Company in the dislocation of service as they were to the insurers, but must be viewed in relation to the enormous amount of mileage logged by the Union fleet which exceeded the distance around the world every month. Bob Logan and his engineers had a stiff task keeping the tough Union squadron in operation through these trying episodes. Minor breakdowns were to be expected in the around-the-clock operation of so many routes, and they were tackled in their stride. When the cruising queen *Chilcotin* was disabled by a hot bearing, near the end of a northern trip while southbound off Texada Island in September 1948, and had to be towed to Gillies Bay by a Powell River tug, the *Lady Cynthia* was despatched to the scene and the 102 passengers, members of an American Shrine group, were returned to Vancouver in time for their train and plane connections.

On July 1, 1949, the Union Steamship Company of British Columbia observed its sixtieth anniversary of service on the B. C. coast. The fleet had grown to an impressive total of sixteen passenger and freight vessels exceeding 18,000 gross tons, an aggregate never surpassed after that date. President Gordon Farrell and Managing Director Gerald McBean launched the Company's Diamond Jubilee in June with a full week of bargain "Jubilee Excursions." These included a "Showboat Cruise" to Bowen Island, featuring singer Betty Phillips and other prominent entertainers from Vancouver's Theatre Under the Stars.

A summer casualty dampened the celebrations and dislocated the northern cruise program for two weeks in July. On Sunday morning July 10, the *Coquitlam*, after backing away from the Masset wharf in the North Queen Charlottes, was blanketed in fog. She was bucking currents from what was described as a 10-knot tide, and struck a rock, damaging her propeller and tailshaft. Gerald McBean was reported in the *Province*:

> The vessel held fast for about thirty minutes then slid off the reef a few moments after Captain William McCombe ordered the ship lightened by pumping out the water ballast. Two lifeboats, each containing about thirty life-jacketed passengers, which had been swung out ready to be lowered at a moment's notice, were brought back to the deck when the ship became free.

The *Coquitlam* was towed back to Vancouver, the passengers being brought back by chartered plane and by other vessels from Prince Rupert.

Senator S. S. McKeen, O.B.E. was elected to the board of directors in August. Stan McKeen had succeeded his father as head of the McKeen & Wilson, Pacific Towing and Salvage firm. He sat as a member of the Legislative Assembly in Victoria before his appointment to the Senate, and was president of Straits Towing & Salvage Co. Ltd. George B. Rea became comptroller and, following his departure to the U. S., was succeeded by W. A. (Bill) Reid, C.A. as administrative head.

Long before the Jubilee year was out, the day-excursion trade showed a sharp decline. The increased use of automobiles for family holidays following the removal of gasoline restrictions cut heavily into local steamer travel. Construction of new roads connecting Horseshoe Bay and the North Shore to ferries serving resorts on Howe Sound and along the Gulf Coast peninsula transformed the local travel picture. It was a natural response of the public to seek new avenues and modes of recreation, and even though more resorts were opened up, the organized picnics and day-trippers no longer provided sufficient volume for the ships except on weekends. Then the Great Lakes steamer *Noronic* caught fire at Toronto on September 17, 1949 and 119 lives were lost. The excellent safety record of the Union fleet counted for nothing as new government regulations relating to fire protection were applied without exception to all coastal ships. The refitting and fireproofing of six vessels of the passenger fleet cost $250,000 and faced the Company with expenditures on old vessels that made their future dim.

Granted that its day-boat fleet had been a marvel of safe transport for a quarter-century, the Union was not blameless in the sharp decline of this side of its business after 1945. It failed to come up with economical and faster replacements for the older carriers, and held off any major plan and investment in ferry transport across Howe Sound. The opportunity was clearly seen as far back as 1924 with the start of a Whytecliff ferry service by the *Comox*, and again with the Whytecliff land acquisition in 1939. The Union's continuing interest is shown by its purchase and takeover of the Sannie Ferry Company in 1944. In 1946, when the Howe Sound Ferries Company was formed under Jack Gledhill, there was an unaccountable partiality demonstrated for small craft; the *Commuter*, built and put into service between Whytecliff and Gibsons, was a 30-foot craft. She was a useful type of boat for the summer or special runs but not for all-weather public transportation. Seven similar types followed for Whytecliff or for charter service, but the equipment was too small to provide an alternative to the direct steamer between Vancouver and Gibson's or the Gulf coast resorts.

Meanwhile, C. G. Ballentine, operating from Gibsons with the *Commuter* under charter for a period, and Mr. Frith organized the Sea Bus Lines Ltd. to connect across Howe Sound with Pacific Stage Lines. In 1943 Ballentine had obtained from the Public Utilities Commission, a franchise for Howe Sound Transport Company on the Gibsons-Horseshoe Bay route. Mr. Ballentine subsequently indicated a readiness to dispose of his ferry interest, but the Union was in no mind and in no position to embark on a large ship-ferry investment. In October 1947, the Company's local services were further affected when *M. V. Bonnabelle*, a small competitor which had been operating between Vancouver and East Howe Sound points, also moved to a ferry run from Horseshoe Bay to Britannia and Woodfibre. In April 1948, the Sea Bus Line was purchased by W. F. Gibson & Sons, who brought into Howe Sound the converted Fairmile *Machigonne*, which had run between Port Alberni and Zeballos. With a licence for 140 passengers, she operated two daily trips between Horseshoe Bay and Gibsons until the American Black Ball line took over the route on August 11, 1951.

Our Howe Sound ferries suffered only one serious mishap. That was on February 18, 1948, when the 35-foot *Island Flyer*, with eight passengers for the upper sound, was missing for nineteen hours before being spotted aground at Douglas Bay. She had been stranded by a gale, after putting in to land a passenger. Skipper Douglas Cook of Bowen Island looked after everyone in two deserted shacks until help arrived.

The Company's small craft operated out of Whytecliff until Labor Day 1950. When Gerald McBean finally withdrew the Howe Sound Ferries as a spearate division, he merged the remaining vessels with the Sannie operation at Horseshoe Bay. The Whytecliff property was sold to the municipality of West Vancouver in 1953, but ownership of the Sannie Ferries remained with the Union until 1956.

The Company performed an unusual connection of another kind when a flash flood washed out a main North Shore bridge, leaving thousands of residents stranded. The Union donated the services of the *Lady Rose* to join other small vessels in ferrying between Vancouver and Dundarave wharf on November 30, 1949. The next day, the *Lady Cynthia*, under Captain R. T. Naughty, on arriving from Squamish was also pressed into service and carried 425 passengers, who were transferred by smaller craft off West Vancouver.

Local passenger service to the gulf coast was curtailed in the fall of 1949, foreshadowing the Union's final withdrawal from the Sechelt peninsula in November 1950. The *Lady Cecilia* and *Lady Rose* were sold to Coast Ferries and Harbour Navigation Company respectively in 1951. Even the popular *Lady Alexandra* was restricted to a short seasonal operation from May 24 to Labour Day between Vancouver, Bowen Island and Gibsons in 1952 before being withdrawn altogether from Howe Sound the next year. Of the original fleet, only the *Lady Cynthia* remained in year-round service after 1951 on the Squamish route, providing connections with the southern end of the Pacific Great Eastern Railway.

In the northerly areas, the Union Company maintained its passenger services to Stewart and the Queen Charlotte Islands, despite intensive competition from the air lines, which had expanded flight schedules to all the chief ports and taken away most of the business

161

travel to Prince Rupert and the Charlottes. The distant outports, however, still relied on the "coast messengers" for their mail, family transport and regular supplies.

In two successive years, the northern ships were faced with Arctic conditions. In January 1949, the *Camosun* was twice turned back from Stewart by thick ice at the head of Portland Canal. On one occasion, Captain Boden arranged to put in to the adjacent American port of Hyder, where, in the emergency, supplies were transferred across the line to the Stewart residents. On another trip, the vessel ground her way through the ice-field to within half a mile of the village wharf and supplies were taken by sleigh and small boats to shore. A letter about this appeared in the *Province* on February 5: "May we from up-North give due credit and blessing to a northbound ship's captain — smiling, silent skipper at the helm of his ship, Captain Boden."

A year later, Captain Harry McLean met the worst ice conditions on record in Cumshewa Inlet, where passengers from Morgan's camp had to walk more than a mile over the frozen sea to board the ship. And at Alice Arm, Captain McCombe was able to dock at the wharf only after a channel had been blasted through the ice. As one commentator wrote about the Union ships' performance: "Through ice and snow the little ships go." The Company made many mistakes getting into areas where it was not experienced, but in the "bread and butter" service, it was never surpassed.

In the waters off the Queen Charlottes, and in those around Wells Pass and Kingcome Inlet in particular, the vessels frequently encountered schools of whales. The late Don Munday F.R.G.S., the well-known mountain climber, told of one occasion when the *Venture* accidentally rammed one of a school of blackfish, and the vessel heeled over when the monster flung half its body across the foredeck. Mr. Munday paid tribute in the *Province* of February 4, 1950, to "the most precise navigation I ever saw when northbound from Rivers Inlet. Canoe Pass offered a short cut only attempted in daylight and clear weather. Captain Boden told us 'we keep the paint scraped off one side of the spar buoy,' and the spar actually did scrape along the *Camosun*'s hull."

As if signalling the end of an era, the grand old *Chelohsin*, after completing 2,800 voyages since 1911, came to the end of her sea-trail shortly after 8 p.m. on Sunday, November 6, 1949. She was inbound from Cortez Island and Westview when "the worst fog of the year" closed in as she headed for the Vancouver harbour entrance. Captain Alfred Aspinall had altered course to clear another ship and log rafts when his vessel ran aground a hundred yards west of Siwash Rock, off Stanley Park, close to where the historic *Beaver* had stranded. The *Chelohsin* impaled herself on a rock, which pierced her hull aft of the stokehold, and the engine room was flooded almost immediately. Lights were extinguished as the water rushed into the aft section. This complicated rescue operations when "abandon ship" was ordered, the crewmen having to work with flashlights to lower the boats and guide passengers through the freight doors. The tide was out and only 75 yards separated the vessel from the rocky beach to which fifty-three passengers were rowed. They struggled ashore and up the steep banks of Stanley Park to the roadway with their hand baggage and several carried pets in crates. The Company had called two buses to the scene, but many passengers flagged down private cars and taxis, and some, a Vancouver *Sun* writer observed, "got home earlier than they would have if the *Chelohsin* had made dock safely." It was 9:20 p.m. when all were safely beached, and Captain Aspinall and his men remained on board until the superintendent, Captain Suffield, arrived with a standby crew. Salvage crews worked for four days to patch holes between the boilers and to pump out the vessel, which at low tide was ashore for 50 feet back. Eight tugs and derrick scows stood by, and pumps were transferred to barges, as the water was too shallow for the tugs to get alongside. Efforts to refloat her were halted on November 12, and two days later she was declared a total loss by the underwriters, the estimated recovery costs being considered too high.

This was not yet the end of the old ship. The wreck was subsequently bought by Victor David of Food Dehydration Ltd. for a reported $1,600; and, two days after the holes had been patched by cement plugs backed by timbers, the vessel was pulled free by two tugs and beached in North Vancouver. The remarkable recovery was the talk of the waterfront. However, David's plan to turn the hull into a food-processing plant was vetoed by the city, and it was sold in 1951 to dismantlers for scrap. The *Chelohsin*'s sea-days were over.

On May 22, 1951, Pat Keatley, Vancouver *Sun* marine editor, wrote the *Chelohsin*'s epitaph when she was towed by her anchor chain, along with the *Cassiar II*, to the ship-breakers:

They humiliated her . . . they dragged her backwards through the First Narrows to die. She boasted an ornate bar in rich Edwardian decor when miners and loggers had to tone down their hilarity if they were to be allowed the privilege of mixing with the other travellers. After a few years . . . the loggers became more possessive. They used to talk about 'going to town' but all that meant was that they climbed aboard when the *Chelohsin* called at their camp, lived six days at the bar and staggered off again when they came round in the circuit to their starting place.

Prohibition days and regulations long ago ended the "circle" route, but not the memories of it.

Changed conditions in the old logging areas now left the *Cardena* alone to service the camps from Toba Inlet as far as Smith's Inlet. A further sign of the times was the inclusion in the 1950 schedule of six Union-Waterhouse cargo routes. One successful move was the use of the *Catala* on two trips weekly: a four-day run to Ocean Falls and Bella Coola via Johnstone Strait, and a two-day run as far as Port Hardy. This arrangement was welcomed by the settlers, and, as always happened when the Union Steamship Company rubbed the magic lamp of community goodwill, it paid off handsomely for the remainder of the *Catala*'s service days.

CHAPTER 11

1951-1955

Cargo Fleet Expansion
Kemano - Kitimat Boom
An Arctic Adventure and a Costly Strike

Never, never let us permit the weight of little things
to bear us wholly down. If any object that these are
vague aspirations, so is the wind vague, yet it is real.
They may direct us as strongly as the wind presses on
the sails of a ship.

RICHARD JEFFERIES
Jefferies "England"

With the indicated expansion of coastal mining and smelting plants, the Company's main effort was now directed to strengthening R. L. Solloway's cargo division. Two vessels were acquired for the Union-Waterhouse operation, the first being a small tanker, the 157-foot *M. V. Argus*, which was bought from Pacific Petroleum in May 1950. Built in 1944 at Stockton for the U. S. Navy, she carried 200,000 gallons of liquid cargo in eight separate tanks, with space for dry cargo in the forward hold. Under Captain Jack Woods, she had a crew of ten.

Then, in August 1950, the Union purchased and transferred from the East Coast a "China Coaster," a 214-foot freighter of 1,327 gross tons, which inherited the historic name of *Cassiar III*. Actually, she was no stranger to the Pacific Coast, having been built by Burrard Drydock in 1946 and launched as the *Ottawa Page* before being sold to Job Brothers of St. Johns, Newfoundland. As the *Blue Peter II*, she served four years in the Atlantic as a supply depot at sea for the northern sealing fleet. When the Union took her over, she had a three-cylinder triple-expansion engine of 1,000 I.H.P. with Scotch Marine boilers. After reconditioning at Pacific Coast Drydock, the *Cassiar* entered service on September 16 to northern ports and Alaska, including Taku Inlet and Skagway.

Captain Fred Talbot, a cheery Irishman, was now looking after the loading and despatch of our cargo vessels. Fred had a fine record as master in the Waterhouse fleet before coming ashore as their marine superintendent; and before emigrating to Canada in 1914, he had spent three years in sailing ships out of the Port of London. He served as an officer in Canadian Pacific's *Otter* and *Queen City* before joining the Frank Waterhouse Company in 1929 as mate on the *M. V. Watco*.

The *Bervin* — formerly the *Coquitlam I* that had been around the coast for sixty years — was sold in July 1950 to the Canadian Fishing Company; and this time there was no fear of the old ship's coming back again as she was converted into a fish barge. That fall, the *Cassiar* was entered in a joint schedule with the Canadian Pacific's *Yukon Princess* to fill a cargo contract with the White Pass & Yukon Railway Company; they were engaged to handle an estimated 25,000 tons of southbound concentrates from the United Keno Hill Mines by the end of 1951. The *Cassiar* commenced this service to Skagway on November 21, and the two vessels continued for over three years with few breaks in the tandem schedule, calling en route at Kemano Bay, Kitimat, Prince Rupert and southeastern Alaska ports. They also took capacity loads north, which might consist of a complete diesel plant or prefabricated houses, and they brought south asbestos products until 1955, when White Pass & Yukon's own container vessel entered service.

Now followed a new phase in the Union's plans for the Waterhouse division, to cater further to the expanding coastal industries. A new barge operation was set up and three old vessels were converted into cargo carriers. First, the old *Southholm* was stripped down and "hulked" in 1950 as *Bulk Carrier No. I*. Then the old CPR *Princess Mary* was acquired, together with a landing ship from Stockton — the former *U. S. S. A. R. R. 742*. These two vessels were converted into *Bulk Carriers No. 2* and *No. 3* respectively. Finally, to complete the group, the famous old *Princess Maquinna*, with nostalgic memories for west coast residents of Vancouver Island, was obtained in 1951 and converted into the *Barge Taku*. These bulk carriers were used in transporting ore from the Tulsequah Mine of the Consolidated Mining & Smelting Company, from the Portland Canal and also from Britannia Mines in Howe Sound. They were employed in a rotating barge pool with tugs and equipment of Straits Towing Company, with the assistance of the *M. V. Veta C* (renamed the *Chelan*), a 145-foot cargo vessel of 541 gross tons which was acquired in 1952. The *Chelan* was originally built as a U. S. Army transport for the Aleutian Islands campaign, and later converted by Captain C. H. C. Clark for cargo carrying.

In 1951, the cargo fleet was again increased by the purchase from

166

Canada Transport Company of the *City of Belleville*, which had been launched by the Port Arthur Shipbuilding Company in 1946 as the *Ottawa Mayferry*. This 145-foot freighter was brought around to the Pacific Coast from the Great Lakes and arrived in Vancouver harbour on October 1. She was renamed *Capilano III*, perpetuating another proud Union name, and was put into the hands of Allied Shipbuilders for conversion to a motorship, with cargo capacity of 500 tons. She made her first voyage under Union-Waterhouse orders on April 24, with Captain W. B. McCartney on the bridge and Chief Engineer John Goodall in charge below.

A fresh lease of life appeared to be in the offing for the Union's northern passenger vessels, as well as for the cargo fleet, with news in the winter of 1949-50 of the Aluminum Company of Canada's mammoth smelter and townsite projects to be built at Kitimat, seventy miles off the main northern coast route at the head of Douglas Channel. The site was almost opposite the ancient Indian village wharf and settlement of Kitimat Mission. Since the early 1900s, Kitimaat village (originally spelled with the double "a") had been a monthly call in the Union Steamship Company's schedule and its northern subsidy contract. At intervening fortnights, the Indians came down to Hartley Bay in their fishing boats to pick up mail and groceries, loading up with huge sides of beef, sugar and gasoline drums at the wharf close to the main channel. I vividly recall standing alongside Captain John Boden on the Kitimat village wharf soon after Alcan's announcement, when he pointed to the low underbrush wilderness across the inlet and indicated the site of the proposed new town — the terminus selected nearly fifty years earlier for the Canadian Northern Railway which failed to materialize.

In 1949 Alcan began planning the most stupendous engineering and construction project seen in Western Canada for half a century. It embraced the building of the Kenny Dam, completed in 1952. This diverted the water flow westward from a chain of lakes through a ten-mile tunnel driven through Mount Dubose into the Kemano Valley, and powered turbine generators housed in an enormous natural cavern. Because Kemano did not have the area for a town such as Alcan envisaged at Kitimat, a transmission line was built through mountainous terrain to bring power to the Kitimat smelter plant and community.

An army of construction workers totalling over seven thousand was engaged in the work at Kemano and simultaneously in building the smelter and townsite at Kitimat. The former showboat *Delta King* was

167

brought up from California to house temporarily the crowd of workmen.

The project included the building of wharves for both deep-sea and coastal vessels. In addition to Morrison Knudsen's contract at Kemano amounting to half a billion dollars, Kitimat Constructors, a consortium of eight companies, was committed to a total exceeding $600 million.

The municipality of Kitimat was established on March 1, 1953 and spread over an area of sixty square miles. P. E. Radley, who frequently travelled to and from Kitimat on our steamers, was manager of the entire British Columbia project. "Rap" Solloway, a man of jovial and irrepressible personality who promised the moon for breakfast but who was a sound cargo operator withal, initiated scheduled freight service by the Union-Waterhouse vessels *Island King* and *Cassiar* in 1951. Ships were loaded to the gunwales at the Union dock and other wharves, just as they were, only on a smaller scale, in the Alaska gold rush days, with bulldozers, shovels, mixers, trucks — every type of heavy machinery — as well as general supplies. Supplementing the freighters, a small fleet of tugs and scows was pressed into service, carrying materials to meet builder and production deadlines as the first of two smelter pot-line units neared completion. Commented Pat Terry in the Vancouver *Sun*: "Kitimat and Kemano are putting the spotlight on barge traffic, lifting these handy old carriers into a multimillion dollar trade, [as] unbelievable quantities of material are being transported." The developers at this time were looking to not only an initial annual smelter output of over 80,000 tons of aluminum oxide and ingots, but also to the eventual movement of newsprint pulp, lumber and other products from the Kitimat area.

The outlook in coast shipping circles swung optimistically and at last there seemed a possibility of the converted corvettes justifying themselves. Following a meeting between officials of the Union and Morrison-Knudsen, Kemano, at the head of beautiful Gardner Canal, was added to the Company's passenger ship schedules in November 1951. Dispatch of many construction crews to Kemano followed, including a number of special charter trips by the *Coquitlam* and the *Chilcotin* that grossed us over $3,000 a day. The growth of Kitimat township, which became a regular call in 1952, brought in badly needed off-season revenue. It took up the slack from the alarming drop in long distance travel and kept the northern passenger vessels busy over the next two years. The Union Company, however, paid a price for the Kitimat extra revenue, the service entailing the changing of one of the

168

passenger sailings to a midweek departure from Vancouver, since Alcan could not accommodate a weekend arrival. This move, which appeared logical at the time, hurt us with the Prince Rupert merchants who had always enjoyed weekend arrival of supplies for Monday store openings. Of course, a freight-boat sailing should have been slotted in right away, and this was done several months later, but in the interval we lost business to a freight competitor. It underlined an earlier belief that the Waterhouse cargo operation should have been kept independent or else completely integrated into the Union's operations.

The Kitimat-Kemano boom days were, however, to be short-lived for the passenger ships, as the air services were expanding rapidly and competing at the Alcan ports for the large Christmas trek with a shuttle service. The coming of Kitimat had deferred but not solved the Union's problems of keeping going over the long winter months after the salmon pack and fishermen had come south and the tourists had returned home. While there were the soundest reasons for expanding the cargo fleet and developing the imaginative and high-revenue Alaskan cruises, it was a mistake to sweep under the rug the key problem of serving more economically the two hundred and more coast communities for which the Union was subsidized. At certain ports, which had been entirely dependent on the Union ships, but where there now was a connecting plane service, only a few families and heavy baggage would be left for the passenger vessel to bring south when seasonal moves took place. A solution should have been found to obtaining one, if not two, ships with minimum passenger space sufficient to serve outlying areas during the quiet season, for I know that Captain J. A. Heenan, O.B.E. and his chief west coast inspector, Commander Frank B. Latchmore, O.B.E. of the Canadian Maritime Commission, would have been sympathetic. Unfortunately, this weakness was partially hidden while the Alcan boom lasted until after 1954.

In August 1951, I had been appointed general traffic manager, with Harold Crompton — unquestionably the dean of the local passenger men — as passenger traffic manager. Jack Buckeridge, a familiar figure for over a decade at the up-town ticket office on Granville Street, was the new general passenger agent. Mike Benson was in charge of the Waterhouse traffic, working directly with "Rap" Solloway and Sterling Beek, assistant manager (Waterhouse division). On schedule matters I dealt mostly with Mr. Beek, but sometimes with Mr. Solloway, who was always prompt with a response. A prominent shipper who had a large consignment aboard the Capilano freighter for Ocean Falls, telephoned "Rap" to find out when it would arrive. "Tomorrow morning at the latest," was the too fast reply. "You're a bloody liar!" said the shipper. "I've just looked out of my office window and the ship's still sitting at your dock!" About this time Gerald McBean, by a strenuous effort, succeeded in getting a notable revision in the subsidy contract. There was no lack of operating keenness, and only time was needed to catch up with the changing conditions in the trade. But time was slipping away fast.

In 1952, the combined Union-Waterhouse fleet, after disposing of old tonnage, was still a sizable one, consisting of seven passenger ships and seven freighters — *Cassiar, Chilkoot, Chilliwack, Island King, Capilano, Eastholm* and the tanker *Argus* in addition to the four bulk carriers. That year Gulf Lines' *Gulf Mariner*, the converted *Bangor* which had been used against us on the Gulf Coast, received a second conversion into a combination tug and freighter. She was chartered by Union-Waterhouse and Straits Towing and operated under Captain Cecil Roberts after being fitted with an electric towing winch and her freight capacity being increased to 300 tons.

Other coastal companies were also expanding. Captain H. J. C. Terry's cargo fleet secured a U. S. minesweeper for conversion to join their *Alaska Prince* (formerly our *Chilkoot I*), *Island Prince* and *Fort Ross*. This company now had a freight route to the logging camps and the *Pacific Prince*, as the converted ship was named, was the first to carry their new house flag in 1952 when the name of the company was changed from British Columbia Steamships to Northland Navigation.

Around 7 a.m. on March 24, 1952, the *Cardena* ran aground on the mud flats at the mouth of the Capilano River after changing course to clear an outbound ship at a time when fog reduced visibility at the entrance of First Narrows. About eighty-six passengers were transferred by tugs to the West Vancouver wharf and bused into the city. Although damage was minor, this mishap indicated the hazard in poor weather to a local scheduled ship through the increased harbour traffic.

During that summer, both the freighter *Veta C*, on charter to Waterhouse, and the *Catala* tilted with heavy U. S. cargo ships. In neither case were our ships at fault, and damages were recovered from the American owners. On June 28, the small *Veta C* had her hit-and-run affair with the 10,600-ton *Marine Snapper* in Puget Sound after discharging at Tacoma. Captain William Murray said: "We chased her [the *Snapper*] for almost thirty minutes before we got close enough to see her name." Although the *Veta C* needed a new stern and frames, this mishap certainly showed the ruggedness of a wooden ship, as a steel one would have been badly buckled. (The original *Cassiar* demonstrated the

170

same resilience where bumps were concerned.) In the *Catala* incident, she was running in fog on July 23, had stopped and was going astern off Helmcken Island near Sayward, when she was struck by the 8,000-ton *Coastal Rambler* and put out of action for a week. The only damage suffered by the big freighter was a shattered port.

A well-known figure in the Union's gulf coast trade, Robert S. Hackett, died on November 1, 1951. He was the resident agent and general factotum for Union Estates at Sechelt for many years. An unassuming man who won the DCM at Paschendaele in 1917, he had latterly taken on postmaster duties.

Caught up in postwar developments, Sechelt was phased out as an Estates resort after 1953. The Company's store, long the district's Indian trading post and managed until 1950 by E. S. Clayton, was closed in 1954 and its stock, which included many Indian baskets, was transferred to Bowen Park. The Sechelt Inn, rebuilt from the old Whittaker home on the beachfront after fire destroyed the Company's hotel in 1935, was also sold. The resort that had once attracted the Union's campers-by-the-sea for $1.80 round trip fare was now a growing community and a mainline bus and truck halt on the Sunshine Coast highway. The recreation grounds and other Estate holdings were gradually disposed of to make way for residential and commercial expansion. The Union directors gave five acres of land to the people of Sechelt for a recreational centre to be known as Hackett Park. Ernie Pearson, the last local agent for the Company and president of the Sechelt Board of Trade, died in 1957.

The summer season of 1953 was the last in which both the *Lady Alexandra* and the *Lady Cynthia* worked together on the diminishing excursion routes. Over a thirty-year period as Vancouver's most popular excursion vessel, the "Lady Alex" transported the equivalent of the city's population several times over on summer picnics and cruises. What a wealth of memories she conjures up for the older residents of the Lower Mainland! All the city's junior bands played aboard this friendly ship and helped to entertain the happy carefree crowds.

This staged withdrawal of the outmoded day-steamers, completed in 1955, was inevitable due to spiralling costs and followed a continental pattern. The Company's exit from mass transportation in local waters was, however, hastened by having moved too late towards large ferries when it ran into a stalemate over terminals and the franchise. For the developer of Bowen Park, the Company's thinking through the years swung between a "Coney Island cum Summer Resort" and a residential spa. The directors preferred to confine the public facilities on its properties to carefully defined areas, and Harold Brown in his regime strove with fair success to keep a middle ground. Consequently, the promotion sometimes fell between conflicting objectives, and the steamer revenues, failing any major change in carrying equipment or fresh resort inducements, passed their peak of profitability before 1937. It was the enforced steamer retirement and economic factors that finally resolved the Company's Bowen Island policy.

In this transitional period the Union suffered the loss by death on May 23, 1953, of Carl Halterman, managing director until 1945 and then operational vice-president. An able businessman, with a merry twinkle in his eye and a dry sense of humour, it was his lot to face many difficult postwar shipping problems. He was more successful in dealing with the Union's cargo expansion on the coast than with the passenger fleet. Gerald McBean, who in 1947 became managing director, had already taken over active control of the Union Steamship's operations with striking success in both the northern cruise and Alcan developments. He was confronted with inflationary problems throughout the postwar period and, despite his strenuous efforts, was long frustrated by government regulations in bringing passenger and freight rates into line with rising costs. It was my impression that he had never been happy with the purchase of the corvettes, yet he made the best use of the converted ships. At this crucial stage he was not in good health, and a further change in ownership took place before he could effect a turn around in the Company's fortunes. Born and educated in Vancouver, Gerry McBean was a tall, handsome man with an arresting personality. Trained in a steamship subsidiary of the H.R. MacMillan Company, he had a fetish for firsthand information and made his decisions only after searching analyses. He was a good administrator, was well liked in the fleet, and established better relations with the government (represented by the Canadian Maritime Commission) than any manager with whom I served.

Another change occurred upon the retirement of Robert Logan in 1953, when Thomas W. Morgan took over as superintendent engineer. Bob, who bore a high responsibility during the war years in maintaining the fleet, died in August of that year.

The *Cardena* had a narrow escape on her logging route early in 1953. The circumstances were quite unusual when, just after midnight, entering Patrick Passage en route to Sullivan Bay with Chief Officer Neil Campbell on the bridge, she struck a rock off a small island in the channel. Although badly holed in the forepeak, Captain Harry Roach managed to keep the flooding under control with the pumps until reaching Sullivan Bay. The vessel was close to the end of her run with twenty-two passengers on board and her crew of fifty-four. Later, with the aid of tugs, she returned to Vancouver under her own steam. The curious fact is that the high mountain peaks caused shadows in this narrow channel and obscured outlines. Immediately after this grounding, the department of transport installed a light on the island.

What might have been a catastrophe struck suddenly at the new Waterhouse tanker *Argus* at 8:30 a.m. on Monday, June 15, 1953, while she was taking on 200,000 gallons of liquid fuel for Victoria and Alberni alongside the Ioco wharf near Port Moody. Only minutes after a breakdown in the pump room, the first in a series of explosions occurred which engulfed the engine-room in flames and seriously injured four seamen whose shipmates, with much difficulty and using great presence of mind, managed to drag them to safety. The *Argus* carried a crew of fifteen but only ten were actually on board when this first explosion took place. Minutes before, a total of 18,000 gallons of high octane gas and 22,000 gallons of fuel oil had been pumped aboard. It was a miracle that the flow of oil from the refinery half a mile away had been momentarily stopped, for otherwise, nothing could have prevented a major conflagration and possible disaster in the entire east end of the harbour and the town of Port Moody.

The situation still remained critical and was saved only by the personal intervention and heroism of Captain W. (Bill) Boyce, who had just returned to the dockside. After accounting for all hands and with the injured men under care, he boarded the burning ship alone, cast a line to the tug *Sea Chief* in charge of Captain John Ryall, and ordered the *Argus* cut loose. Then, notwithstanding the heat of the flames less than fifty feet away, he steered the vessel into midstream, hacking the tow-line before jumping aboard the tug. Chief Engineer Walter Hasket had been equally alert in closing the hatches to seal off the gas and oil, and in starting up the emergency carbon dioxide system before abandoning the ship.

Meantime, police had closed off two miles of the highway along the south shore of Burrard Inlet. The Vancouver *Sun* headline of June 16 read: HERO SKIPPER RIDES SHIP AS FLAMES MENACE HARBOR. Captain Boyce had been master of the *Argus* for two years, and George Kelso, Ioco marine superintendent, was quoted in the *Province* as saying that he "couldn't think of praise high enough for the heroism of Captain Boyce, whose courage had saved the situation." Two further explosions at about 10:30 a.m. rocked the *Argus*, now isolated in the middle of the inlet and described as "a floating bomb," but eventually the burnt-out hulk was towed to a tidal flat and grounded. No attempt was made to rebuild the vessel, and her hull was later sold to Straits Towing and turned into a transport barge.

After a wonderful coasting career of forty-eight years, Captain John Boden finally "swallowed the anchor," stepping ashore from the *Camosun* on arrival from Stewart on October 1, 1953, with his cap at its customary jaunty angle. The next day special presentations to the senior mariner were made in the Company's office by Gerald McBean on behalf of the directors and by Captain Eric Suffield for the employees. Tributes came from all quarters. The Vancouver *Sun* noted that "The veteran skipper commanded everything from the *Cassiar* to the latest vessels." Norman Hacking, marine editor of the *Province*, recalled: "For nearly half a century Captain Boden has been a familiar figure to every logger, fisherman and miner on the coast. There is not a navigable nook or cranny as far north as Alaska that he has not entered."

Through the years, the Union was well served by its pursers or business agents aboard ship, who acted as personal links with many coastal consignees. Several left to become prominent in industry and business. M. J. (Mike) Lucas became an executive and later general manager of Crown Zellerbach, as well as honorary chairman of the Vancouver Maritime Museum. Denis (Danny) Shaw, our city representative, and Don MacLeod both pursued successful real estate careers.

Two collisions within range of the harbour entrance and in October fogs marred the winter record in 1953. In the first, the *Cardena* — involved in more than her share of troubles at this time, perhaps because she was the busiest workhorse — was proceeding inbound with fifty passengers through the First Narrows on October 23 at 9:30 a.m., when she was struck almost head-on by the Nanaimo-bound *Princess Elizabeth*. The vessels collided almost directly under the Lions Gate bridge and, after opening a gaping hole of 20 feet in the *Cardena*'s bow, the *Elizabeth* hooked fast into her. Two seamen were knocked from their berths in the forecastle of the Union ship and were later taken to hospital, but damage to the *Elizabeth* was superficial. The accident had its lighter moments. Captain Harry Roach related an incident that occurred while the two vessels were locked together, the bridge of the *Elizabeth* only a few yards away from him: "From the CPR vessel came the voice of Captain Stewart McGillivray, who leaned over the rail and passed a piece of paper: 'Sign on the bottom line, Harry please, while we're waiting for a tug.' " The paper turned out to be a form nominating Captain Roach as next president of the Officers'

Guild, and Captain McGillivray needed his acceptance signature. A tug towed both vessels, still fast together, into English Bay where a barge cut them apart. Two questions were later raised: the existence of a possible blind radar spot under the bridge; and the operation of a dredge in the Narrows, which restricted the channel. Both matters had the effect of further tightening harbour control following strong protest.

The second collision occurred within a week, on October 28, when the *Lady Cynthia* cut into and sank the tug *Dola* which was towing the PGE Railway barge loaded with box cars for Squamish. The tug went down in five minutes, but the nine-man crew was rescued and taken aboard the Union vessel.

The old cargo vessel *Chilliwack II*, obtained in 1927 and which had rendered splendid service, was now sold and her name was preserved and transferred to the motor vessel *Island King* — henceforth the *Chilliwack III*. Alcan and Skagway cargo continued to tax the resources of the Waterhouse freight division, and three appointments relating chiefly to cargo were made: Charles Guy, who had served in the pursers' department and on the traffic staff, became wharf freight agent; Alfred W. (Al) Newman was appointed freight traffic representative; and L. J. E. (Les) Smith took charge of the Prince Rupert office when Frank Skinner joined the Straits Towing operation.

A shocking tragedy befell the cargo tug *Chelan*, in command of Captain Cecil Roberts, on Thursday morning, April 15, 1954. She had left Skagway loaded with 450 tons of sacked lead and silver concentrate and towing a barge — the 240-foot hull of the former *Princess Mary*, known as *Bulk Carrier No. 2* — fully loaded with 1,900 tons of zinc concentrate from the United Keno Hill mine. The first and only direct word of the disaster was the radio message "Sinking Abandoning Ship," but two U. S. lighthouse men later reported having seen the vessel in distress at 7:16 a.m., four-and-a-half miles off Cape Decision. They said she went down by the stern at the entrance of Sumner Strait. It was snowing with poor visibility and winds exceeded fifty miles an hour when the *Chelan*, heavily punished by the gale, was evidently driven off course onto a submerged reef and swamped, with the loss of all fourteen crewmen. They included Captain Roberts, Chief Officer David A. MacDonald, Second Officer Richard Childs and three engineers.

An extensive search by the Coast Guard and a sweep of the area by planes found only debris and an empty lifeboat. The sunken wreckage of both tug and barge was located later, but only two bodies were recovered. Larger freighters were generally used in the southbound ore movement, but the barge had been called upon in this instance owing to a heavy backlog that had piled up at Skagway.

Early in 1954, a changeover took place in the direction of the Union Steamship Company when a substantial minority interest was obtained by a group headed by Senator Stanley S. McKeen OBE and including Fred B. Brown and F. Ronald Graham. Final negotiations for the takeover by this group continued for another year before the controlling block of shares was purchased from Canadian Pacific Railway. This was the fourth and last transfer of ownership of the Union fleet, and it portended a radical swing away from the traditional community-oriented policy.

The Frank Waterhouse name, which had been retained for the cargo division, was dropped and all vessels were integrated into the operating company of Union Steamships Limited. The Union-Waterhouse ships, which had carried the Waterhouse colours since 1939 — a black funnel with the letter "W" on a star superimposed on a white circle — now took on the familiar Union red and black-topped funnels.

President Gordon Farrell, a director since 1929, retired from the board after contributing a great deal to the Company's success over a difficult period. He was succeeded as president and chairman of the board by Senator McKeen. Both the Hon. W. C. Woodward and W. G. Murrin also retired at this time, after serving as directors for sixteen years.

An active management change also occurred when Gerald McBean resigned on May 31, 1954, to enter into partnership with E. A. Riddle as vice-president and manager of Canada Shipping Co. Limited in Vancouver. The last several years had been a strain on Mr. McBean, and I gathered that he did not see "eye to eye" with the prospective new owners. Although not as close to him as I was to earlier managers, I greatly respected his integrity and prodigious industry, and regret that he did not survive by many years his departure from the Union Company.

Philip B. Cooke, a shipping man of wide experience both coastal and deep-sea, came out of retirement for a limited engagement as general manager of operations for the balance of 1954. By a coincidence, "P. B.," as he was known among the shipping fraternity, served in the vessels and head office of the Union Steamship Company of New Zealand, of which he became general manager. He came to Vancouver in 1920 for several years, and again in 1936, as principal officer for the Canadian Australasian Line on the Pacific Coast. Having a familiarity with all phases of coastal shipping, he placed his finger with unerring accuracy on our weakness — the age and unsuitability of most of the ships, about which his comments were caustic. Tall and of distinguished appearance, "P. B." feared no man and spoke his mind. His priority was that of streamlining the fleet, but he did not overlook the welfare of shore employees during his brief tenure and set up the first pension fund, a matter that had been long deferred. He certainly "let in the breezes" during the ensuing six months, dealing directly, as did the old-time managers, with every department.

For special purposes, in August Mr. Cooke obtained the handy 139-foot freighter *Northern Express* (300 tons capacity including reefer space) from General Sea Transportation Ltd. The vessel was renamed *Chenega* and fitted in 1956 with twin G. M. diesel engines for a speed of 12 knots. (I was always interested in Indian names, and learned that *Chenega* means "the gathering of a tribe," being taken from the name of an Alaskan village.) Before the end of Mr. Cooke's stay with us, R. L. Solloway retired as head of the cargo side, which had now become fully meshed with the general operations, and Captain Fred Talbot, who had been supervising the cargo ships, took over from Captain Suffield as marine superintendent of the united fleet.

John F. (Jack) Ellis, a native son of Prince Rupert who was superintendent of marine operations of B. C. Packers for fourteen years, was appointed general manager of Union Steamships on January 1, 1955, upon the conclusion of Mr. Cooke's "trusteeship."

On Mr. Cooke's recommendation, I was appointed assistant manager under Jack Ellis. Harold Crompton succeeded me as general traffic manager, with Mike Benson as assistant for the cargo ships.

A difficult engineering project began on April 26 when the *Cassiar* was converted from steam to diesel. This was carried out by Superintendent Engineer Thomas W. Morgan and his staff and involved removing all the steam equipment and gutting the engine and boiler rooms completely. The feat was performed on the east side of the Union pier, except for the installation of the 1440-B. H. P. diesel engine from Springfield, Ohio, which was done in False Creek by the Arrow Transfer, under Tom Morgan's supervision, the engine being lowered into the *Cassiar* with only inches to spare. Two new motors and a generator were fitted for electric power, and the steering gear and windlass were converted to hydraulic. Six 5-ton electric winches were also fitted on deck.

In the meantime, and this was a compelling reason for expediting the work, the vessel had been chartered by the department of transport

177

to carry supplies, mainly fuel oil in barrels, to Cambridge Bay for the Arctic posts of the RCAF. The *Cassiar*, with her long cruising range and cargo capacity increased in the conversion by 7,500 cubic feet with 35 tons reefer space, was considered the most suitable Canadian ship for this important national defence assignment. Many preparations were needed, and two lighters, the *U. S. L. Nos. 1 and 2*, had to be specially constructed for unloading and taking on supplies at Arctic ports without harbourage, as well as a self-propelled pusher, called the *Midget*, for the lighters. The general manager had his hands full with almost daily communications about the *Cassiar* voyage with the department of transport pressing for her earliest departure. In the midst of it all, there came the threat of a seamen's strike. Although the Arctic contract for over $200,000 had been insured, this gave rise to considerable anxiety; hence the *Cassiar* was moved as a precaution from Union pier to an adjoining wharf in the latter part of June.

Direct negotiations with the local Seamen's International Union continued through June, and it is tragic even now to recall that a strike could possibly have been averted by a quick adjustment of the wage scale. Jack Ellis, who handled our side of the negotiations, had good reason for believing a compromise agreement was near at hand. Then, without warning, the basis of previous discussions was dropped; and on twenty-four hours' notice, we were forced to pay the same hourly wages as those paid by a small Montreal shipping company, of which we had never heard. We learned that this company had only one sightseeing vessel which ran with a small crew for several summer months.

Union Steamships was struck on July 3, with no further opportunity for discussions, and there seems little doubt that the Union fleet was singled out as a target. It was a heavy blow to the renewed hopes of the Company, resulting in the loss of gross seasonal earnings of a million dollars, with the regular vessels being tied up until September 3. The settlement imposed an entirely new set of operating conditions on Union vessels, the nature of whose routes depended on the facility to unload without restrictive costs by night or day at up-coast ports. These new conditions became operative despite warning from the Company that they would mean a reduction in the number of ships that could be operated. They undoubtedly hastened the decline of the coast shipping industry, already badly hit by other competitive factors.

There was no interference with the government-chartered *Cassiar*, whose job, originally expected to take five months, was completed in

Ferries carried large volume of passengers across to Snug Cove, Bowen Island.
(above) The *Bowen* and other Howe Sound Ferries operated
mainly out of Whytecliff.
(Union Steamships collection)
(below) Horseshoe Bay terminal of Tommy White's popular *Sannies*,
later joined with Union's other small craft.
(Vancouver Maritime Museum)

The *Coquitlam II*, a "white lady" at first, passing under Prospect Point, Vancouver's beautiful harbour entrance, outward bound for northern British Columbia in 1947.
(James Crookall collection)

Standard Main Deck Rooms 58 and 59. Hot and cold running water, upper and lower berths and Settee Berth. (Three Berth rooms)

Standard Main Deck Rooms 52, 53, 54, 55, 56, 57, 60, 61, 62, 63, 64, 65, 66, 67, 68, 69, 70, 71, 72, 73, 74, 75, 76, 77, 78, 80, 82, 84, 86. Hot and cold running water, upper and lower berths.

Standard Upper Deck Rooms 2, 3, 4, 5, 6, 7, 8, 9, 10, 11, 12, 14, 15, 18, 19, 20, 21, 22, 23, 24, 25. Hot and cold running water, shower and toilet, upper and lower berths.

Standard Upper Deck Rooms 26 and 27. Hot and cold running water, private tub bath and toilet, upper and lower berths.

De Luxe Upper Deck Rooms 16 and 17. Hot and cold running water, private shower and toilet, twin Beds.

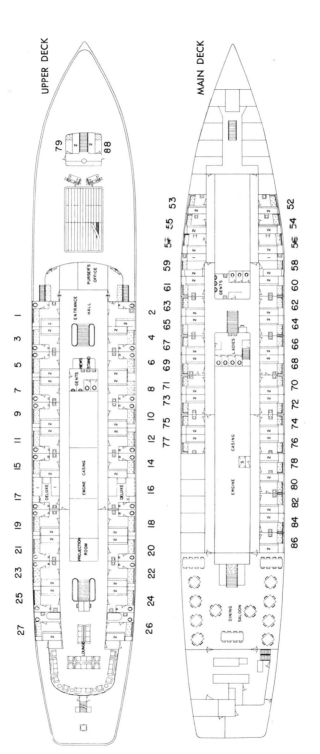

Berthing Plan: *S. S. Coquitlam II* and *S. S. Camosun II*

(above) H.M.C.S. St. Thomas, before conversion as *Camosun III*
(below) S.S. Camosun III, converted at Burrards', North Vancouver;
entered service November 1946.
(Vancouver Maritime Museum)

Four ships loading weekenders on a Saturday afternoon;
Union Pier resembled "Central Station."
(Note signboard directing passengers to *Lady Pam* on West dockside.)
(Union Steamships collection)

M.V. Bowen coming into Union Steamships ferry landing at Whytecliff, August 1946.
(Vancouver City Archives)

Five veteran mariners with a combined total of more than two hundred years in Union Service.

Captain Robert Wilson (*top*).

Captains William McCombe and Ernest Sheppard (*middle, l-r*).

Captain John Boden and Engineer Robert Logan (*bottom, l-r*).

The *S. S. Chilkoot II*, a "China-coaster" being built in Victoria,
was taken over and completed for a Waterhouse cargo route in 1946.
(Union Steamships collection)

(opposite) The *Lady Cecilia* ashore on Tattenham Ledge, Buccaneer Bay,
December 23, 1947, refloated a few days later.
(Vancouver Maritime Museum)

(above) The *S. S. Chilcotin* began northern and Alaska cruises, May 1947.
(Warner F. Clapp, photographer; Union Steamship collection)
(below) The *Chilcotin* as *H.M.C.S. Hespeler* in wartime service.
(Vancouver Maritime Museum)

Union staff celebrates company's Golden Jubilee, July 1949.
(above, below banner on bridge of *Lady Alexandra, l-r)*
E. G. Eakins (Director Personnel); John H. Gilligan (Asst. Supt. Eng.):
Captain W. L. Yates; Capt. E. W. Suffield (Marine Supt.), and author.
(below, l-r) Capt. Suffield; C. W. (Chuck) McLean (Asst. Gen. Mgr.)
and Harold N. Crompton.
(Union Steamships collection)

The *S. S. Capilano III* following conversion to a motorship in 1951,
loads at CPR Pier H for Alcan's Kemano project.
(Vancouver Maritime Museum)

The *M. S. Cassiar III*, northern cargo vessel, purchased in 1951, accomplished
an historic Arctic voyage after being dieselized in 1955.
(Union Steamships collection)

The *M. V. Argus*, bought as the "Argo" by Waterhouse for carriage of liquid fuel, was gutted in an explosion at IOCO wharf near Port Moody, June 15, 1953. A disaster was averted by the heroism of Capt. William Boyce.
(Vancouver Maritime Museum)

The cargo tug *M. V. Chelan* (ex-*Veta C*) was lost with all hands on
April 15, 1954, off Cape Decision, Alaska, while towing
Bulk Carrier No. 2, loaded with ore from Skagway.
(Union Steamships collection)

The small motorship *Chenega* was obtained
for southern B.C. cargo routes in 1954.
(Vancouver Maritime Museum)

The *Chilkoot II* loading heavy cargo for Union-Waterhouse west coast routes. (Vancouver Maritime Museum)

The *Chilliwack III* was a busy Union-Waterhouse carrier in
the Alcan-Kitimat boom. Her name was changed from
Island King in 1954 after *Chilliwack II* was retired.
(Union Steamships collection)

M. S. Redonda, small "landing ship" obtained in late 1955
for "roll on-roll off" heavy loads to camps and project bases.
(Vancouver Maritime Museum)

eighty-five days by July 20, thanks to the efforts of the men who worked on her, including fitters, electricians, carpenters and welders. Because of the urgency, the usual trial period was dispensed with and the bugs had to be ironed out by the competent crew she had on board. The *Cassiar*, after completing the loading of 1,219 short tons with 8,363 drums of petroleum, general voyage supplies and the three auxiliary craft, sailed under the Lions Gate on Wednesday afternoon, July 27, 1955, for Canada's Arctic seaboard. It was almost the last possible date that permitted her to make deliveries and return past Point Barrow without being caught in the icefields. On her bridge for the 12,000-mile voyage was Captain Fred L. Coe, veteran Arctic skipper with the Hudson Bay's *Baychimo*. The deck officers, appointed by Captain Talbot, were Chief Officer C. C. Wilson, who had served in several Union cargo ships; and L. Thompson (from the *Chilcotin*) and G. Hunter (from the *Coquitlam*), as mates. Engineer officers were Chief Engineer R. Macdonald, and G. Beckett and J. M. Speers, second and third engineers respectively. The crew comprised a bosun, nine able-bodied seamen, three oilers, two cooks, a steward and a messman. The *Cassiar* also carried Surgeon Commander W. M. Greer, former Royal Navy doctor who was loaned by the federal department of Indian affairs. The total complement of the vessel was twenty-five.

The *Cassiar* arrived at Dutch Harbour on August 4 on the first leg of her adventurous trip. She then experienced rough weather through Bering Strait to Icy Cape, encountering her first ice on August 8 with some fog most days. Averaging 11 knots, she gave her position on August 9 as off Point Barrow. From here, constantly meeting ice and fog, her progress was very erratic. On most nights, Captain Coe had to anchor in a heavy ice pack, while he prayed for an easterly from Siberia. Then, on August 15, the *Cassiar* came into company with an American convoy, and a party came over from the transport vessel *Merrick* and rendered valuable help by repairing the ship's radar. Thick fog held up her passage through the ice with the U. S. vessels: then the *Cassiar* suffered her first mishap, touching bottom off Barter Island on August 18 while skirting the ice pack at slow speed. She managed to get clear and stopped off the RCMP post at Herschel Island on August 20.

After leaving Herschel, the *Cassiar* was clear of ice for several days, but ran through drizzle and fog; and for a second time she struck bottom, this time off the west end of Lambert Island. Fifteen minutes later she grounded for the third time, in 15 feet of water. With a rough sea running, Captain Coe launched a lifeboat to survey the area. Five

179

hours later the vessel worked free and proceeded through snow flurries and continuing heavy weather before her master again lowered a boat to survey the route into Cambridge Bay. While manoeuvring into the bay entrance, the *Cassiar* struck bottom twice more but was refloated with the aid of a tow-line from the *U. S. S. Storis*, a lifeboat being swamped in the process. She finally made the dock at Cambridge Bay on August 24 and was discharging there until August 30.

The vessel was scheduled by the department of transport to deliver supplies at Tuktoyaktuk before shuttling back to Cambridge Bay, but because of the damage to the ship's hull and the extreme lateness of the season for an ice-free return passage, Captain Coe advised that the ship should not proceed further to Tuktoyaktuk, and this was agreed to by the department.

Thus, with 300 tons of Arctic mud for ballast, the *Cassiar* headed westward and homeward on September 8, soon encountering frequent snowstorms. It was touch-and-go whether she could make it, as the ice was drifting south early that year. Six days later she was once more held fast in the ice pack. Film taken at the time showed the incredible conditions the vessel had to battle in her struggle to keep going. Captain Coe managed to make slow speed through a field of heavy broken ice, eventually passing Icy Cape on September 21 and making a landing at Dutch Harbour on September 27.

The *Cassiar*'s return to Vancouver on October 6 was heralded with sighs of relief. The message from the department of transport was a model of official understatement: "I think you have carried out a good job . . . and under very difficult conditions." The vessel had been delayed and held stationary in ice for a total period of nine days and sixteen hours. I was with Manager Jack Ellis when the *Cassiar* was drydocked in North Vancouver for major repairs, and her keel for two thirds of its length reminded me of a jagged concertina. Only a courageous crew and a very staunch ship could have withstood such a hammering sustained over five Arctic strandings. The $108,000 repair bill at Burrard Drydock did not seem excessive to anyone who had seen the battered and torn hull.

The triumph of the *Cassiar* and several improvements in operating plans were marred by the effects of the summer strike and resultant higher costs facing the Company. As was to be expected, this hastened the withdrawal of our last day steamer, the *Lady Cynthia*, which did not resume Howe Sound sailings in September 1955. With the impending completion of the Pacific Great Eastern rails between Squamish and North Vancouver, the *M. V. Hollyburn* was chartered in the interval for connecting railway passengers and express until the line came through in 1956.

A major change was effected by the new board at this time in the structure and financial setup of the Company. Active steamer operations had been carried on since 1926 under the name of Union Steamships Limited, to which the assets of the parent company had been transferred, following various corporate reorganizations at different periods. In April 1956, Union Steamships Company of British Columbia Ltd., which had functioned for several years as a holding company, was wound up. It was agreed that the shareholders would relinquish their shares in the old parent company in exchange for common and preferred shares of Union Steamships Limited. During 1955, when serious losses were incurred owing primarily to the strike, Union Steamships Limited had obtained additional capital funds by way of a five-year bank loan of two million dollars secured by the Company's 5 per cent debentures. In this story I am concerned with the background of events only as they influenced the steamer operations, and this had the effect of putting the ships "in pawn to the future." It was later the subject of some comment in the House of Commons because of the Company's contractual situation, and had a definite bearing on events two years later when the Company failed in its effort to recover losses by obtaining an increased subsidy.

In November 1955, the Victoria *Daily Colonist* quoted Mr. Ellis to the effect that "the (Union) Company had under consideration two general purpose ferry ships as big [as] or bigger than the *Chinook* to maintain eight round trips daily between a Saanich peninsula terminal and the mainland." Earlier, I had been assigned to report on the potential of a Sidney-White Rock crossing, and I returned a highly favourable answer provided a breakwater was built and access obtained to an assembly area at White Rock. Nothing further developed about such a project at this time.

Not long afterwards, it became known to the operating officials, for it was impossible to keep such matters entirely secret, that a Dutch line was considering taking a majority interest in the Company. As it turned out, negotiations broke down at a late stage, but other policy changes were to occur before the Union story would end.

CHAPTER 12

1956-1959

New Brooms Sweep the Decks
Passenger Ship Withdrawals
The Catala's *Last Stand*
End of a Saga

> It was the custom to Whistle a Wind when becalmed
> in a sailing ship; if perchance a gale ensued the
> assumption was that they overdid it! Another ancient
> superstition for producing wind was the knotting of
> a short length of rope, a single knot for a light breeze,
> two for fresh breezes and three for strong winds.
> *Union Steam*, July 1957 (adapted from *Seaports and*
> *the Transport World* — Lieut. A. D. Taylor, RCN)

The loss of the 1955 seasonal earnings because of the strike and resultant higher costs tempered the optimism of the new owners of the Union fleet. An intensive reorganization followed in the spring of 1956, in the apparent belief that efficiency experts with slide-rules could measure success or failure on trade routes that had been nurtured for half a century. Some new ideas were undoubtedly good; but others, such as repainting the ships to create a more dashing appearance, were costly and, to my mind, unfortunate. The three-tone colour scheme of the *Coquitlam*, for example, was copper, cream and turquoise. At some angles, the face-lifted vessels looked exactly like the camouflaged ships that docked in the Mersey and Clyde after eluding enemy submarines. On the first voyage that Captain McNeill took the newly disguised *Coquitlam* alongside Sandspit wharf in the Queen Charlottes, an old Indian on the dock shouted up to the bridge: "Say, Cap'n, where did you get the war canoe?"

The same expert who dreamed up the gaudy colours tackled one of the senior masters as to why he had shut off the loading of his vessel at the Union wharf while cargo space still remained in the hold. The veteran skipper, whose ship was already "down by the head," turned on his heel when he realized that the time and motion man did not grasp the significance of a Plimsoll line!

It was unfortunate that as a consequence of several internal

182

shuffles, the Union lost such experienced operators as Harold N. Crompton (to Coast Ferries) and Captain Fred Talbot (to the White Pass & Yukon Company). Only Jack Buckeridge, in charge of the passenger end, and Charles Guy, traffic manager, remained of my original staff. But the freight department was strengthened by David McGowan in the city, and N. E. (Norrie) Wood to look after the up-coast needs. Mr. Enwright was moved from the Estates to Prince Rupert as general agent for northern B. C. Alf Conklin, chief accountant and the Union's office manager, was appointed secretary in 1957. Despite the uneasy spring, the cruise vessels had another bumper season; and even after severe streamlining in service, the Union still had four passenger and three scheduled cargo routes in existence.

A major change followed when Tidewater Shipping Company was taken over and merged with Union Steamships on September 1, 1956. Captain J. A. Macdonell, who came to us with the Tidewater vessels, became executive vice-president and manager of the amalgamated fleet. A successful operator of small coastal ships, including the *Troubadour* (formerly *Gulf Wing*), the *Tournament* and the *Triggerfish*, and with a distinguished naval record, Jim Macdonell had the reputation of a shrewd trader. He brought his own team of Captain David Roberts, who was appointed marine superintendent, and his engineer, Jack Scagel. The latter took over several months later as superintendent from Tom Morgan, who had executed the fine *Cassiar* conversion job. Dave Roberts, a Liverpool *Conway* boy, saw action in North Atlantic convoys during the war, and was with Marine Express before it was absorbed with Gulf Lines into the Tidewater Company. Jack Scagel had been with the department of transport before joining Captain Macdonell. Jack Ellis became head of the Estates section of the Union Company. I was retained as assistant manager until November 1957, then replaced by Captain Roberts, and created director of public relations, which kept me in contact with the coast settlements until almost the end of the Company's existence. Captain Macdonell restored all the ships' funnels to their original red and black colours, and with seven motorships now included in the Union Tidewater fleet, set up a diesel department under engineer Hugh Connacher with the steam vessels continuing under the supervision of Duncan McGregor.

Some may have wondered how these switch-overs in control — the fourth in twenty years for a company that had only one ownership change in its first half-century — affected the morale of its personnel. But only a handful of seniors had had any personal association with the Welsford regime. Then again, the Union was closest of any coast line to being a transportation utility, and its mariners were professionals with allegiance to the Union service ideal rather than to any group. The only general complaint was not against such changes but against the policy of not developing top management from among the Union's own experienced men. They might not have had the flair of the deep-sea men who were brought from outside; but they would certainly have avoided the tonnage errors and have obtained economical coasters that could have kept the Union flag flying for another quarter-century.

Somewhat incongruously, I am reminded of the East Anglian coasterman who was seated at dinner alongside the captain of a crack ocean liner. The great man asked him if he knew "the sextant," and the local skipper replied that he'd had a pint in most of them from the Tyne to the Thames but couldn't recall a pub of that name. "Well, what on earth do you do when you lose sight of land?" asked the captain, somewhat taken aback. "Same as you fellows when you see land, I shiver and shake." Left to their own devices the Union coaster-men might sometimes have shivered but would likely never have strayed very far off course!

Tidewater sailings were continued from their Coal Harbour wharf, and the services were not physically integrated into the Union's. However, the calls at some ports were redistributed and a reconditioning got the *Camosun* back to her top performance of 14 knots on the Stewart route.

To counteract increasing cargo rivalry in the north where North-land Company vessels were providing aggressive competition, two Union cargo motorships were double-headed every Friday night. The *Capilano*, with her new refrigerator space, was scheduled to Kitimat; while the *Cassiar*, with packaged frozen foods, went non-stop to Prince Rupert. After making Arctic history and getting a newly plated bottom as a reward, the *Cassiar* was now the cargo mainliner, making up to 13 knots.

At 11 p.m. on Sunday, November 30, the *Cardena*, under Captain Sheppard ran aground in light rain and mist at Duval Point soon after leaving Hardy Bay wharf. She was en route to Bella Coola, and most of the passengers had disembarked at Johnstone Strait stops. The Vancouver *Sun* reported that "Two shuddering jolts roused sleepy passengers when she rammed ashore." Two launches arrived on the scene from Port Hardy, the RCMP launch *M. L. 15* and a forestry department vessel, and took off thirty passengers, who stepped directly over the aft rail of the *Cardena* into the rescue boats, as the vessel's stern was so low. The following morning, tugs pulled the *Cardena* free.

She was not holed or damaged seriously enough to prevent her returning under her own steam to Vancouver for a full survey.

Some days later, on October 6, 1956, the little Tidewater craft *Triggerfish* capsized off Point Atkinson, with the loss of three of her eight-man crew. Heavy cargo had apparently shifted in the weather, but there was no evidence of overloading. She was promptly replaced by the *Chenega* in the Tidewater schedules.

When the mill at Silbak Premier Mines near Stewart burned down on November 20, Captain Angus McNeill of the *Chilcotin* was diverted from the Queen Charlotte Islands to pick up the employees, made homeless by the fire. Chief Engineer Jack Munro got his ship to top speed and made the emergency run without loss of an hour, and with a vote of thanks from the Stewart community.

With fewer ships on the passenger runs, the load naturally fell more heavily on the *Cardena* when the logging camps on Johnstone Strait were shut down before Christmas. In a single day, the *Cardena*, under Captain Harry Roach, shuttled more than four hundred loggers from the Port McNeill and Englewood camps by means of a short run into Sayward, and a second trip direct to Vancouver. Earlier in the season, the *Cardena* made the headlines when a passenger claimed a flying saucer sighting off Ripple Rock — an event certainly not included in the Union's usual list of tourist attractions.

Locally on Howe Sound, Sannie Ferries, which had kept up the connection with Bowen Island after the *Lady Cynthia* was tied up, were withdrawn. In tribute to Tommy and Mrs. White — "the only lady skipper on the Howe Sound run" — the Vancouver *Sun* of December 10, 1956, said that Sannie Ferries "had carried one-and-a-half million passengers on thirty thousand crossings without a major mishap."

With the start of Captain Alex Peabody's Blackball ferry, a new era began for the Bowen Island suburb. The inaugural run of *M. S. Bainbridge* from Horseshoe Bay at noon on December 7, 1956, was followed by a welcoming luncheon at Evergreen Park Lodge (the former Bowen Inn). The transformation of the "peoples' playground" into Evergreen Park Resort, catering to selective tourist tastes, was perhaps an outward symbol that the excursion dream, which had stimulated the lower coastal growth thirty-five years earlier, had ended.

It was an oldtime custom for the Union's office Christmas party to be joined by as many of the wharf staff as could be spared and by crewmen of all vessels in port. The last such gathering was in 1956 and was held in the *Camosun* alongside the wharf, with Captain Ernest Sheppard as master host and Captains McCombe, McCartney, Swank,

Morrison and Billy Yates among the "crew." Someone reported that Santa Claus was carrying Neptune's trident, but this was only figuratively speaking, as "tridentos" was an old Cretan word in that ancient maritime hub for "a hollow leg" or "tall jug."

An impressive innovation for the Union ships in early 1957 was the container method of shipping. Although used in many European ports and by the White Pass & Yukon for their Skagway cargo, Union Steamships were the first to bring containerized freight to the B. C. coast. Under the plan devised by Captain Roberts, special use was made of sealed plywood containers, the panels of which were easily replaceable, and were light yet very strong. MacMillan & Bloedel Limited, in their *Sylvaply News*, said of our innovation: "Union Steamships Limited have developed a new approach to more efficient, more profitable freight handling — containerized freight. The idea is as simple as it is revolutionary. They supply their shipping customers with handy-sized plywood containers . . . the customer loads the container instead of loading a truck." An initial supply of one thousand, standard units for two tons weight of general merchandise, was built at Union dock under the supervision of Captain Thomas Lucas, who was now assistant superintendent. Tom Lucas joined the first *Camosun* as a deckhand in 1921, and his commands included all the passenger ships. The new program was well received, and there was a gain in the cargo volume.

In the tramp category, the small motor vessel *Redonda*, 125 feet in length and of the landing-ship type, had been purchased in late 1955. Built in 1944 at Portland, Oregon, she was equipped with tanks to carry 50,000 gallons of liquid fuel and could handle 200 tons of deck cargo. Her landing ramp provided roll on-roll off facilities practically anywhere on the beach, and made her very useful in handling tractors and heavy loads. On her second trip in April, she "rolled on" at Maple Bay, Gilford Island, a 28-ton log loader, driven from the beach by one man instead of the eight men needed to load it on a scow; then one man drove it off at Attwood Bay in Homfray Channel.

It is ironic that at this time of new cargo methods, a combination of different factors — changing markets for several big companies on the coast and cargo competition, but chiefly unacceptably high costs — forced a reduction in the tonnage committed to the oldtime routes. Whether it was carried out altogether wisely is another matter. To begin with, the Port Alice route operated by the *Chilkoot* under Captain D. A. Connell had to be withdrawn following a realignment of the plant's pulp and export contract. Then, after a series of managerial meetings that blamed the traditional Union routes, rather than the

186

expensive equipment, as the source of the problem, passenger vessel schedules were further restricted. In fact, the streamlining of the main routes portended a breakaway from the intimate service to the smaller ports with which the Union name had always been associated. It was the first stage in a progression of passenger vessel curtailments that was to bring the Union into conflict with the views of the Canadian Maritime Commission and into a subsidy battle within twelve months.

In the eventful 1957 season, only one passenger unit, the *Camosun*, was assigned to look after the main northern services. She departed Vancouver every Monday at 8 p.m., with stops only at Ocean Falls and Kitimat on a fifty-hour run to Prince Rupert. The *Camosun* proceeded on alternate weeks beyond Prince Rupert either to Stewart or to Masset Inlet, Queen Charlotte Islands. At the same time, it was arranged for a cargo vessel, on opposite weeks to the passenger ship, to serve either the Queen Charlotte Islands or Stewart. This ensured uninterrupted weekly supplies and mail to both areas. The *Cardena* was employed as a back-up ship, making a weekly sailing as far as Butedale via the small intermediate ports. The old logging camp routes of the *Cassiar* and *Chelohsin* eras were abandoned. Three of the settlement ports, Sullivan Bay, Simoon Sound and Minstrel Island, were now included in the *Catala* run to Alert Bay, Port Hardy and Bella Coola. Other logging ports were transferred to schedules of the small Tidewater vessels. In a nutshell, the policy was "Fast to the main centres, links to outlying areas." In principle it had merit; but, with the absence of economical replacements for the subsidized routes, it meant fitting the ports to available equipment and this was to prove costly.

The two remaining passenger units, *Chilcotin* and *Coquitlam*, were assigned to Alaska cruising service. Both vessels were slated to sail out of Vancouver, but the *Coquitlam*, with Reg Stover, our senior purser, was placed in the hands of Charles West's Alaska Cruises Inc. in Seattle for service to Juneau. The *Chilcotin* sailed on June 7 for the first of her ten-day cruises under Captain Ernest Sheppard, and was fully booked for the season. She was the only Alaska tourist ship to include a cruise around Glacier Bay in her itinerary. New faces had appeared in the cruise preparations since the forties: assisting Jack Buckeridge, the passenger chief, were George Greig, who dealt with a mountain of tourist mail; Andy Urquhart of the purchasing office; and Harold Humphries, the brisk port steward. In season, these cruise ships were the equivalent of floating hotels and required round the clock servicing.

One unscheduled stop by the *Coquitlam* in the course of an Alaskan cruise quite angered "Chuck" West, the charterer, when a passenger remarked to him, on the vessel's return, how much he had enjoyed a conducted tour of the Bella Bella cannery. On enquiry, it turned out that a Union freight official, who urgently needed to get out a load of fish fertilizer, had cajoled the captain into stopping at Bella Bella on the pretext that the cruise passengers could inspect a B. C. cannery. While this was going on, the mate quietly loaded the fish products, the flavour of which stayed with the vessel for another round-voyage!

On its scheduled services, though, the Union still specialized in British Columbia coast trips. Requests for information about the Canadian fjords came from as far away as San Salvador, C. A., and Indonesia. One letter arrived addressed to "The World's Best Steamship Co., Vancouver, B.C." — an efficient post office knew where to deliver it! A large number of visitors, including many from the prairies and eastern Canada, as well as from Southern California, came to sample the different and inexpensive trips known as "freight boat" or "vagabond" cruises aboard the *Catala* and the *Cardena*. They wanted to see the tiny landing and houses on floats in Simoon Sound, the falls of Butedale, or the enterprising Scandinavian village of Bella Coola.

Much developed from the days of Tommy Walker's trail rides, Bella Coola now had a moderately good gravel road to Williams Lake that was started by the residents of Bella Coola themselves and which was passable for cars in the summer. Cliff Kopas, photographer and tourist booster of the community, once described its progress: "Starting at Bella Coola dock there is fifty miles of valley road with high mountains on either side, deep forests and waterfalls . . . at Mile Fifty it is a ten-mile climb to five thousand feet . . . at Mile Sixty commences a 250-mile trip through parklands and ranch country of the Chilcotin down to the Fraser." The Union ships brought tourists to the entrance of this beautiful land.

With the withdrawal of the last excursion steamer on the local routes, Harbour Navigation Company ran a limited number of picnics to the Evergreen Park facilities at Bowen Island. On October 5, 1957, the dismantled *Lady Cynthia* and the old *Southholm* left Vancouver harbour under tow of Straits Towing for break-up in Seattle. Also marking the close of long service, four "steam" chief engineers retired after completing between them a total of 165 years with the Company. This must surely constitute something of a record in coastal shipping. John T. Hogan, who joined in 1911, was that legendary type of Liverpool engineer whose machinery was his pride. He served many years in the old *Venture*, and was a familiar figure in the *Lady*

Alexandra and the *Lady Cynthia* before taking over the *Cardena*. Fred E. Smith, who hailed from Gloucester, England, came in 1915 and served in every steam vessel of the fleet. His enthusiasm and ready wit will not quickly be forgotten. Frederick Matheson, born in Norway, came to the Company in 1918; and, after being in most of the steam vessels was latterly "chief" of the *Camosun*. Robert Whitelaw, a quiet Scot, was in the steam vessels (except the corvettes) for thirty-eight years, his last assignment being in the *Chilkoot*.

At this juncture, in November 1957, R. Glenn Chestnut was appointed executive assistant. He had an industrial engineering background, after having graduated from the University of B. C. and serving two war years with the R.C.E.M.E. Latterly, he was assistant to the vice-president (operations) of Canadian National Railways. D. A. (Dave) McGowan, who had spent nearly ten years on the Waterhouse staff, became traffic manager, the last official to hold this position.

A great effort was underway to turn the tide of events. The containerized loading was meeting with success, and the wharf staff knew by their chart where every container was located, using the same principle as that in controlling railway box cars. In August, the *Redonda* moved the heaviest piece ever handled by a Union vessel — a 72-ton Northwester shovel, which was "rolled on" at Deas Island for the new airport at Digby Island, and "rolled off" three days later. In *Union Steam* (October 1957) I wrote: "There can be no finality in transportation equipment . . . as much thought and testing [are] being devoted now to blueprinting new plans as in supervision and maintenance of our present service."

Meantime, in an endeavour to reduce the cost of carrying surplus tonnage, the *Chilkoot II*, the last of the steam freighters in the fleet, was sold to Mexican buyers, Navieros Unidos Del Pacifico S. A. of Mazatlan. She was a fine vessel but had been idle since the west coast pulp contract ended.

At this time, Captain Macdonell began, with the assistance of Captain Roberts, a feasibility study about operating either without subsidy or with reduced passenger tonnage committed to the routes involved. For nearly a year before this issue came to a boil, I had been relieved of any operating responsibility but made clear my view of the dangers involved in cutting back the service too far. Since 1946, I had supplied all trade information and revenue estimates on the Company's routes for the Maritime Commission. Apart from this close contact with their officials, I knew well that the subsidized line always had an edge on business to the ports concerned.

On a lighter note, my ability to forecast closely our revenues on the various subsidy routes for the succeeding year was long a private joke between the Union's management and the Maritime Commission. I was permitted a margin of not over 5 per cent from the actual results and my projections invariably came within 2 per cent. One late spring the Vancouver *Province* ran a baseball results competition for a prize of $100, which I won by not only giving all correct results but also the exact score of the clincher game. Gerald McBean promptly sent particulars to the Commission as certain evidence of my uncanny skill, and received a most amusing acknowledgement.

In the late fall of 1957, the Company entered the final phase of its struggles to continue operations with an application to increase its subsidy to offset losses sustained during the year. The president stated that the $325,000 received in 1956 would scarcely go halfway in covering the losses suffered in 1957 on these routes. When negotiations with the Canadian Maritime Commission broke down, I urged that the Company propose continuing service with at least two passenger ships including a limited schedule by a northern vessel. I felt a higher subsidy was essential and well justified, but was not alone in believing that a withdrawal beyond this point was courting serious trouble.

Suddenly, an unexpected decision was made at the top level to withdraw all subsidized passenger service at the end of the year. The news was conveyed to a tense meeting of the senior staff, and the Company's official announcement followed on December 18, with January 2, 1958, being the effective date for curtailment service. With mounting losses, the situation was certainly critical; but this arbitrary move to cut the subsidy painter altogether ran contrary to both the concept under which the routes had grown since 1892 and the spirit in which the Union's coastal links had been so magnificently forged. Perhaps it was too late for the fleet to be redeployed without suitable units, but it was unfortunate that a minimum, even token, passenger connection was not maintained to the northern ports during the inter-regnum, which might have served the purpose of a compromise. This is particularly so as Captain Macdonell, in a frank message to the Company's up-coast customers, stated in *Union Steam* (January 1958): "We are still in the passenger business" and that if an analysis worked out satisfactorily "we intend to proceed with our new equipment and construction program and assign our old friend *S. S. Catala* to an interim passenger route until her replacement is ready." He further deplored "the conditions that made necessary the recent cancellation of services on the subsidy routes." So it came about that the Company put into effect a provisional and reduced cargo schedule on January 6, 1958 to the main northern ports, including the Queen Charlotte Islands, with the freighters *Cassiar* and *Chenega*. The latter was assigned to the Johnstone Strait-Alert Bay-Bella Coola route. This was supplemented by sailings of two Tidewater vessels, which continued their freight and passenger service to the logging camps as far as Kingcome Inlet.

To say that the Company's withdrawal from coast passenger service caused consternation and amazement is putting it mildly. On January 4, 1958, the Prince Rupert *Daily News* said:

> Three times at least . . . people of this city have stood on the docks or on the high places around town to witness the end of an era. Last night it was the *Chilcotin*, tidy little coast steamer of the Union Steamships Ltd., which sailed away to mark the end of that Company's forty-eight years of service for passengers from this port . . . Thousands of Prince Rupert residents will have fond memories of the leisurely voyage down the coast, the good meals, the fellowship on board, the excellent service, going down for the midnight snack . . ."

The Vancouver *Province* on January 9, 1958, reported:

> Captain Harry Roach, veteran of forty years with Union Steamships, nosed his ship *Catala* in to [the] wharf Wednesday afternoon to join the five-ship 'Mothball Fleet.' It was the end of an era which began before the turn of the century. 'There's a lot of sad faces in the settlements along Johnstone Strait,' Captain Roach said, as he gathered his belongings from his cabin.

In Ottawa it was stated in the House of Commons that $300,000 in addition to the $325,000 already provided would be required to continue Union service until the end of March, and probably a total for the subsidy year of more than $700,000. Federal subsidies to the Union over the preceding forty-five years had approximated five million dollars, and the supplementary amount the Company was asking for was considered to be "an unjustifiable expenditure." It was announced that the Government was arranging for another company to take over the service. One can only comment that, considering the increase in shipping costs by at least 150 per cent since 1940, a subsidy of five million to guarantee mail, passenger and freight service for almost half a century to three-fourths of the coast settlements of British Columbia was not a high figure by any means for essential services. In comparison with other expenditures, there are those who would call it one of the best and cheapest investments ever made on behalf of the coastal inhabitants and industries of Canada's westernmost province.

From communities, business leaders and organizations, protest letters and telegrams poured in to Ottawa and our head office in Vancouver, especially from the Indian settlements. Father J. L. Bradley, superintendent of Indian Missions wrote: "The passing of the Union Steamships is not only a very great inconvenience to me; it is also a very great sorrow. For nearly twenty-five years the Union boat has been the nearest thing to home for me in this country . . . I am still hoping this may not be my last trip on the *Catala* after all." From almost every industry and community board of trade the protests mounted, and Ottawa was kept closely informed.

Before the end of January 1958, Captain Macdonell made an approach to the Maritime Commission to resume passenger-ship service to the southern and intermediate section of the coastal run, which included all the Johnstone Strait ports up to Port Hardy and the ports beyond as far as Bella Coola, for a subsidy around $175,000. The application was strongly supported by the communities and the Native Brotherhood of B. C. Simultaneously, the Company went ahead with plans to provide minimum passenger accommodation on the freighter *Cassiar*, which was continuing to serve the northern ports including the Queen Charlotte Islands. Marine editors of both Vancouver dailies made separate visits to the coast communities and returned with the same message. Les Rimes of the *Sun* (February 27) wrote: " 'We want Union Steamships!' — that's the cry I heard all along the coast from here to Bella Coola." Norman Hacking of the *Province* (March 7) commented: "I have just returned from a trip up the coast in the *Chenega*, and I can report that up-coast people are hopping mad because of the dearth of passenger ships."

On the morning of April 5, 1958, the world's greatest non-nuclear blast to that date removed Ripple Rock in the 800-yard wide Seymour Narrows, which have a tidal current that sometimes exceeds 12 knots. The event came late in the day to be of benefit to the Union steamer operation, but it cleared away one of the Pacific Northwest's worst marine hazards. Like the Columbia River bar which was such a danger to the Hudson's Bay ships in the early days, Ripple Rock claimed many lives and ships. Union captains who traversed Seymour Narrows in the following weeks concurred that while the currents and eddies had not appreciably changed, the greater manoeuvrability and freedom afforded were a great boon and time-saver in navigating this key tidal channel.

On March 31, 1958, Union's Tidewater subsidiary moved "lock, stock and barrel" from their Coal Harbour location to resume business at the Union pier terminal. While the Tidewater identity was preserved, its freight and passenger bookings were merged with the main Union operation.

It was good news for many coast settlements when, on April 21, the passenger vessel *Catala* was returned to service as promised, after reconditioning, to make two trips weekly on her familiar Johnstone Strait, Port Hardy and Bella Coola routes. One practical economy consisted of a self-service cafeteria to replace her original dining saloon. The new schedule provided a total of ten Union-Tidewater routes and included well over 150 ports of call. There was now limited passenger accommodation on the *Cassiar* and the *Chilliwack*, both of which were servicing the northern ports, Prince Rupert and the Queen Charlotte Islands. The Company stated, however, that it could not consider "the extended scope of previous passenger schedules which required the maintenance of three to four large passenger vessels the year round," and which entailed steaming 200,000 sea miles annually on the subsidy routes.

I was delegated to accompany Captain Ernest Sheppard on the *Catala* when she resumed service, and the welcome mat was put out for the favourite Union ship at every port from Campbell River to Bella Coola and Ocean Falls. A chamber of commerce delegation awaited Captain Sheppard in the early morning at Campbell River to express the good wishes of the community. Seldom in the Company's long connection with the coast was such a reception accorded to one of their vessels as to the *Catala* at Alert Bay. The vessel was heralded by Indians in ceremonial costumes aboard a seiner. At the government wharf, several hundred Indians, and other residents, assembled to greet our vessel with ancient tribal dances in costume. Welcoming speeches were made by Chiefs James Sewid and William Snow, and by Mr. J. A. Findlay of the Alert Bay board of trade. Greetings of the Indian Nation were conveyed to the Union "in appreciation of its long service to our people in isolated places." It was the same all along the route, and the *Catala* continued to be well supported in the succeeding months under Captains Ray Perry and Harry Roach.

Further lengthy negotiations followed with the Maritime Commission; and R. G. Chestnut, who was ably carrying the Union banner in Ottawa, only narrowly failed in having the *Catala* route restored to subsidized service at an annual cost of $150,000. The Company president had said that, if the subsidy were to be granted, the *Cardena* would be reconstructed and converted to diesel power. The decision was in fact so close that two telegrams to Captain Macdonell arrived from the chairman of the Canadian Maritime Commission within a day.

193

The first, dated August 8, intimated that the *Catala* would be restored to subsidy; the second, on Monday, August 11, cancelled the advice concerning the proposed new contract, which was intended to run until March 31, 1959.

An interim payment had earlier been authorized to the Canadian Pacific for one ship to call at certain ports, the annual cost of which was estimated at around $190,000. This did not of course compare with the year-round coast calls, including the Queen Charlotte Islands, by three Union ships. The Company might have survived this disappointment, but the fatal blow when it came was from another direction. While the Union was engaged in its subsidy battle with Ottawa, Captain H. J. C. Terry, president of Northland Navigation Company, the Union's chief freight competitor, offered to take over service to the coastal ports "with or without subsidy," and was in fact already converting his cargo ship *Alaska Prince* for carriage of thirty-five passengers. Then came a new development in the middle of a strike by the SIU which had tied up the Canadian Pacific's coastal fleet. Captain Terry announced on August 2 that Northland had purchased two of the CP passenger ships, the large *Queen of the North* (former *Princess Norah*) and the small *Princess of Alberni*. These acquisitions provided Northland with the means and qualifications for subsidy; and it was the re-arrangement of schedule allowing the larger vessel to make a stop at Bella Coola en route to Prince Rupert that decided the issue against the Union's proposals, and changed the decision of the Maritime Commission over a fateful weekend.

I should like to lay one ghost to rest. There are those who have said that politics had a lot to do with the loss of the coast contract by Union Steamships under the new government; and certainly earlier debates in the House of Commons, when the Liberals were in office, did not betray any particular love on the part of the Opposition for Senator McKeen who was one of the Union's owners. It is also likely that a friendlier atmosphere at Ottawa might have tilted the balance and returned the *Catala* to subsidy. Granting all this, and the fact that for a long period the Union services were much undervalued, to my knowledge the government of the day invariably supported the assessment of the Maritime Commission's highly qualified inspectors. This was always scrupulous and friendly, and if a less obdurate policy had been followed within the Company, the Union's position could scarcely have been challenged. It seems fairly obvious now that a costly fumble occurred in dropping "the subsidy ball," and the alert Northland Navigation was quick enough to pick it up.

While all these problems were being thrashed out, the Union fleet had become further depleted. In February 1958, our Tidewater vessel *Troubadour III*, which had earlier competed against us as the *Gulf Wing*, was wrecked off Powell Point, Gilford Island. The four passengers and crew of nine were all rescued, and the ship was eventually recovered and returned to service. Then, on February 7, the *Chilcotin* was sold to the Sun Line of Monrovia and sailed as the *Capri* for Teneriffe. It was announced at the time that the *Camosun* was the vessel disposed of, but because cruises had been sold under the *Chilcotin* name, and also to retain goodwill, the *Camosun*'s name was changed to that of her now-departed sister ship, the *Chilcotin*. The two corvettes retained were also sister ships and had the advantage of being readily interchangeable.

Next, the *Coquitlam*, which had provided the summer link for Charles B. West's Alaskan Tours, was sold. As the *Glacier Queen*, she became the nucleus of Alaska Cruise Lines. On June 4, completing an ambitious program, "Chuck" West announced his purchase of the *Chilcotin* (formerly the *Camosun*), which sailed as the *Yukon Star* on June 9. Both vessels remained under Union management and in command of veteran skippers Ernest Sheppard and Billy McCombe. The Union line had come full-circle with the three corvettes obtained after World War II being all sold as cruise ships. Apart from the corvettes, no large passenger unit was custom built as a replacement for Union's regular trade, or got beyond the drawing board, in twenty-five years of fruitless planning.

Notwithstanding this fleet cut, the *Catala* and remaining cargo vessels continued to serve 150 coastal ports for the rest of the year, even resuming a modified postal arrangement for the Queen Charlotte Islands. On the main routes, the Company now felt the effects of serious inroads by the Northland vessels, operating with a fraction of the older line's overhead. It had become apparent to the local shipping fraternity that, with increasing labour costs, there was no possible room for two major coastal operations in the same general area. The disposal by sale of so much tonnage also made our position less credible. All the same there still was talk of new moves by the Union owners, and I was even sent north in the fall of 1958 with Traffic Manager McGowan to further bolster the communities.

It was with shock and considerable sadness, that the general public received news on January 14, 1959 of the sale of Union's fleet and floating equipment to the Northland Navigation Company headed by Captain H. J. C. Terry. The Bowen Island Estate properties were exempted from the sale. Further coastwise operations, however, were transferred to the Northland Navigation terminal at Commissioner Drive. At the time of the takeover, the Union had four vessels in active operation, the passenger ship *Catala* and three freighters, the *Cassiar*, the *Capilano* and the *Chenega*.

The last passenger ship to return to Vancouver in Union colours was the *Catala* under Captain Angus McNeill, who was met on arrival by Captain Harry Terry with the comment: "You'll be working for us now." This was Captain McNeill's first intimation that the Union operation had ended. He went over to Northland for seven years, together with Captain Tom Lucas and other personnel, and served as relief master on the *Canadian Prince*, as the *Queen of the North* had been renamed. Two other Union men who transferred were J. B. Buckeridge and N. E. (Norrie) Wood of the freight staff. No former Union passenger vessel was returned to service by the Northland Navigation Company. Instead, Captain Terry absorbed into his operation the pick of the Union's cargo fleet — the *Cassiar III* as the *Skeena Prince*, the *Capilano III* as the *Haida Prince* and the *Chilliwack III* as the *Tahsis Prince*. The era of the Union's special brand of all-round services was over.

Norman Hacking, marine editor of the Vancouver *Province*, summed it up well in a column headed "Heavy Pall Hangs Over Union Wharf." His last paragraph read: "In one respect Union Steamships has fallen a victim of progress. Roads and planes have taken away traffic. Out-of-date and uneconomical ships were not replaced . . . Big business stepped in and the Company became a casualty. Many, like me, will miss the old house flag and funnel." Captain Terry later sent me the water colour paintings of the early Union fleet done by S. P. Judge of the Vancouver Art School in 1905. They had hung in the board room and in my office, and it was a gesture I appreciated.

There remains a danger that one can become too dramatic about events that affected one's daily existence. Any such feeling I might have had of overdrawing the picture of the passing of Vancouver's pioneer line has been completely dispelled by reinforcing comments from many diverse sources. In "Days of the Gypo Logger" (*The Fisherman*, June 1970), Harold Mulyea said:

> Sailing from the old Union dock were the ships that hauled the logger and his varied complement of equipment, and fishermen were also dependent on [their] coming and going. . . . Not until these steamers were drawn out of service did we realize how big a role they

played in our everyday lives . . . We have all at one time and another marvelled at these skippers of the Union boats who sailed in thick weather by the seat of their pants aided by a deep-throated whistle.

He expressed it well, although in fact most Union ships gave out a sharp penetrating whistle that rebounded with great clarity from the walls of the "sea canyons."

Reminiscing in 1971 to the late Charles Defieux, then *Sun* marine editor, about the "drummers" (travelling salesmen), O. R. Ellis wrote:

From 1927 until a few years before the Company stopped operations, we enjoyed the freedom on board . . . the ships all had their own characteristics and peculiarities and the colourful officers and men did a fantastic job. . . . I would leave my trunks on a remote cannery dock in Rivers Inlet and they would be promptly delivered to me somewhere. . . . The passing of Union Steamship Company was a great loss to Vancouver, almost a calamity.

Finally, from David Greenlaw of Berkeley, California, who recalled "sailing as a lowly deckhand" aboard the first *Camosun* into China Hat, before it was called Klemtu, came this nostalgic recollection:

When the ship gave one blast of the whistle . . . the old trapper came out in his rowboat with a bundle of furs. We would give him his carton of groceries and then be on our way, leaving him to the solitude of the north. Nothing too small for the Union to handle — they really were part of the life line on the B. C. coast.

The strength of the Union in its heyday rested solidly on its diverse trade and comity of interest with both the main ports and isolated settlements. In a long period of years under bold leadership, the search for a legitimate commercial profit coincided with the natural development of the coast. There is no virtue in being "old established" unless one can offer the best; and, with the gradual unhinging of half a century's coast monopoly, the end result was certain.

In April 1958 I had written: "This life-line cannot be supplanted 'holus bolus' on this rugged coast for many moons to come." In a factual sense I was wrong, but I added something that was true and cannot be erased.

In reviewing changing conditions in the coastal trade there is always the danger of focussing too close a glass upon passing events. This becomes more obvious when it is remembered . . . our first mail contract dates from 1892, exactly three hundred years after Juan de Fuca discovered the Strait which bears his name and just one hundred years after Captain Vancouver entered Burrard Inlet. And a great deal has happened passenger-wise since 1892. In these same waters we have transported over two-thirds the present population of Canada without the loss of a passenger on a scheduled route in the last forty-five years. The Northwest has no like record.

Captain Jock Muir wrote to me in 1958, concluding his letter as follows: "This history of the grand old Company will now be handed down to posterity in just as glowing a manner as that appearing in Canadian school books of the Hudson's Bay Company."

I believe he was right.

APPENDICES

UNION STEAMSHIP CO. OF BRITISH COLUMBIA LTD.
(UNION STEAMSHIPS, LIMITED)

CHAIRMEN AND/OR PRESIDENTS

1889 (Nov.)	- 1893	A. St. George Hamersley (Chairman)
1893	- 1911 (Sept.)	Gordon T. Legg (also Manager from March 1900)
1911 (Sept.)	- 1917	Francis Carter-Cotton (Chairman)
1911 (Sept.)	- 1917	J. H. Welsford (President)
1917	- 1929	Grange V. Holt (Chairman)
1922	- 1931	R. A. H. Welsford (President)
1929	- 1936	R. Kerr Houlgate (Chairman)
1936	- 1943	J. K. Macrae K.C. (Chairman)
1938	- 1942	Harold Brown (President)
1943	- 1954	Gordon Farrell (President & Chairman)
		(Carl Halterman, Vice President 1945-1953)
1954	- 1959 (Jan.)	Senator S. S. McKeen O.B.E. (President & Chairman)
		(Captain J. A. MacDonell, President July, 1957)

MANAGERS AND/OR MANAGING DIRECTORS

1889 (Nov.)	- 1893 (Apr. 30)	Captain William Webster
1893 (May)	- 1893	Captain Donald McPhaiden
1893	- 1894	Walter F. Topping
1894	- 1900 (Feb.)	Henry Darling
1900 (Mar.)	- 1911 (Sept.)	Gordon T. Legg
1911 (Sept.)	- 1920	Ernest H. Beazley
		(J. H. Wrigley, Joint Manager 1911-1912)
1920 (Aug.)	- 1924 (Aug.)	John Barnsley (Managing Director Oct. 1922)
1924 (Aug.)	- 1938	Harold Brown
1939 (Feb.)	- 1945	Carl Halterman (Managing Director 1943)
1945	- 1954 (May 31)	Gerald O. McBean (Managing Director 1947)
1954 (June)	- 1954 (Dec.)	P. B. Cooke
1955 (Jan.)	- 1956	J. E. Ellis (Estates Manager 1956 - 1958)
1956 (Sept.)	- 1958	Captain J. A. MacDonell (Executive Vice Pres. & General Manager) (President, July 1957)

UNION WATERHOUSE CARGO DIVISION

1939   - 1954   R. L. Solloway (Manager)

ASSISTANT MANAGERS

1911 (Oct.)	- 1917	John Galt
1917	- 1920	John Barnsley
1923 (Oct.)	- 1924	Harold Brown
1926 (Jan.)	- 1937	A. L. Clements
1938 (Mar.)	- 1939 (Feb.)	Carl Halterman
1941	- 1945	Gerald O. McBean
1947 (Sept.)	- 1954	C. W. McLean
1955 (Jan.)	- 1957 (Nov.)	Gerald A. Rushton
1957 (Nov.)	- 1958	Captain D. Roberts

EXECUTIVE ASSISTANT

1957 (Nov.)   - 1959 (Jan.)   R. G. Chestnut

MARINE SUPERINTENDENTS

1907	- 1938	Captain Alexander S. Walker
1938 (June)	- 1947	Captain John Muir (General Supt. until 1948)
1947	- 1954	Captain E. W. Suffield
1954	- 1956	Captain F. Talbot
1956 (Sept.)	- 1957	Captain David Roberts
1957	- 1959 (Jan.)	Captain T. Lucas

SUPERINTENDENT ENGINEERS

1891	- 1894	Henry Darling
1894	- 1914	James Frith
1914	- 1923	A. S. De Gruchy
1923	- 1938	George H. Foster
1938	- 1953	Robert M. Logan
1953	- 1956	T. W. Morgan
1956	- 1958	J. Scagel

MASTER MARINERS * OF THE UNION STEAMSHIP FLEET

(* Served as Captains, in command of Union ships, including Union-Waterhouse and Union-Tidewater vessels, between 1889 and 1958)
M — designates Master of particular named ships
c — indicates an approximate date or dates only

The following list has been compiled according to information presently available.

Alfred Aspinall — Born Liverpool, served 1924-49, M *Lady Pam, Chelohsin* and others

Francis Bannerman — Born Phoenix, U.S.A. (from Empress of Japan), served 1911 27, incl. war service, 1st officer *Camosun*, M *Lady Cynthia*

James J. Bartlett — served 1898-c1905 and 1918-23, M *Comox* (1903)

Robert E. Batchelor — served 1904-c1910, M *Camosun*, before going to Pilotage

Kenneth Bennett — served Union-Waterhouse 1939-c1944, M *Eastholm, Northholm*, going to Pilotage Authority

John (Jack) Boden — Born Glasgow 1882, served 1905-53 (exc. brief period towboats 1912), M *Cassiar* (1916), *Cardena, Catala, Venture, Lady Alexandra, Camosun III* and others, Senior Captain before retirement

William Boyce — Union-Waterhouse service, M several vessels including *Argus* (burnt 1953), later joining Pilotage service

C. Brown — Born Newfoundland, M *Comox* (1911), joined the Government Marine service

John H. Browne — Born Belfast and came in *Cariboo (Cowichan)* from Scotland, served 1908-32, M *Camosun*

John R. (Buster) Browne — son of above, born Rothesay, served 1921-45, M *Capilano, Catala* and others, joined Pilotage service

Neil Campbell — Born Isle of Skye, Scotland, served c1935-58, M *Chenega*

John Cockle — Born Whitehaven, England, served 1905-17, died on overseas service, M *Comox, Capilano* and *Cheslakee*

Frederick L. Coe — (From Arctic service), M *Cassiar III* on Arctic voyage (1955)

H. George Coles — Born Elliston, Newfoundland (from Canadian National S.S.), served 1940-45, M *Camosun II*, going to Pilotage service

Donald A. Connell — Union-Waterhouse service 1939-c1956, M *Chilkoot II*

John Cowper	— Born Isle of Man 1852, M *Comox* and *Chelohsin* (1911)
F. R. Davies	— Union-Tidewater service 1956-58, M *Chenega* and *Triggerfish*, joined Pilotage Authority
A. W. Dawe	— Born New Westminster, M *Capilano* (1899)
Alfred E. Dickson	— Born Antigonish, Nova Scotia, served c1895-1935 inc. war service, Senior Captain for many years, principally on northern routes, M *Camosun, Cardena, Catala* and others
D. Donald	— served c1904-10, M *Coutli, Camosun* and others, transferred to Grand Trunk Pacific S.S.
James Donnelly	— Union-Tidewater service 1956-58, M *Tournament, Troubadour III*
Dean F. Eaton	— Born New Westminster, served in Union ships, also Union-Tidewater 1956-58, M *Troubadour III* and *Tournament*
Jack T. Edwards	— Born in Ontario 1874 (from White Pass S.S.), served 1907-19, M *Coquitlam, Cassiar, Chelohsin, Venture*, joined Pilotage
James Findlay	— Born Portessie, Banffshire 1873, served 1911-38, ferried *Catala* and *Chilliwack II* from Scotland, M *Coquitlam, Cassiar, Chilkoot, Cardena* and others
A. Freeman	— served c1890-1901, M *Skidegate, Capilano, Comox* and *Cutch*
E. Fulton	— Born in Nova Scotia 1862, M *Capilano* (1896) and *Coquitlam*
George Gaisford	— Born Chelsea, Eng. 1864, served c1898-1933 mainly on logging routes, M *Cassiar* (1908), *Cowichan, Chelohsin, Lady Alexandra* and nearly all passenger ships
Edward Georgeson	— Born Galiano Is., B.C., served 1910-35, M *Chasina, Camosun, Chilkoot, Catala, Cardena* and others, joined Pilotage service
F. W. Gilbert	— (from Terminal Steam Navigation Co.), M *Cheam* 1921-22
William Gleeson	— Union-Waterhouse service 1939-c1955, M *Chilkoot II* and *Chilliwack III*
Lorne A. Godfrey	— served 1917-47, principally on freight routes, M *Lady Pam, Lady Cecilia, Chilliwack II* and others
John F. Gosse	— M *Coquitlam* (1901)
J. R. Grauer	— M *Capilano* (1901)
Neil Gray	— Born Argyll 1870 (from Clyde excursion steamers), served 1906-39, M *Coquitlam, Chilco, Lady Cecilia* and six other passenger ships

John J. Halcrow	— Born Shetland Is., served c1923-57, M *Lady Rose, Cardena, Coquitlam II* and others
M. J. (Paddy) Hannigan	— served c1930-58, M *Venture, Cardena, Catala* and others
V.D. Hayman	— Born Nova Scotia 1896. served in ships 1928-50, on wharf to 1954, M *Lady Rose, Capilano II* and others
Walter Holmberg	— Born Vancouver 1917, served Union-Waterhouse 1943-51, M *Southholm, Eastholm, Island King, Chilliwack II*, joined Pilotage Authority
William E. Holmes	— Born London, Eng. 1857, served c1890, M *Leonora* and *Senator*
Charles Holt	Union-Tidewater service 1956-58, M *Tournament, Chenega, Redonda* and others
James House	— served c1905-06, M *Chehalis* (sunk 1906)
James (Jimmy) Hunter	— Born Shetland Is., served 1920-55, M *Cardena, Coquitlam II* and others
Albert Johnson	— Union-Waterhouse service, M *Capilano III, Cassiar III* (1957)
Bernard L. (Barney) Johnson C.B.E., D.S.O.	— Born Birkenhead 1878, served 1895-1906, M *Comox, Capilano* and *Camosun* (1905), joined Boscowitz Line and later the Grand Trunk Pacific S.S., going to Pilotage service in 1913, Naval service first war and Senior Naval officer, Port of Vancouver in World War II
P. H. Johnson	— Born in Sweden 1862, served c1889-96, M *Leonora, Skidegate* and *Cutch*
Andrew (Andy) Johnstone	— Born Dalton, Dumfries 1887, served 1909-32 (inc. war service) and best known of the 'cannery skippers', M *Coquitlam* (1912), *Venture, Catala* and *Cardena*, going to Pilotage Authority
Howard E. Lawrey	— Born at sea (Cornish family), (from Great Western Railway steamers and All-Red Line), served continuously as Union master 1917-45, M *Chilco, Lady Cynthia, Lady Cecilia, Lady Evelyn* and others
Thomas Lucas	— Born Newcastle, Eng., served 1921-59, coming ashore in 1955 as Assistant and (1957) Marine Superintendent, M various passenger ships including *Cardena, Chilcotin* and *Camosun III*
E. McCaskrie	— served c1894-96, M *Skidegate*
William McCombe	— (from Glasgow in *Cardena*), served continuously 1923-58, also relief duty as Marine Supt., going to Alaska Cruise Lines 1958, M *Lady Alexandra, Cardena, Catala, Coquitlam II* and others

J. McKillop	— served 1917-c1943, 1st Officer *Venture* and M several day steamers
A. McKinnon	— Union-Waterhouse service 1939-58, M *Chilliwack III*
Henry C. (Harry) McLean	— Born Sydney, Australia, served 1917-c1955, well known on cruise ships, M *Cardena, Camosun III, Chilcotin* and others
E. E. McLellan	— Captain of *Coquitlam* on Alaska sealing charter 1892
A. C. McLennan	— Born Kyle, Ross 1887, served 1920-50, M *Chilco, Cheakamus, Camosun II, Cardena* and *Chilcotin*
Frank McMahon	— Union-Waterhouse service, M *Northholm* (lost 1943)
Angus McNeill	— Born Waternish, Isle of Skye, (came from Scotland in *Chilliwack II*), served continuously 1927-59, M *Coquitlam II, Camosun III, Catala* and others
J. D. McPhee	— served from c1911-28, including war service, chiefly on cargo vessels, first master *Chilliwack II*
W. B. McCartney	— Born San Francisco 1891, served Union-Waterhouse 1939-58, M *Eastholm, Island King, Capilano III* (1951)
John L. Malcolmson	— Born Lerwick, Shetland Is., served continuously 1917-47, M *Lady Pam* (1936), *Capilano II* and other day steamers
Douglas Manuel	— Union-Tidewater service, M *Triggerfish* (sunk 1956)
John Mercer	— Born Newfoundland, joined *Venture* (1923) and served to c1940, M *Lady Cynthia* and others
F. Monk	— Born Newfoundland 1865, served c1898-1903, M *Leonora* and *Chehalis*
Charles Moody	— Born Newfoundland 1868, coming to Vancouver 1890, M *Skidegate, Comox, Cowichan* (1908), going to Pilotage 1917
Walter Moorhouse	— (from Boscowitz Line), served 1911 to c1914, M *Venture* before joining Pilotage service
Patrick Morrison	— Union-Waterhouse service c1939-55, M *Chenega*
William W. Mounce	— Born Blaine, Wash., served 1919-37 before joining Pilotage, M freighters *Chilkoot* and *Chilliwack II*, also *Lady Pam, Capilano II, Lady Cynthia* and *Cardena*
John (Jock) Muir	— Born Campbeltown, Argyll, 1885, served continuously 1913-48, M *Cassiar, Coquitlam, Cowichan, Chelohsin, Chilkoot, Catala, Cardena* and total of twelve ships on all routes, appointed Marine Superintendent 1938 and General Supt. 1947

206

William Murray	— Union-Waterhouse service, including M *Veta C* (1952)
R. T. (Bob) Naughty	— Joined *Cheakamus* (1916) and served to c1948, M *Chilco, Capilano II, Lady Cecilia, Chelohsin, Venture*
Robert Naughty	— (son of above), served c1935-58, M *Chenega*
Samuel Nelson	— Born Ireland, 1st Officer *Camosun*, M *Capilano* (sunk 1915)
Holmes Newcombe	— Born New Brunswick 1859, coming to Vancouver 1889, M *Comox, Skidegate* and *Cutch* (1898-1900), going to Canadian Government Marine service
James E. Noel	— Born Newfoundland, (joined from Boscowitz Line), served 1911-22, M *Venture, Vadso*, later going to Pilotage service
W. D. Owen	— Union-Waterhouse service, including M *Southholm* (1946)
John Park	— Born Aberdeen 1880, joining Union S.S. 1910 from deep-sea ships, M *Capilano* and *Venture*, later going to the Pilotage Authority (Retired as Senior Pilot 1948)
Fred H. Parker	— (Joined from All-Red Line), served 1917-c1930, M *Cheakamus* and other logging route vessels
Garfield Pengally	— Union-Waterhouse service 1939-c1955, M *Chilliwack III*, later joining the Pilotage Authority
Ray W. Perry	— Served with Union-Waterhouse, as well as passenger ships, 1939-57, M *Catala*, also *Camosun III* and cargo vessels
Ernest A. Powys	— Born Sydney, N.S.W. 1867, joining Union S.S. from deep-sea ships, served c1890-c1902, M *Senator, Capilano* and *Comox*
J. Richardson	— Captain of *Vadso* (1914)
Henry (Harry) Roach	— Born Cardiff, Wales 1898, (Joined Union S.S. from All-Red Line), served continuously 1917-58, M *Lady Cecilia, Lady Pam, Chelohsin, Cardena, Catala* and others
Cecil Roberts	— Union-Waterhouse service, M *Chilliwack II, Gulf Mariner* (tug) and *Chelan* (lost 1954)
Frank T. Saunders	— Served c1897-1910, M *Coquitlam* (1903), and *Camosun* (1905), later joining G.T.P. Steamships, and subsequently the Pilotage
Ernest M. Sheppard	— Born Harbour Grace, Newfoundland 1894, joined Union S.S. 1911 and served continuously to 1958 (incl. World War I) M *Chilliwack II, Cardena,*

207

	Catala, Chilcotin and seven other vessels, before going to Alaska Cruise Lines
Andrew Sinclair	— Born Shetland Is., joining from Boscowitz Line and serving 1911-23, M. *Venture*, later going to Pilotage service
Charles B. Smith	— Born Weston-Super-Mare, Eng., brought *Camosun* across Atlantic (1905) and ferried both *Lady Alexandra* and *Lady Cecilia* to Pacific coast, M *Chilliwack, Cardena* and others, later joining the Pilotage service
R. Stacey	— Served c1911-c1928, M *Chelohsin* (1922)
Hugh Stalker	— Pioneer of Moodyville Ferry, served 1889-c1900, M *Senator* and *Leonora*
H. Stephens	— Born Vancouver, served with Union-Waterhouse 1939-51, M *Chilkoot II, Southholm, Eastholm, Island King* and *Chilliwack II*, later joining the Pilotage service
L. Stephens	— Born Vancouver, serving with Union-Waterhouse 1939-42, M *Northholm* and *Gray*, later going to the Pilotage Authority
A. (Al) Strang	— Served c1930-53 in Union and Waterhouse ships, M *Gulf Mariner* (tug)
Eric W. Suffield	— Served continuously 1921-55 (including service both world wars), M *Lady Evelyn, Venture, Lady Cynthia, Lady Alexandra* and other passenger vessels, appointed Marine Superintendent 1947
J. E. Summerfield	— Served c1923-50, M *Lady Pam* and others
Edward Swank	— Union-Waterhouse service 1941-57, M *Cassiar III* (1956)
Frederick (Fred) Talbot	— Joined Union S.S. with Waterhouse fleet 1939, Assistant Superintendent cargo vessels, becoming Marine Supt. 1955
Michael Uldall	— Union-Waterhouse service 1939-c1942, M *Chilkoot II*, joining the Pilotage service
John J. Veal	— M *Skidegate* in 1894
Donald Wallace	— Union-Tidewater service, M *Troubadour III, Tournament*
A. E. (Wally) Walsh	— Served 1926-1957, Shore (Terminal) Captain for several summer and other periods, M *Lady Cecilia* and other passenger ships
John Walters	— Served c1895-1901, M *Coquitlam*
James Watt	— Joined Union S.S. with Canadian National ships (1940), served 1940-44, M *Camosun II*
George Whalen	— Born Newfoundland, served c1908-21, M *Capilano II* (1920)

208

J. W. (Chips) Williams	— Served c1911-28 (incl. war service), M *Chilkoot*
Robert (Bob) Wilson	— Born Shetland Is., served continuously 1910-47, best known Captain on the logging camp routes and Senior master in latter years, M *Comox* and six other passenger ships including *Venture, Cowichan, Chelohsin* and *Cardena*
Jack Woods	— Union-Waterhouse service, M *Argus* (1950), going to the Pilotage
W. L. (Billy) Yates	— Joined Union S.S. 1907 and served on day steamers until 1957 (except for periods with Marine Express between 1914-22), M *Lady Alexandra* (1937-52) and six other passenger ships
Arthur Young	— Union-Tidewater service 1956-58, M *Triggerfish, Tournament*

UNION STEAMSHIPS FLEET
All Time Roster — 1889 to 1959

53 Vessels excluding chartered ships (see note)

Note: The following list of Union owned and operated vessels includes 3 motor-vessels which operated on Union-Tidewater Schedules between 1956-1959 (Jan.)

Name of Union Vessel (Previous name/s in brackets) *Indicates Diesel Powered	Period In Union Service	Tons Gross Net	Dimen's Length Beam Depth Feet	Capacity Passengers Licence Berths Deck Acc'm	Cargo Tons (Approx.)	Speed Knots	Built (or Converted) *Date Dieselized
*Argus (Ex-Argo)	1950-1953	517 344	157.3 27.2 19.9	None	800 (Bulk Liquid Cargo)	10½	1944 Kyle & Co., Stockton, California (For U.S. Navy)
Camosun I	1905-1936	1369 793	192.7 35.2 17.9	199 68 120	300	14 (Max.) 12 (Avg.)	1904 Bow McLachlan & Co., Paisley, Scotland
Camosun II (Ex-St. Margaret Chieftain Prince Charles) From C.N. Steamships	1940-1945	1344 767	241.7 33.1 11.1	178 (150 Licence Q. Charlotte Is.) 87 (berths) —	150	13	1907 Ailsa Shipbuilding Co., Ayr, Scotland
Camosun III (Ex-H.M.C.S. St. Thomas)	1946-1958	1835 1012	235.7 36.6 25.5	200 114 16	250	15 (Max.)	1943 Smith Dockyard, Middlesbrough, Eng. 1946 - Converted Burrard Shipbuilders, North Vancouver, B.C.

Name of Union Vessel (Previous name/s in brackets) *Indicates Diesel Powered	Period In Union Service	Tons Gross Net	Dimen's Length Beam Depth	Capacity Passengers Licence Berths Deck Acc'm	Cargo Tons (Approx.)	Speed Knots	Built (or Converted) *Date Dieselized
Capilano I	1891-1915	231 157	120.0 22.2 9.6	25 (deck) (Carried additional in Alaskan Service 1897) after passenger alterations)	300	17 (Max.) 12 (Avg.)	1891 J. McArthur & Co., (Eng. Bow McLachlan) Glasgow, Scotland. Assembled 1891 Coal Har., Vancouver, B.C.
Capilano II	1920-1949	374 200	135 B.P. 26.9 8.2	350 150 (Winter)	50	13½ Max.	1920 B.C. Marine, Vancouver, B.C. (Eng.-Ex-Washington)
*Capilano III (Ex-Ottawa Mayferry -City of Belleville)	1951-1959	530 360	145.0 27.1 8.0	None	500	11 (Max.)	1946 Port Arthur Shipbuilding Co., Ontario. *Dieselized 1951
Cardena	1923-1959	1559 842	226.8 37.1 18.4	250 132 60	350	14 (Max.)	1923 Napier & Miller, Old Kilpatrick, Scotland
Cassiar I	1901-1923	597 384	120.6 29.0 6.9	144 42 —	110	9	1901 Wallace Shipyard, False Ck., Vancouver, B.C. Hull – Ex.-J.R. McDonald Ballard, Washington Engines – Bow McLachlan, Paisley, Scotland

Name of Union Vessel (Previous name/s in brackets) *Indicates Diesel Powered	Period In Union Service	Tons Gross Net	Dimen's Length Beam Depth Feet	Capacity Passengers Licence Berths Deck Acc'm	Cargo Tons (Approx.)	Speed Knots	Built (or Converted) *Date Dieselized
Cassiar II (Ex-Amethyst -Prince John) From C.N. Steamships	1940-1949	905 540	185.3 29.6 10.9	85 38 —	400	11	1910 Scott & Sons, Bowling, Scotland
Cassiar III* (Ex-Ottawa Page -Blue Peter II)	1951-1959	1377 971	214.1 36.7 19.8	4	1500	13	1946 Burrard Shipyards, North Vancouver, B.C. *1955
Catala	1925-1959	1476 851	218 B.P. 37.1 18.4	267 120 48	300	14 (Max.)	1925 Coaster Construction Co., Montrose, Scotland
Chasina (Ex-Santa Cecilia -Selma)	1917-1923	258 139	141.8 22.1 11.6	200 153 (Winter) —	40	13½ (Max.) 11½ (Avg.)	1881 J. Elder & Co., Glasgow, Scotland
(1) Cheslakee Lengthened and Renamed	1910-1913	526 261	126.0 28.1 17.1	148 56	120	12	1910 Dublin Dockyard Co., Dublin, Ireland Engines - MacColl & Co., (Belfast)
(2) Cheakamus	1913-1942	689 403	145.3 28.1 17.0	148 56 —	120	12 (Max.) 10½ (Avg.)	1913 Lengthened and re-built Wallace Shipyard, North Vancouver, B.C.

Name of Union Vessel (Previous name/s in brackets) *Indicates Diesel Powered	Period In Union Service	Tons Gross Net	Dimen's Length Beam Depth Feet	Capacity Passengers Licence Berths Deck Acc'm	Cargo Tons (Approx.)	Speed Knots	Built (or Converted) *Date Dieselized
Cheam (Ex-City of Nanaimo -Bowena)	1920-1923	821 558	159.0 32.0 9.4	500 (Day Lic.)	200	10½	1891 McAlpine & Allen, False Ck., Vancouver, B.C.
Chehalis	1897-1906	54 —	59.7 13.3 6.5	Limited to Charter only	Tow Boat Service	—	1897 C. McAlpine, False Ck., Vancouver, B.C. (Engines - Ex-Skidegate)
Chelan* (Ex-Veta C)	1952-1954	541 235	148.0 33.3 15.6	None	450	12	1944 Northwestern Shipbuilding, Bellingham, Wash. (For U.S. Navy)
Chelohsin	1911-1949	1134 597	175.5 35.1 14.0	191 81 95	150	14 (Max.) 12½ (Avg.)	1911 Dublin Dockyard Co., Dublin, Ireland (Eng. - MacColl & Co., Belfast)
Chenega* (Ex-Lighthouse Tender Rose -Northern Express)	1954-1959	381 179	129.3 24.6 11.0	None	350	10	1916 Anderson Steamboat Co., Seattle, Washington *1954
(1) Chilco (Ex-Santa Maria) Renamed	1917-1935	305 166	151.0 22.0 12.6	200 144 (Winter)	40	13½ (Max.) 11½ (Avg.)	1883 J. Elder & Co., Glasgow, Scotland
(2) Lady Pam	1935-1946	Same	Same	130 (All year)	Same	11½	1935 Accommodation modernised

Name of Union Vessel (Previous name/s in brackets) *Indicates Diesel Powered	Period In Union Service	Tons Gross Net	Dimen's Length Beam Depth Feet	Capacity Passengers Licence Berths Deck Acc'm	Cargo Tons (Approx.)	Speed Knots	Built (or Converted) *Date Dieselized
Chilcotin (Ex-H.M.C.S. Hespeler)	1947-1958	1837 990	235.7 36.6 25.5	200 106 Nil	250	15½ (Max.)	1944 Henry Robb Ltd., Leith, Scotland 1946 Converted West Coast Shipbuilders, Vancouver, B.C.
Chilkoot I	1920-1934	756 411	172.6 30.2 12.9	12 2 (1 cabin) —	800	12 (Max.) 10 (Avg.)	1920 Wallace Shipbuilding Co. North Vancouver, B.C.
Chilkoot II	1946-1957	1336 782	214.1 36.7 19.9	4	1500 (China-Coaster)	11	1946 Victoria Machinery Depot, Victoria, B.C.
Chilliwack I (Ex-Onyx -British Columbia)	1919-1926	557 219	170.7 27.1 10.5	10 (deck)	750	9	1903 Scott & Co., Bowling, Scotland
Chilliwack II (Ex-Ardgarvel)	1927-1954	834 397	200.3 30.2 12.8	10 4 (berths)	1100	10	1917 Ferguson Bros., Port Glasgow, Scotland
(1) Island King (Ex-Granit -Columba)	1944-1954	591 291	165.1 28.2 12.4	4	800	10	1920 Trosvik Mer. Verk., Brevik, Norway
Renamed (2) Chilliwack III*	1954-1959	Same	Same	Same	Same	11	*1954

Name of Union Vessel (Previous name/s in brackets) *Indicates Diesel Powered	Period In Union Service	Tons Gross Net	Dimen's Length Beam Depth Feet	Capacity Passengers Licence Berths Deck Acc'm	Cargo Tons (Approx.)	Speed Knots	Built (or Converted) *Date Dieselized
Comox I	1891-1919	101 / 60	101.0 / 18.1 / 5.2	200 / 40 (berths) (Cabin acc'm increased 1897)	150	12 (Max.)	1891 J. McArthur & Co. (Eng. - Bow McLachlan), Glasgow, Scotland Assembled, Coal Hbr., Vancouver, B.C.
Comox II*	1924-1943	54 / 36	54.0 / 15.5 / 7.2	25	20	7	1924 Wallace Shipbuilding, North Vancouver, B.C. (Eng. - Atlas Imperial)
Coquitlam I	1892-1923	256 / 166	120.0 / 22.0 / 9.6	24 (deck) (license 157 for period from 1897) 93 (berths) 64 (steerage)	300	9	1891 J. McArthur & Co., (Eng.-Bow McLachlan) Glasgow, Scotland Assembled, Coal Hbr., Vancouver, B.C., 1892
Coquitlam II (Ex-H.M.C.S. Leaside)	1946-1958	1835 / 1009	235.6 / 36.6 / 25.5	200 / 114 / 24	250	15 (Max.)	1944 Smith Dockyard Co., Middlesbrough, Eng. Converted 1946 West Coast Shipbuilders, Vancouver, B.C.
Coulti	1904-1909	99	71.4 / 18.8 / —	None	Tow-boat Service	—	1904 C. McAlpine, False Ck., Vancouver, B.C.

Name of Union Vessel (Previous name/s in brackets) *Indicates Diesel Powered	Period In Union Service	Tons Gross Net	Dimen's Length Beam Depth Feet	Capacity Passengers Licence Berths Deck Acc'm	Cargo Tons (Approx.)	Speed Knots	Built (or Converted) *Date Dieselized
Cowichan (Launched as Cariboo)	1908-1925	961 520	156.1 32.0 13.5	165 73	125	11	1908 Ailsa Shipbuilding, Troon, Scotland
Cutch	1890-1900	324 123 (676 163 1898)	180.0 23.2 11.7	150 200 (1898) (60 berths) (140 deck)	150	14 (Max.) 13 (Avg.)	1884 J. Bremner & Co., Hull, England (Rebuilt and re-engined in 1898)
Eastholm (From Waterhouse Fleet)	1939-1957	174 85	93.0 24.3 6.8	None	250	8	1913 A. Moscrop, Vancouver, B.C.
Gray (From Waterhouse Fleet Ex-Petriana)	1939-1944	707 280	182.7 27.9 12.3	None	650	—	1909 R. Williamson & Son. Workington, England
Island King	1944-1954		Refer to particulars included with *Chilliwack III* (later name).				
Lady Alexandra	1924-1954	1396 678	225.4 40.1 9.7	1400 (Howe Sound) 10 (berths)	300	14	1924 Coaster Construction Co., Montrose, Scotland
Lady Cecilia (Ex-H.M.S. Swindon)	1925-1951	944 382	219.5 28.6 16.3	800 (900 excursions) 500 (winter) 3 staterooms	75	15½ (Max.) 13½ (Avg.)	1919 Ardrossan, Scotland Converted, 1925 Coaster Construction Co., Montrose, Scotland

Name of Union Vessel (Previous name/s in brackets) *Indicates Diesel Powered	Period In Union Service	Tons Gross Net	Dimen's Length Beam Depth Feet	Capacity Passengers Licence Berths Deck Acc'm	Cargo Tons (Approx.)	Speed Knots	Built (or Converted) *Date Dieselized
Lady Cynthia (Ex-H.M.S. Barnstaple)	1925-1957	950 390	219.3 28.6 16.3	800 (900 excursions) 500 (Winter) 4 staterooms	75	15½ (Max.) 13½ (Avg.)	1919 Ardrossan, Scotland. Converted, 1925 Coaster Construction Co., Montrose, Scotland
Lady Evelyn (Ex-Deerhound)	1923-1936	588 249	189.0 26.1 9.5	480 200 (Winter)	100	14 13 (Avg.)	1901 J. Jones & Sons, Birkenhead, England
Lady Pam	1935-1946			Refer to particulars included with *Chilco* (previous name).			
Lady Rose (Launched as Lady Sylvia)	1937-1951	199 110	104.8 21.2 14.3	130 70 (Winter)	20	11½	1937 A. & J. Inglis Ltd., Glasgow, Scotland
Leonora	1889-1904	33 18	57.0 9.0 5.3	Not Known (similar type to Senator)	5	Engine (15 NHP)	1876 J. Spratt, Victoria, B.C.
Melmore (Ex-Wolfhound)	1914-1916	424 180	156.0 26.0 11.3	200	100	13	1892 D.J. Dunlop & Co., Port Glasgow, Scotland Converted for pass. service 1914
Northholm (Ex-Robert H. Merrick) (From Waterhouse Fleet)	1939-1943	447 229	150.2 25.2 11.9	None	550	10	1924 J. Towers Shipbuilding, Bristol, England

Name of Union Vessel (Previous name/s in brackets) * Indicates Diesel Powered	Period In Union Service	Tons Gross Net	Diemen's Length Beam Depth Feet	Capacity Passengers Licence Berths Deck Acc'm	Cargo Tons (Approx.)	Speed Knots	Built (or Converted) * Date Dieselized
Redonda* (Ex-Y.T.C. No. 501-52)	1955-1958	185 —	125.0 23.6 6.6	None	225 Cargo Tanker	7	1944 Portland, Ore. (U.S.L.S.)
Senator	1889-1904	31 21	51.5 12.0 4.5	30 (license) 12 (cabin)		8	1880 Henry Maloney, Moodyville, B.C. Rebuilt 1896
Skidegate	1889-1897	37 28	76.0 12.5 6.0	20 (Org.) (Pass. accm. rebuilt 1891)		9 11 (after 1891)	1879 Victoria, B.C. Rebuilt 1891 with Bow McLachlan Engines
Southholm (Ex-E.D. Kingsley) (From Waterhouse Fleet)	1939-1950	1029 541	200.0 32.0 14.5	None	1100	10	1919 Canadian Car & Foundry, Fort William, Ont.
Tournament* (Ex-Jervis Express) (From Tidewater Co.)	1956-1959	149 101	108.0 18.4 7.0	101	40	15	1942 Annapolis Boatyard, City Island, New York
Troubadour III* (Ex-Gulf Wing) (From Tidewater Co.)	1956-1959	103 33	107.6 17.9 6.0	95	25	12 (Avg.)	1944 as Fairmile Star Shipyards, New Westminster, B.C.

Name of Union Vessel (Previous name/s in brackets) *Indicates Diesel Powered	Period In Union Service	Tons Gross Net	Dimen's Length Beam Depth Feet	Capacity Passengers Licence Berths Deck Acc'm	Cargo Tons (Approx.)	Speed Knots	Built (or Converted) *Date Dieselized
Triggerfish* (From Tidewater Co.)	1956-	149 101	108.0 18.4 8.0	None	100	10	Built by G. Hittebrant, Kingston, N.Y., U.S.A.
Vadso (Ex-Bordeaux) (From Boscowitz Fleet)	1911- 1914	908 698	191.2 28.7 21.7	50	400	11	1881 Motala, Gothenburg, Sweden
Venture (From Boscowitz Fleet)	1911- 1946	1011 580	180.4 32.0 17.0	186 60 85	550	13 12 (Avg.)	1910 Napier & Miller, Glasgow, Scotland
Washington	1918- 1919	306 185	125.5 25.8 7.3	350 (operated on Sechelt Route)	100	12 (Avg.)	1914 Dockton, Washington By John A. Martinolich, for Washington route

BULK CARRIERS: (Barges)
Bulk Carrier Union No. 1 Ex "Southholm"
Bulk Carrier Union No. 2 Ex "Princess Mary"
Bulk Carrier Union No. 3 Ex U.S.S. A.R.R. 742 (landing ship)
Bulk Carrier Barge "Taku" Ex "Princess Maquinna"

INDEX

222

223

Farris, W. B., KC 131
Felice (ship) 2
Ferguson Bros. (Port of Glasgow) 108
Financial Post, The 148
Findlay, Alexander (Chief Eng.) 143
Findlay, Capt. James 41, 84, 101, 108, 116, 128, 134
Findlay, J. A. 193
Fisherman, The 196
Fisherman's Cove 87
Fleck, Bryce 106
Fletcher, Bill 149
Fletcher, J. G. 76
Food Dehydration Ltd. 163
Foreman, Provost (Montrose) 97
Fort Camosun (Bay of Camosack) 4, 149
Fort George 3
Fort Langley 3, 4
Fort McLoughlin 4
Fort Ross, S.S. 170
Fort Simpson 4
Fort Vancouver 3, 4
Fort Wrangell 35
Foster, George H. 41, 52, 58, 91, 97, 113, 134
Fox, Alderman 14
Frank Waterhouse Co. of Canada Ltd. 136, 166, 176
Fraser River 3, 5, 6, 9, 11, 12, 18, 64, 126
Fraser, Simon 5
Frederick Arm 41, 42
Freeman, Capt. A. 36
Freeman, T. 20
Frith, Mr. 160
Frith, James 20
Frizelle, George 53
Fry, George H. 17
Fuller, G. 20
Fyson, O. 72

Gaisford, Capt. George 41, 55, 93, 98, 103
Galbraith, Chief Officer James 154
Galloway, D. E. 110
Galt, John 53, 63, 79
Galveston (Texas) 59, 60
Gambier Island 123
Gardiner, William 127
Gardner Canal 150, 168
Gastown (Vancouver) 7
Geddes, Sir Auckland 95
Georgeson, Capt. Edward 92, 122

Gerbrandt, A. H. 143
Gibson, Mr. (Gibsons Landing) 30
Gibson, Rev. Mr. 65
Gibson, George 123
Gibson & Sons, W. F. 161
Gibsons (Landing) 25, 30, 81, 105, 160, 161
Gig Harbour 12
Gilbert, Capt. F. W. 86
Gillies Bay 159
Gilligan, John H. 153
Gillis's Camp 9
Gilmore, Mr. (Oceanic Cannery) 66
Glacier Queen, S.S. (ex *Coquitlam*) 195
Glasgow (Scotland) 12, 16-18, 20, 24, 90, 108, 129, 130
Gledhill, Jack 136, 160
Glenora 37
Godfrey, Air Vice-Marshal Earl 154
Godfrey, Capt. Lorne E. 77, 81, 129, 139, 154
Goodall, John 167
Goose Bay (Anyox) 58
Goose Bay Cannery 122
Gosse Packing Co. 108
Gower Point 81, 106
Governor Douglas, S.S. 5
Gracie, Beazley & Co. (Liverpool) 57
Graham, F. Ronald 176
Grain Trade (Picnic) 106
Granby Bay 69
Grandholm, S.S. 18-20, 24, 29
Grand Hotel (Vancouver) 44
Grand Trunk Pacific Railway 45, 50, 51, 53, 69
Grand Trunk Pacific Steamships 53, 54, 62, 71, 73, 95
Granite Bay 44, 88, 103
Granite Falls 40
Grant, Alexander 43
Grant, Miss Flora 43
Granthams (Landing) 105
Grassey Bay 88
Gravesend (UK) 4
Gray, S.S. 136, 146
Gray, Capt. Neil 55, 76, 77, 102, 104
Gray, Capt. Robert 2
Greene, Canon Alan G. 79
Greene Point (also Green Point) 26, 31, 44
Greenlaw, Dave 197
Greer, Surgeon Cmdr. W. M. 179
Greig, George 187

226

236